OPERA WORKSHOP

In the aria 'Non disperar' from Handel's *Giulio Cesare* Cleopatra (Valerie Masterson) is seen taunting Ptolemy (James Bowman) from behind the couch where he is sitting. She has moved across to this position (marked as 7 in Diagram 1.2, p. 7) in the final ritornello of the 'A' section of the aria and is now singing the 'B' section during which, in the ENO video recording, the long roulade on 'consolar' (*consolation*, see p. 18) is made especially provocative. *Photograph Catherine Ashmore*

OPERA WORKSHOP

Studies in Understanding and Interpretation

RAYMOND WARREN

Published by
SCOLAR PRESS
Gower House
Croft Road
Aldershot
Hants GU11 3HR
England

Ashgate Publishing Company
Old Post Road
Brookfield
Vermont 05036
USA

British Library Cataloguing-in-Publication data

Warren, Raymond
Opera Workshop
I. Title
782.1

Library of Congress Cataloging-in-Publication Data

Warren, Raymond
Opera Workshop: studies in understanding and interpretation /
Raymond Warren.
p. cm.
Includes bibliographical references and index.
ISBN 0–85967–970–5
1.Opera. 2. Opera—Production and direction. I. Title
ML1700.W3 1995
782.1′143—dc20 94–13604
CIP
MN

ISBN 0 85967 970 5

Typeset in Times by Photoprint, Torquay and printed in Great Britain at the University Press, Cambridge

Contents

Preface and Acknowledgments

If the book had a dedication it would be to the memory of Benjamin Britten whom I met in 1960 when he gave me a lesson, very kindly going over with me the score of my first opera. His teaching method was to ask the most searching questions of each passage: how was it to be sung and acted, how paced, how related to other passages, etc. And when a general problem was isolated he referred at once to something relevant in the classics. I remember that one such problem, how to handle a change of level from recitative into aria, led to a memorable analysis of the interaction of melody, harmony and rhythm in the Countess's 'E Susanna non vien' from *The Marriage of Figaro*. I think that is the only bit of Britten analysis actually to find its way into this book, though I hope that something of his penetrating understanding of opera pervades the rest too.

At the time, of course, there was no thought of a book. That idea entered my mind much more recently while I was watching Andrew Shore working with students in *real* opera workshops. He showed such understanding (musical as well as dramatic) in bringing opera scenes to life on the stage, that I wondered if anything of his approach could be put into writing. I certainly owe him a lot. I am also very grateful to Janet Price for some sensitive and helpful comments, to David Selwyn for helping me to argue things through, and to many other friends. I acknowledge, too, generous help from the scholarly community, notably the late Denis Arnold, Brian Trowell, Winton Dean, Philip Pickett, John Whenham, Michael Robinson and, above all, to Nigel Davison who kindly read the manuscript and made a number of helpful suggestions. I would also like to express my gratitude to Felicity Firth and David Higgins for their help with translating the Italian libretti. The translations are literal rather than elegant and are not meant for singing.

For the illustrations my first thanks must go to Sylvia Bramley for her sketches: there are some fifty of them, all executed with great skill and much loving care. They are valuable not least because they can give views of the whole stage, which the quality of the video stills rarely allows. I am grateful nevertheless for permission to use the latter: from films of *Carmen*, *La Bohème* and *Peter Grimes* by courtesy of NVC Arts, and from *The Marriage of Figaro* and *The Magic Flute* by courtesy of RPTA. I acknowledge with gratitude help with the cost of the illustrations from the Arts Faculty Research Fund of the University of Bristol. The musical extracts from *Wozzeck* are reproduced by kind permission of Universal Edition A. G. Vienna, and those from *Peter Grimes* by kind permission of Boosey & Hawkes Music Publishers Ltd. I owe many thanks to Derek Bourgeois for help with the setting up of the music examples.

Last but not least I must thank my family, especially Christopher for drawing the diagrams and Roberta for helping in countless ways.

RW

Introduction

Much has been written on the meaning and history of opera, but comparatively little on how in practice the medium actually works. This is an attempt to tackle the question by studying scenes from some of the great operas of the repertory, looking in particular at how their workings are to be understood by those involved: the singers, conductors and producers. But if it is a 'user's guide' for them, I hope it will also appeal to a more general readership wanting to share in the quest for a more intimate understanding of this most exciting but elusive of musical forms.

It is a fascinating and complex subject. There is not only the subtlety of the interactions between the different elements of opera, the words, the music and the stagecraft, but in addition, within the dimension of the music itself, there is the continually fluctuating relationship between what is sung on the stage and played in the pit: and the stagecraft, the magic of the theatre, is constantly compromising that very relationship. In the first topic of Chapter 1, Handel's recitative, it is the words which are of the first importance. The singer is dominant and is supported by the pit musicians only in the lightest way. Then, in the ritornello of the aria immediately following, the tables are completely turned: music takes over from the words, the singer for the moment is silent and the orchestra posits a new dimension of feeling, buoying up the singer so that he or she can feel (or at any rate beguile the audience into feeling) that, as Dent memorably puts it, 'it is the singer's inward emotion which causes the orchestra to play the appropriate phrase'.[1] There are things to be said about the purely musical relationships here, and how in performance the one type of movement can lead smoothly into the other. But over and above that, the theatre can weave its spell too. The singer who can add to the required range of vocal colouring a good stage presence and appropriate actions can weld a whole scene into an integrity not to be revealed by an analysis of the musical notes alone.

Handel's organisation of words, vocal and orchestral music, and theatre is the first of many operatic amalgams whose processes I am trying to understand. His approach is analysed first because its logical separation of verbal and musical levels makes it a useful yardstick for understanding the others, both historically earlier and later. In Part I all of these amalgams have it in common that the orchestra is entirely concerned to support the singer. In Part II, there are other roles for the orchestra in 'enlarging the stage', suggesting a dimension to some extent independent of the singers. The Handelian forms still provide useful criteria for much of Part III. In separating out the operatic occasions for action and contemplation, they make a good starting point for a more general discussion of action in opera: they also provide a useful comparison in considering those opera traditions where spoken dialogue and melodrama appear in the place of recitative.

Within this framework each topic has a short introductory essay followed by a study of some selected scenes, whose music examples are sometimes illustrated with sketches and sometimes with synchronised stills from opera productions on video (listed below), making possible a discussion of a producer's or a singer's particular response to the music and the dramatic situation. As this is an innovative feature of the book, it calls for some further explanation. When, as is often the case, the video production seems to me to work well it is sufficient to give a brief description of the staging and its relationship with the music: such description is necessarily selective, choosing those features where relevant points can be made. At other times an aspect of the music or its interpretation may call for a wider or more critical discussion. I am aware, of course, that there are many different ways of doing things and so I should explain that in choosing one particular interpretation of each scene, not because it is typical or even necessarily good, but simply because it is available on a video film, I have two objects in mind. In the first place it is possible for readers, if they so wish, to follow up any points raised by referring to the film, though I trust that what is said here is complete in itself without such reference. Secondly, simply because it is a verifiable and concrete realisation, it can be examined and used as material for a more general discussion of the relationship between music, words and staging. If that is found to be helpful to the understanding of opera in performance then the object of the book will indeed have been fulfilled.

Readers who refer to the video films should remember that they constitute an art form in their own right, and may sometimes work differently from that which they seek to portray: for example the small screen seems to demand more constant movement than the opera house. In essence there is a different balance between the visual and the aural in the two mediums, and certainly it is true of the musically heightened passages, such as the arias in Handel or Mozart, that visual stasis is easier to accept in the theatre. Wagner's celebrated advice to Nietzsche, who was to see *Tristan and Isolde*, 'Off with your spectacles! You are only to listen to the orchestra.' would be anathema to most video producers. It is also true that the position and angling of the camera may, in altering a perspective, change an interpretative emphasis. Yet despite these reservations the video film is a very useful resource for the study of opera performance. Sylvia Bramley's sketches are generally based on the named video productions: however, their function is not to depict the production in any literal way but simply to illustrate the points being made.

It will be evident that the degree of detail of the actions and the reasons for suggesting them will vary from example to example. The very first, an aria from Handel's *Julius Caesar*, is more detailed than most for several reasons: being the first example it could expand on certain principles, such as the use of orchestral ritornelli to change stage positions, which didn't then need to be worked out in every later example. Moreover there was the particular point to be made that although the words of Handel's libretto suggest little action, the music's characterisation is so vivid as to make a 'modern realistic' stage interpretation viable, even if perhaps anachronistic. On the other hand, the reason behind giving the detail in the very last example of the book, a scene from Berg's *Wozzeck*, is that much of the action is programmed into the music and is therefore mandatory. There may be some choice as to how and where on the stage these actions are made, but none at all as to what they should be and when.

Readers will need a certain basic technical knowledge of music to follow what is said here, and the understanding is important because music is ultimately the dominant dimension in opera. Producers must never, I believe, go against the music: the date, place, costumes, scenery, actions and general staging can differ from the original intentions of the composer and librettist only so far as the music allows. Indeed, a prime concern of mine is to explore just what the music does allow (or imply), both in its own dimension, in such matters as pacing and vocal intensity, and also at its interface with the other elements of opera, notably the action on the stage.

In beginning at a point chronologically nearly half-way between Monteverdi and Berg, it will be evident that this is not primarily an historical treatment of the subject, and indeed, even with an approach which is often concerned in a practical way with performance, I have not gone into matters of historical performance practice more than necessary. Of course, where the results of historical research are directly relevant to the argument in hand (as in the achievement of pace in Handelian recitatives) I have been grateful to use them. On the whole, though, my concern is less with historicity than simply to show how the operatic amalgam works and in particular how a sensitive response to the music can be wedded to stage action; this is something that can underly different approaches to historical authenticity.

I cannot claim that this is a comprehensive treatment of what is a vast subject, though I hope its selection of topics will at least cover a good range of the big issues. It seemed sensible to be selective too in the list of works to be used as material for the illustrations: so, although other works are discussed, I have for convenience concentrated on the operas listed below. They are not what I would have chosen to represent the history of opera; they are too idiosyncratic for that. I am also aware that their composers did things differently, and even in some cases more expertly, elsewhere. But they have all stood the test of time, they exemplify techniques which have been proved viable in countless productions, and there are scores and recordings of them readily available.

The video films to which reference is made are given below. Those with an asterisk are illustrated with stills in the book, the other operas with sketches by Sylvia Bramley. Singers taking the principal roles on the video stills are named in the List of Illustrations.

Monteverdi *L'Orfeo*, (1607), Harnoncourt, Decca.
Monteverdi *L'Incoronazione di Poppea*, (1642), Harnoncourt, Decca.
Handel *Julius Caesar*, (1724), Mackerras, Virgin Classics.
* Mozart *The Marriage of Figaro*, (1786), Pritchard, Longman Video.
* Mozart *Die Zauberflöte*, (1791), Haitink, Longman Video.
Beethoven *Fidelio*, (1805/14), Haitink, Southern Television Limited.
Verdi *Rigoletto*, (1851), Elder, Thames.
Wagner *Das Rheingold*, (1854), Boulez, Philips.
* Bizet *Carmen*, (1875), Haitink, The National Video Corporation.
* Puccini *La Bohème*, (1896), Gardelli, The National Video Corporation.
* Britten *Peter Grimes*, (1945), Davis, The National Video Corporation.

Note

1 Quoted from Dent (1940) p. 141. The impression is rather spoilt by what Dent goes on to say: 'What generally happens is that when the orchestra plays the phrase the singer is caught napping and suddenly remembers he has some gesture to make at this point – half a bar too late.'

Part I
The Orchestra Supports the Singer

A painting by Pietro Domenico Olivera shows the Teatro Regio Turin on the opening night (26th December 1740) of an opera seria *Arsace*, Francesco Feo's setting of the libretto by Antonio Salvi. The close relationship between the subject of the opera and the moral concerns of the audience is reflected in the way in which the stage is seen to be an extension of the auditorium. The position and elevation of the orchestra facilitates a close rapport between singers and players (see p. 4). (*Museo Civico, Turin*)

1 Recitative and Aria in Handel and Mozart

I Handel

Criticisms of late Baroque opera have so often concentrated on the abuses of opera seria[1] that one can easily forget that the rigid division into recitative and aria was a very sensible way of dividing the honours between words and music. The greater part of the verbal text was set to simple recitative (recitativo semplice, later called secco), which had little melodic distinction in the vocal writing, with the singer adopting a flexible parlando style not generally using the full voice. Indeed, such recitative had very little musical interest at all though, as we shall see, it was not without certain structural virtues. Its sparse continuo accompaniment (harpsichord with solo cello), helped to ensure that it was a good vehicle for the clear projection of the words, an issue of importance not only because these words often had literary merit, but also because they provided the necessary details to enable the audience to follow the dramatic situations and to understand the motivations of the characters.

Then, in the aria, the music took over, doing that for which it is arguably best fitted, exploring the emotional response of the character. For the singer, the shift to musical dominance in the aria would involve a new concentration on vocal colouring and shaping of phrase so as to add a deeper musical dimension to the emotion and the characterisation. If this and the generally slower pace of the word setting made the words less clearly discernible to the audience, there was some measure of compensation in their repetition: the aria words were in fact usually short rhyming verses designed for such treatment. (See for instance page 6, giving the words of Example 1.1.) The drama, too, now had to yield to the music, and indeed when the aria took the form of a soliloquy addressed not even to another character but to the audience, the dramatic momentum was in effect frozen. As Grout well puts it, this kind of opera is 'the classical compromise of operatic form, in which drama and music each yield certain rights and thereby find a means of living together compatibly'.[2] However, compatibility does not mean equality. The arias, despite their fewer words, were of longer duration than the recitatives, and in effect they (and the musical dimension generally) could be said to dominate the form.

But how does the scheme work in practice? On closer examination it often turns out to be less rigid than our brief description implies. Arias will have moments when the words need especially clear articulation (the aria in Example 1.1 is a case in point), and recitatives will have passages when the musical intensity increases, notably at the end, at the lead into the aria. Such refinements are especially appropriate in Handel, who infused much subtle characterisation into the opera seria forms.

Handel's recitatives mostly consist of verbal exchanges which need to get through the words virtually at the pace of spoken dialogue, and that, in musical terms, is quite fast. The writings of the time (and our modern experience confirms it) insist that the preservation of pace is paramount,[3] but that this must go hand in hand with a certain flexibility;[4] for instance there are words or phrases which need to be taken more slowly, as any good actor knows. What often happens in opera is that the slower words will come at cadence points, and any feeling of loss of momentum can be avoided if the quicker tempo is resumed immediately on the last chord of the cadence. Since the cadences often finalise modulations, pointing them in this way helps to make musical sense too, by articulating the tonal structure and so giving a clearer preparation for the more sustained tonal areas of the coming aria. It should be borne in mind that the rhythmic notation of this type of recitative was conventional and need not always be taken literally: often it was intended to indicate the stress of the syllables rather than their duration or the precise lengths of the articulating rests. However, there are some places where the notated rhythm is mandatory, e.g. at certain cadence points, and our examples will identify such places.

At the end of the recitative, as we have seen, the singer must fashion the way it leads into the aria; how this is done will depend on the context. Very occasionally, when the aria is particularly fast, it is effective to go headlong into it without preparation; but in most cases there will be a certain firming up of the tempo and a fuller, more cantabile style of singing; in other words, a move towards the condition of the aria. Often the composer gave a hint of at least a modest allargando in the penultimate bar, by giving a greater melodic interest not only to the voice but also to the continuo line: an invitation for it to be played so as to match the singer's cantabile. Such sharing of the change of level by singer and accompaniment is further enhanced by the stabilisation of the tonality at the approach of the aria. And if, as occasionally happens in Handel, the following aria begins with the voice, without an opening ritornello, it is even more important that the recitative should move towards the aria's condition (rhythmic firmness and sustained vocal and continuo lines) as it approaches it. A further modification of the general rule about the pace of a recitative may be necessary when the following aria is slow. In that case, the slowing may well begin earlier in the movement, which, if it is short, may even appropriately be taken slowly throughout.

The moment of the join into the aria needs careful thought in the staging too, because a suitable action or gesture, or even the freezing of an expressive stance, can further suggest a connection between the two musical sections, making it visually clear that the move into the aria is simply the intensified continuation of the singer's feelings from the recitative. It is one of the miracles of opera that by such means the apparent extreme artifice of this moment can be made to seem so natural, involving, as it does, not only a change of musical dimension from voice domination to orchestral ritornello, but also a change of the music's place of origin, from stage to pit.

When the words of the recitative were of exceptional intensity or emotional range they would be set as 'accompanied' recitative, and in Handel's time that usually meant string accompaniment. Although at any moment such a setting could be as passionate as an aria, it was emotionally more flexible, and indeed it could embrace stark changes of mood. This was musically possible because the figurations representing the different emotions did not need to be reiterated over such a wide span as in a strict aria form. Metastasio, the most famous of the opera seria librettists, drew attention to the fact that the pace of the word setting was generally slower than in secco recitative,[5] though there can still occasionally be fast passages. So in performance, as with secco recitative, flexibility of pace and tone is called for, an attention to the form and tonality of the movement, and, of course, a handling of the ending to give an appropriate lead into the following aria. A movement of this type is the subject of Example 1.2.

Handel's arias are underpinned by the basic assumption that the unwavering role of the orchestra is to support the singer: every note of the orchestral music becomes an immediate expression of the singer's innermost feelings, buoying him or her up and bridging the gaps between vocal phrases so as to maintain musical intensity and continuity throughout the movement. Usually the identity between the vocal and instrumental sections is quite evident, both of them being based on the same musical figure.[6] Thus the singer can feel the ritornelli simply as extensions of the vocal line and act accordingly. Of course, the ritornelli may be the occasions for more action than when the singer is actually singing: they are often useful for moving from one part of the stage to another, as is illustrated in Example 1.1. All this is equally true of that minority of arias (which includes Example 1.1) where the main ritornello material doesn't actually appear in the voice part: the figurations in the orchestra are still integral to the singer's character and feelings.

A more subtle musical link between stage and pit is to be found in those many arias where the main musical figure of the ritornello returns *piano* as accompaniment in the vocal sections. The singer must be aware of this and feel it as further emotional support. Such close musical liaison was more feasible in the opera houses of Handel's day when the pits were generally shallow enough for the singers on stage to be able both to see and hear the orchestral players[7] (see illustration on p. 2). The typical modern opera house's deeper and more distant pit is less conducive to sensitive Handel performances.

Like much other eighteenth-century music the operatic aria enshrined the idea that there should be a growth to a climax or a point of greatest fulfilment at the end of the movement. This might seem to be contradicted by the symmetrical ABA structure of the Da Capo form, but it could still be realised to some extent through the use of two conventions, the first of which was musical: the singer would heighten the main section of the Da Capo form by ornamenting the vocal line when it was heard for the second time in the reprise. Since the ability to improvise such ornamentation was an expected part of every singer's musicianship, the composers did not normally provide the notes, though Handel and others did on occasions do so, and have left us some excellent models.[8] The ideal, not always achieved in the eighteenth century, was of course to intensify the emotion and characterisation, rather than to impress with virtuosity.

The other convention was dramatic: the singer was normally required to leave the stage at the end of each aria, and so the action in the closing ritornello and the manner of the departure would set the seal on the character portrayal of the aria. In our Example 1.1, the Cleopatra of the ENO (English National Opera) production achieves this by walking ostentatiously right across the stage in front of Ptolemy, whom she has been taunting. The exit is generally best timed to coincide with the end of the ritornello. If it is significantly earlier than this, the music will seem redundant,[9] if later, the singer, suddenly left with no supporting music, has the difficulty of continuing the action without losing momentum. Should a producer of a modern performance feel the need to keep the character on the stage, then at least the music's pull towards the end should be respected and matched with a strong closing movement or stance.

One of the problems in understanding opera seria today concerns how a complete character is built up. The theory of the time was that each aria should concentrate on a single affection, with perhaps a second one in its 'B' section, and the character would emerge facet by facet in the course of successive arias until by the end of the opera it was completely revealed. This description certainly indicates the formal structuring of a character in an opera, and to my knowledge that is the extent of any theoretical or critical writings of the time. But a modern singer preparing a Handelian role will surely feel the need to absorb the whole from the outset, in order to convincingly project the parts. The kittenish Cleopatra of her first aria (Example 1.1), must be the same person who later shows bravery, love and grief. There is evidence that Handel himself must have thought along these lines too, because signs of a more pervasive characterisation are to be found in his music. It can hardly be accidental that six of Cleopatra's scenes are in the sharp keys of E and A, that several of them exhibit her mercurial changes of mood, and that there are melodic connections between her arias e.g. a later reappearance of the repeated note figure from the first aria, and the use in several movements of pithy short phrases of 2–4 notes.

The suggestions in this chapter are very far from being a blueprint for a producer grappling with the considerable problems of staging a Handel opera so as to be acceptable at the present time. For one thing, our whole theatre tradition and audience expectations are so different from those of the baroque period that success is hardly likely to be achieved simply by aiming for historical authenticity. Such an aim would in any case be elusive since the general style of the staging of opera seria was by no means uniform. In court theatres on the continent there was a high degree of formality, Metastasio on one occasion stating a preference for stage positions, presumably static, reflecting the social rank of the characters.[10] It was the abstract qualities of duty, love, etc., which were depicted, rather than realism of character, and performances were in effect ritualistic re-enactments of aspects of the courtly society from which the audience came.[11] Handel's own base in London, the King's Theatre, was nearer to our modern theatre in that its productions reflected some influence from the English spoken theatre, but the partly aristocratic audience still accepted conventions that would now be regarded as stultifying. We know too that the events on the stage did not always receive the undivided attention of the audience. The theatre lights were kept on, enabling them to read their libretti, but also giving the opportunity to engage in social activities during the performances. The music simply wasn't written for the demanding realism of the twentieth-century theatre.

Nevertheless Handel's operas have often proved to be viable for transposition across the centuries into our different theatrical tradition: for without transcending the integrity of the opera seria disciplines, they infuse new life into the old forms and transform potentially stereotyped characters into credible human beings. The aria of Example 1.1 might seem at first glance to be a conventional exploration of the single affection of the opening ritornello music, suggesting the scorn which Cleopatra feels for her brother. But Handel expands this into a wider and more lively character portrayal in which her mood ranges from mock consolation to a fine regal imperiousness. And the function of the roulade on 'amor' is more than simply to bring the 'A' section of the aria to a lyrical climax at the end, though it certainly achieves that. It is surely not fanciful to find in it sexual innuendos, for which Valerie Masterson's mock-caressing hand to Ptolemy's face (see frontispiece) is an appropriate gesture. Such an aria seems positively to invite a more naturalistic staging.

Example 1.1
Handel Recitative and Aria, 'Non Disperar' from *Giulio Cesare* Act I, Scene 5

This is the last section of a secco recitative and the whole of the aria which follows it, except that, as in Handel's score, the music of the Da Capo is not written out again. The stage diagrams and the positions in the sketches are based on John Copley's ENO production on the Virgin Classics video film which is given the English title, Julius Caesar. As this is a longer example than most, we shall consider some aspects of it as a whole before giving a detailed run through.

Firstly the libretto is given with a translation. The recitative, with its long lines, is in the style of the spoken drama of the time, and for the most part its pacing and dramatic production can be treated accordingly.[12] It is the aria, despite its shorter lines and more compact verse form, which takes up the major part of the scene. The much greater importance of the music calls for a different approach to the staging, based on the music as well as the words. Of its six lines, the first three are used for the 'A' section of the aria, the second three for the 'B' or middle section.

Libretto with Translation

Recitativo

Cleopatra: (*a Nirenus*) Egli è il germano, e la regina io sono. (*Entra Tolomeo*)
Tolomeo: Tu di regnar pretendi, donna superba e altera?
Cleopatra: Io ciò ch'è mio contendo; e la corona dovuta alla mia fronte giustamente pretendo.
Tolomeo: Vanne, e torna omai, folle, a qual di donna è l'uso, di scettro in vece a trattar l'ago, e il fuso!
Cleopatra: Anzi tu pur, effeminato amante, va dell'età sui primi nati albori, di regno in vece a coltivar gli amori!

Aria

Non disperar; chi sà?
Se al regno non l'avrai
Avrai sorte in amor.
Mirando una beltà
In essa troverai
A consolar un cor.

Recitative

Cleopatra: (to Nirenus) *He is my young brother and I am the queen.* (Ptolemy enters)
Ptolemy: *You demand to rule, proud and haughty lady?*
Cleopatra: *I fight for what is mine; and I justly claim the crown which is owed to my brow.*
Ptolemy: *Away with you, and return, a fool, to what are the ways of a woman, to ply the needle and the shuttle in place of the sceptre!*
Cleopatra: *No, rather you go, womanish lover, in the early dawn of your youth, and instead of governing, look after your amours!*

Aria

Don't despair; who knows?
If you find no fortune in government
You may be lucky in love.
Gazing upon some beauty
You may find in her
A heart for consolation.

The following schedule of actions summarises the main action and stage positions on the video stills, showing in particular how these bring out the musical structure of the aria. Each ritornello has stage movement to new and strong positions for the following vocal section, the strongest action of all being reserved for Cleopatra's exit at the end.

Summary of the Main Movements of *Giulio Cesare* Act I, Scene 5

Below is a simplified schedule of the actions in this scene: Cleopatra in solid lines, Ptolemy in dotted. Position numbers correspond to the numbering of the sketches in the main commentary.

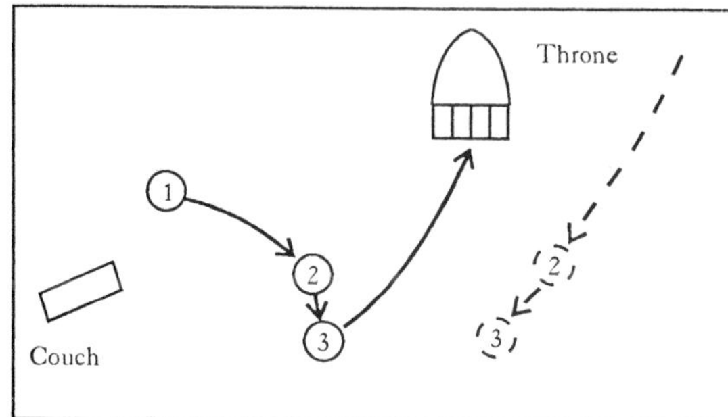

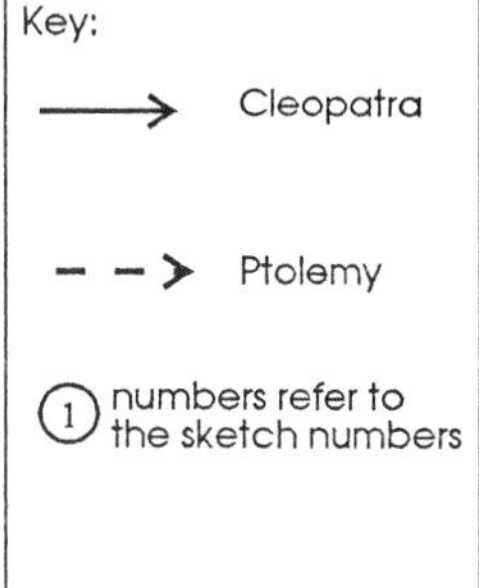

Diagram 1.1
Recitative

Cleopatra at ①
Ptolemy enters from back, and moves to 2
Cleopatra to ②, moving forward to ③ for the end of the recitative.

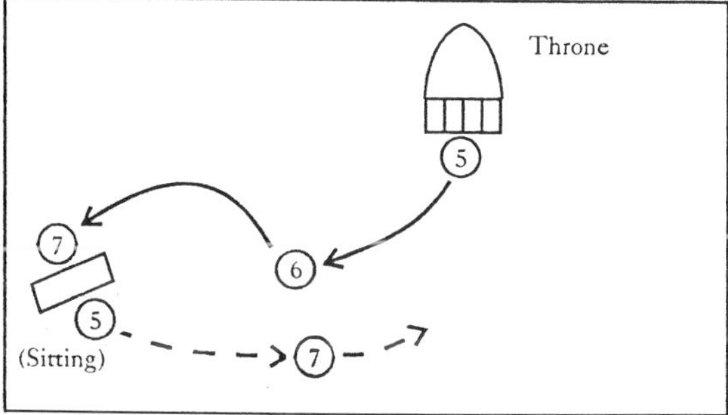

Diagram 1.2

Aria

Aria	Section A	
Ritornello		Cleopatra back to throne ⑤
		Ptolemy moves to 5 and sits
1st vocal section		Cleopatra seated on throne
Ritornello		She stands
2nd vocal section		She walks slowly ⑤to ⑥
Ritornello		She moves ⑥to ⑦
	Section B	
		Cleopatra at ⑦(behind Ptolemy)

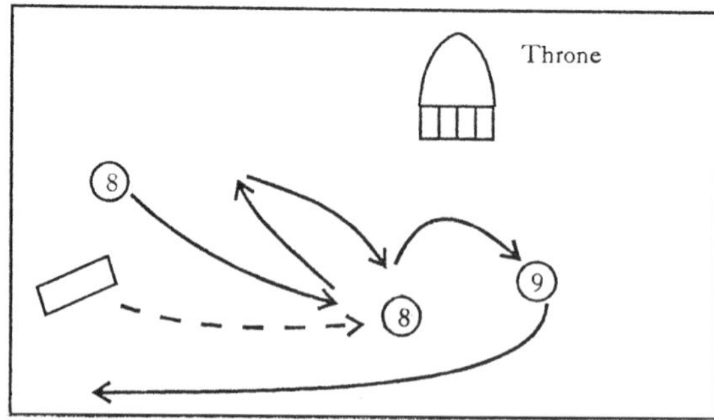

Diagram 1.3

	Section A Reprise	
Ritornello		Cleopatra moves back to ⑧
		Ptolemy moves across to 8
1st vocal section		Cleopatra at ⑧ Ptolemy at 8
Ritornello		She walks back again to Nirenus
2nd vocal section		She slowly returns to ⑧
Final Ritornello		Cleopatra walks right round in front of Ptolemy, going off stage right from ⑨ Ptolemy remains at 8

Music, Sketches and Commentary

The musical analysis is related particularly to the pacing and staging. In the earlier part of the recitative, prior to the beginning of this extract, Cleopatra had learnt from her servant Nirenus of Ptolemy's treachery in murdering Pompei. Her reaction to this irresponsible deed is to resolve the more firmly to resist his claim to the Egyptian throne: hence her own regal claim with which the extract begins, words of such weight that they must surely be sung with full, sustained voice and in a firm tempo. The sustaining of the B flat continuo harmony in the first full bar confirms this gesture, which could be further supported by a well spread continuo chord. The bracket around the rest is an editorial suggestion that it could be omitted to give better pace and continuity. The passage will grow naturally towards its heightened ending at the F major cadence, where the continuo should give support by playing the cadential chords firmly in the singer's tempo and on the beat as indicated.[13] The sketch shows a suitable position for Cleopatra's conversation with Nirenus when, in a typical and effective operatic gesture, she turns away from him towards the audience to make her assertion.

Cleopatra
he is my younger brother
and I am the queen.
(enter Ptolemy)
e — gliè il ger- ma - no, e la re - gi - na io so - no.
6
4
2

1. 

At this moment Ptolemy suddenly enters and overhears her. He comes forwards quickly to rebuff her, singing as he moves, and the faster recitative pace will best be resumed at once on the last chord of the cadence. The flexibility referred to earlier will mean that the editorially bracketed rest is almost certainly best omitted in the interests of maintaining pace, making in effect a 3/4 bar. She turns to him and in a small gesture to mark the moment in which she begins her reply, she moves a step towards him. There is little musical interest here, the words are paramount and pace continues to be of the essence.

Ptolemy
You demand to rule, proud and haughty queen?
Cleopatra
I fight for what is mine
Tu di reg - nar pre - ten - di, don - na su - per - ba e al - te - ra? Io ciò ch'e mio con

Ptolemy
and I justly claim the crown which is owed to my brow
Away with you
ten-do; e la cor-ro-na do-vu-ta al-la mia fron-te giusta men - te pre-ten do. Van-ne, e tor-na o -

2. 

The key now changes remarkably quickly, modulating sharpwards towards the tonal area of Cleopatra's coming aria, and indeed of her subsequent arias in the opera. For this reason it is appropriate that while Ptolemy is singing, it is she who moves, walking forwards to a more commanding position for the start of her next section, which will bring the whole recitative to its fulfilment and lay the musical foundation for her aria.[14]

and return, a fool,
to what are the ways of a woman,
to ply the needle and the shuttle in place of the sceptre.
Cleopatra
mai, fol-le a qual di donna è l'u-so di scet-tro in ve-ce a trattar l'a-go e il fu-so. An-zi tu

3.

As the dominant key (B) of the aria's E major is established, the singer's intensity of tone and legato will increase and the tempo become a little firmer. In the ENO production the singer, having earlier turned away from Ptolemy, now emphasises the importance of this last phrase by turning back towards him. At the end of the recitative her stance is maintained for a moment across the division of the music. She could have moved straight away: what is important is that it should clearly be felt by her, and be evident to the audience, that the new music of the orchestral ritornello arises directly out of the final phrase of her recitative and refers to her feelings. Equally, it is important that Ptolemy should not move at that point lest the ritornello music might be taken to refer to him. The musical 'comma' between recitative and aria will be best if shorter than the conventional minim rest shown.

In this production, very soon after the start of the ritornello, she moves towards her throne at the back of the stage, beckoning to Nirenus to join her there. Ptolemy watches her for a moment and then moves over to the opposite side of the stage with his entourage, getting there in good time before the end of the ritornello. Since the aria is addressed to him, his role must be to react to Cleopatra in a natural way, but without distracting too much attention from her, for the music is entirely hers and she must hold the floor throughout. In this instance, a simple movement on his part later in the very busy ritornello seems perfectly consistent with this.

4.

The sketch on page 14 shows the start of the first vocal section. Cleopatra's sitting position is arguably not a strong one for the very lively affection of the aria, but the fact that she is on her throne does visually stress her regal claim. Moreover it is part of a well considered overall plan, being a good starting point for her later actions which increase in intensity towards her dramatic exit at the end of the aria. Bar 13 sees the first of the violin entries of ritornello material in an accompanying role, and the singer will feel it as supporting her. However in this case the violin line poses a certain element of competition with her, for although it is soft, it is somewhat astringent in nature and is pitched higher than her melody. If she can hear and feel that, and is provoked into adding just a sufficient matching astringency of tone herself to bring out her

5.

vocal line against the violins, it will surely add a nice edge to Handel's intended characterisation. Comparatively little action is necessary in the vocal section, when the attention of the singer and the audience are largely focussed on the music. Gestures with head, hands or arms give sufficient visual interest to enable the singer to point her emotions in a natural way.

A short cadenza, such as that suggested, is evidently invited by the composer at the cadence in bar 20, to bring the vocal section to a final climax. This, in turn, makes a good springboard for further action in the following short ritornello. Cleopatra rises and steps down from the throne.

She is seen slowly approaching Ptolemy as she sings the next vocal section. As she closes in on him he turns impetuously and looks away from her, an excellent movement because, being only a reaction to her pressing proximity, it does not detract from her necessary dominance in this, her aria. Musically it works well that his gesture comes not as a distraction in the middle of a phrase, but to coincide with the C sharp minor cadence in bar 28.

6.

Non dis-pe-rar, chi sà? Se al re- gno non l'a - vrai, a - vrai sor- te in a - mor,
25
p

a-vrai sor- te in a- mor, non dis-pe-rar,
p

non dis pe-rar, chi sà? se al re-gno non l'a-vrai, a- vrai sor te in a - mor, se al re - gno non l'a -
30

The main 'A' section of the aria comes to a fine climactic ending with a voluptuous vocal roulade on 'amor' (*love*), suggesting that she could even taunt him with a mock caressing hand towards his face. The roulade leads to a strong cadence in the home key, strengthened further by the orchestral re-entry which overlaps with the final note of the voice. The sheer musical force of this seemed to call for another reaction from Ptolemy, who makes a threatening gesture, again at the cadence. As he gets up Cleopatra smilingly moves to avoid him, using the music of the short ritornello to place herself in a new position behind him.

35
vrai a - vrai sor- te in a - mor, a - vrai sor- te in a - mor, chi sà? a - vrai sor-te in a
mor a - vrai sor-te in a -
40

7.

The abrupt change of key from E major to C sharp minor seems to reinforce the need for a new position like this. Although there is not a strong change of affection in this middle section, the use throughout of minor keys, C sharp, F sharp and B, suggests a more expressive aspect which will be the more tormenting for Ptolemy. As is common in Handel this section begins with a one-note-per-syllable underlay of the text. The singer will use a full voice, but there is no reason for the words not being clearly enunciated: indeed a certain stressing of them gives ironic force to Handel's change of key. The lovely roulade on 'consolar' (*consolation*) can of course be pointed with a smile, but as earlier, the vocal interest of this section is such that any large scale stage movement is unnecessary.

Fine
Gazing upon some beauty you may find in her a heart for consolation.
Mi - ran - do u-na bel-ta in es-sa tro-ve-rai a con-so-lar un cor, a
p
con - so - lar un cor, a con - so -
50
lar un cor, in es-sa tro ve-rai a con - so-lar un cor, a con - so-lar un cor.
55
Da Capo

In this production Cleopatra uses the opening ritornello of the Da Capo to move to a new position, rejoining her female servants, in order now to address Ptolemy from there. This position, backstage from Ptolemy, enables the producer to place more emphasis on his reactions, which are still stances (perhaps changing at the ends of her phrases or in the ritornelli) rather than movements which would in the fuller sense upstage her.

8.

Later in the Da Capo she moves over towards him again and then at the very end, in the final ritornello, she makes her required exit suitably ostentatious by coming with her entourage right across the stage in front of him, timing it so that her disappearance from view roughly coincides with the end of the music.

9.

Example 1.2
Accompanied Recitative
from *Giulio Cesare* Act II, Scene 8

In a mere 18 bars of accompanied recitative Handel gives a vivid sketch of his heroine at a moment of crisis: her fears are quickly overcome, and then a brave new resolve is balanced with her loving concern for Caesar. She was with her beloved Caesar when they learnt they had been ambushed by a large force of Ptolemy's men. As Caesar went off to join battle with them, she heard their shouts from offstage (Handel sets this in a confident B flat major). Now, at the start of the recitative, she realises that he may well have gone to his death. The key suddenly changes to a pathetic G minor and she suggests her concern for him by moving across the stage as if to follow him. Then she stops as she realises her own danger, expressing this further by looking down. The urgency of this whole situation seems to imply that this first section of the recitative should not be slow, though there can be some freedom of tempo.

At bar 4 she suddenly pulls herself together. Handel introduces a new assertive repeated-note figure in the orchestra and the key jumps sharpwards to A minor. Such a violent change of mood within a movement was only possible for him in an accompanied recitative. The singer can express it gesturally by turning back again and looking up. The tempo is best centred around the fixed tempo of the orchestral figure (say ♩ = 80). Of course, phrases will be sung freely so as to draw the maximum of intensity from them, but it is helpful to the cohesion of the music if the last few notes of certain phrases are sung rhythmically and in tempo (e.g. di-car-mi of 'vendicarmi'), so that the entries of the semiquaver figure in the orchestra are given a good rhythmic springboard. The orchestral music, which is more than a mere accompaniment, will then sound as an integrated part of the singer's feelings.

The sudden *piano* (Handel's marking), and the striking modulation to F sharp minor, the key of the coming aria, mark another change of mood as her thoughts turn to prayer for Caesar's safety. The key is only one of several elements taking this last part of the recitative forwards into the aria. The tempo, possibly slower, can be geared to the aria, and there is even a motivic link which will be clear if the quality of singing, now very close to that of the aria, brings out the beauty of the falling phrases (bracketed in the music example), which are taken up by the violins in the following ritornello, and later by the singer herself. Moreover a good singer will be able both to observe Handel's rests and also to feel a continuity through them so that the vocal line coheres into a single melody projecting forwards into the beautiful counterpoint between the violins and bassoons.

In the ENO performance Cleopatra hardly moves at all now, only employing small gestures of face or hands, for it is an inner intensity that is to be conveyed. In particular she is quite still at the moment of the break between the movements, where her gestural stasis matches Handel's tonal stasis; and so the aria is felt to be the natural outcome of the recitative.

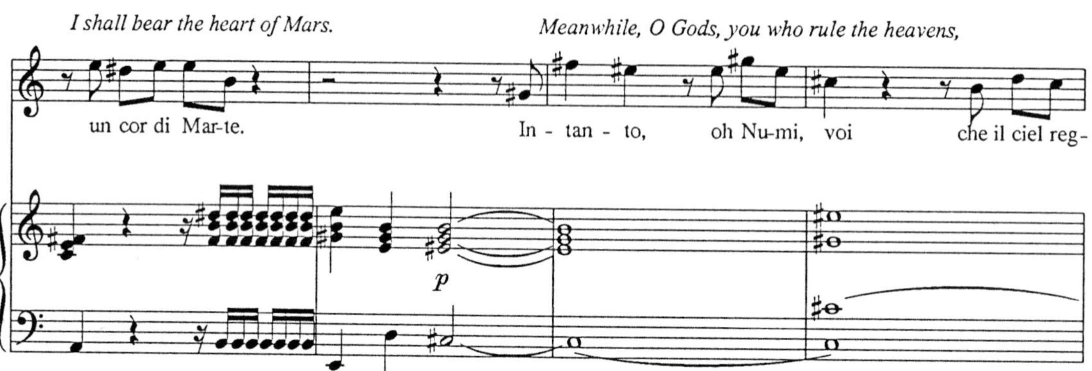
I shall bear the heart of Mars.
Meanwhile, O Gods, you who rule the heavens,
un cor di Mar-te.
In - tan - to, oh Nu-mi, voi che il ciel reg-
p

protect my love! For he is my consolation and hope.
ge -te, difen-de -te il mio be-ne! Ch'e-gli è del se-no mi-o con-for-to e spe-me.
p

II Mozart

Although Mozart's most popular Italian operas are in a different genre, opera buffa,[15] it is still useful to apply to them some of the criteria of the opera seria tradition, especially in thinking of the recitatives and arias, and perhaps it is worth mentioning at the outset some of the differences of most practical interest to the performers. Mozart brought to the opera aria some of the techniques of his symphonic music, notably an ability to incorporate into a single movement a body of much more contrasted musical material than would be found in a baroque movement. So, in place of the exploration of a single affection, there is often a multi-faceted characterisation.[16] We saw Handel moving in this direction, incorporating into a ritornello several different figures (though all related to the main affection), and making creative use of the traditional cadential formulae. All this he managed to do without going outside the opera seria disciplines. Mozart, on the other hand, went a good deal further, using a richer diversity of elements to create his very human characters. In his buffa works the Da Capo form, a constraining feature of opera seria, is not strictly used, and where he comes nearest to using only a single affection, he either keeps the aria short, as in Barbarina's little Cavatina at the beginning of Act 4 of *The Marriage of Figaro*, or he adds a concluding Allegro to make a 'double' aria, as in the Countess's 'Dove sono'. This form, with its potential for bringing a scene to a climax at the end, had become very popular by the 1780s. The singers in Mozart must be aware of a more complex reliance on the orchestra than in Handel, involving exchanges that are sometimes very quick indeed, and with a new subtlety arising from the more fluid orchestration, another link with the symphonic music.

However, in our starting point, the secco recitative, the stylistic conventions used by the two composers were very similar. In particular Mozart, like Handel, was a master of the art of underlining dramatic moments with changes of key. This is evident in Example 1.3, part of the recitative leading into the Trio in Act 1 of *Figaro*. The example also illustrates Mozart's care with timings. At one point he adds a little modulating phrase in the continuo to cover a prescribed movement (round a chair in this case) that will take a few seconds, and there are other moments where the music and the drama seem to suggest a little time can be taken by the singer. For the most part, though, these generally more lively buffo situations make the maintenance of pace in the recitatives even more paramount than in Handel.

The Mozart recitatives are full of passages like Example 1.3, showing ingenuity in their renewal of the very restricting musical conventions; full of little touches to enhance wit and characterisation. The ingenuity is invariably evident in the endings, in the ways in which he leads into the following set pieces. Example 1.4 gives the ending of the same recitative, typical in its brilliant use of conventional material. It is only fair to say that the skill here belongs as much to Da Ponte as to Mozart. Often at this point in a recitative he will contrive a twist in the plot or a surprise action that will raise the dramatic tension at the crucial moment. In this particular case it is an action, the appearance from behind the chair of the Count, whose indignation, matched of course in the music, will propel the recitative forwards into the ensuing movement.

The two examples of accompanied recitative are chosen to explore the extremes of Mozart's range, classical poise in the first and volatile anger in the second. The Countess's lovely 'E Susanna non vien!' provides an object lesson in the way that right from the start it can be felt to be moving towards its aria. This it must do with more certainty than usual because 'Dove sono?' dispenses with the opening ritornello, the conventional way of indicating the start of the aria. Yet the audience must still know that the aria's first note is not just a continuing of the recitative. Example 1.5 examines how Mozart achieves this, looking particularly at the shaping of the vocal line (and its associated levels of sostenuto), the harmony/tonality, and the control of rhythm. There are also some suggestions for the musical realisation of these components in performance. Like Cleopatra's 'Che sento?', the drama is of an interior nature and does not call for much action, so that only a very few stills are necessary to illustrate the main stage movements of the video production.

For the most part the conventions used in Mozart's accompanied recitatives are similar to those of Handel, but there are certain differences of language, both in the harmony and the orchestral textures. In the Count's 'Hai già vinto', the subject of Example 1.6, the initially wayward tonal scheme (going from C to F sharp minor in the first few bars), might just have been possible for Handel, and perhaps even the potent augmented 6th chord in bar 3 too, though this was not a usual feature of the older composer's vocabulary. However, the sudden E major outburst in bar 5 is decidedly unlike Handel, its brusque triadic motif and rather rough wind scoring coming from the world of the classical symphony. Taking into account also its abrupt move sharpwards, it shows Mozart using the strongest language he knew to portray a violent change of mood. The performers must be sufficiently aware of this to project an appropriate intensity in their interpretation, both musically and gesturally. The Count, in Mozart's portrayal, is aggressive and emotionally volatile though, as the overall logic of the musical form shows, his scheming is held in purposeful control. Another very Mozartian feature of this recitative is the extent to which the orchestra takes over towards the end, interposing quite long rising passages between the vocal phrases (beginning at bar 30). The singer will feel his own temper rising through these passages so that each time he enters he is already on the crest of an emotional wave, and when the last cadential chord is elided into the first chord of the aria (a characteristically original manipulation of the convention), it is as if his temper positively boils over into that fiery movement.

After the start of the aria, Example 1.6 only gives a list of the main vocal phrases. In their sheer variety, major and minor, loud and soft, smooth and jagged, they show something of the depth and richness of the characterisation. The Count's thoughts change quickly from moment to moment, but as in the recitative there is a purposeful overall musical control implying in the dramatic dimension his determination that his plans should succeed. Da Ponte was praised earlier for his recitative words. In the aria words he tends to fall back on standard clichés, such as might have been set to baroque music with a single affection. Certainly in this case the performers would get a very superficial idea of the Count's personality from reading only the words: it is the music which conveys the pulse of the man.

As in many other Mozart arias, the orchestral figures are by no means all related thematically to the vocal lines. The opening of the ritornello at the beginning of 'Vedrò mentr'io' is a tempestuous cascade of notes of a highly unvocal nature. In this instance the singer is helped to feel them as his own by the fact that the second time round his vocal line rises to their first note. As with Handel, the singers need to have an intimate rapport with the orchestra and vice versa.[17] *The Marriage of Figaro* was written for performance in Vienna's old Burgtheater where the relative positions were similar to those of Handel's period. We know that the increased size of the orchestral wind section sometimes caused balance problems and that at least one German theatre tried to solve the problem not by the more modern expedient of hiding the orchestra (and so diminishing the rapport with the singers) but by hanging curtains at the side of the players to absorb some of the woodwind sound.[18]

Example 1.3
Extract from *The Marriage of Figaro* Act I, Scene 6

This is an example of how Mozart underlines and paces a very intense few seconds of action.

The Count is talking to Susanna; the key of F is established. Earlier in the scene, when Cherubino had been with Susanna and she had heard the Count approaching, she hid the young man behind a chair, from where he is no doubt listening to the present conversation.

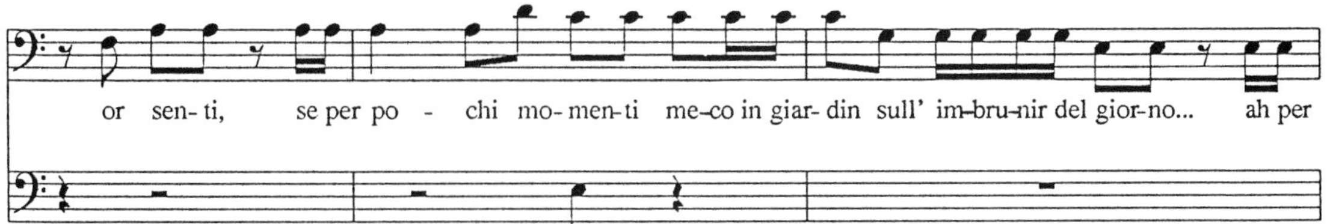
Count
Listen, if you'll spare me a few moments in the garden at dusk....
or sen- ti, se per po - chi mo- men- ti me-co in giar- din sull' im-bru-nir del gior-no... ah per

The conversation is interrupted by the approach of Basilio, whose offstage phrase might seem to be in B flat, but in the context it relates to the dominant chord of F: in other words Basilio does not yet cause the tonality to change. The harmonic stasis is a further hint that although this interruption is a dramatic surprise, it doesn't call for more than a momentary slackening of the pace. Susanna reacts very quickly and we see the look of alarm on her face at the moment Basilio's voice is heard.

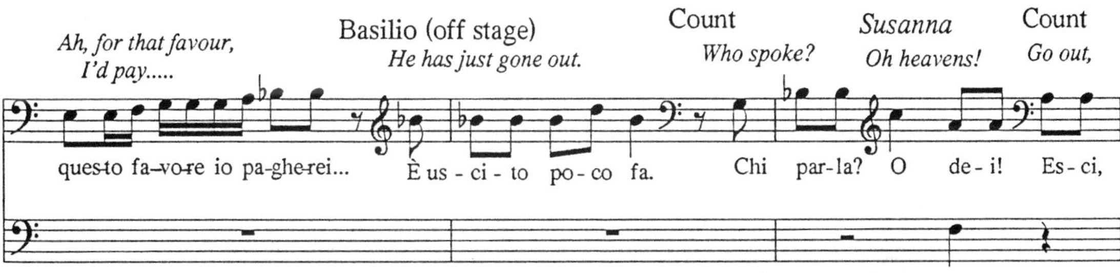
Ah, for that favour, I'd pay.....
Basilio (off stage)
He has just gone out.
Count
Who spoke?
Susanna
Oh heavens!
Count
Go out,
ques-to fa-vo-re io pa-ghe-rei... È us - ci - to po - co fa. Chi par - la? O de - i! Es - ci,

Basilio's imminent arrival forces the Count and Susanna to think quickly. He decides that she must go off to prevent Basilio from entering. His pointing to the doorway reinforces the order, to which Mozart assigns a strong F major arpeggio. But she must contradict this, knowing that she can't leave him in the room alone with Cherubino, and her greater authority (in this situation) is expressed in the musical modulation to C. The crucial modulating note, the B natural of 'solo', is made all the more tense by being approached from the tritone below. The singer's pace and tone must be such that the note and the tritone, which are articulating the key change, should make their due, if brief, musical impact, and this probably means singing the B's with a fuller voice. Basilio, still offstage, picks up the B natural, as he had the Count's B flat earlier, a nice touch suggesting his close proximity.

The Count concedes defeat and decides to hide behind the chair, towards which he now moves. Susanna takes charge again in directing him, and again it is she who effects the new modulation to G. Again her passage should be sung, with a slight stressing of the A on ce-la-te, so that the tonal point can be clearly heard.

The tiny continuo solo provides music for the action: the Count moves over to the chair and crouches behind it, Susanna meanwhile interposing herself between him and Cherubino so as to enable the page to sidle into the front of the chair without the Count seeing him; Susanna is seen covering him with a dress. The continuo solo also has the practical function of allowing a little time for the audience laughter which can sometimes hold up proceedings here. The action, as so often in Mozart, is clinched musically with a modulation. The new key is D, whose dominant chord sets the musical stage for Basilio's entry and greeting, at which point the pace can immediately be picked up.

Example 1.4
The End of the Same Recitative

Basilio prattles on, unaware of the presence of the Count, whose emissary he is in seeking Susanna's affections; but he can't resist gossiping about Cherubino too. Susanna, knowing that the Count can overhear, is a most reluctant listener. Da Ponte is on fine form here. He keeps close to the Beaumarchais play, the small changes he makes being mostly concerned to tighten it up. Mozart for his part doesn't need

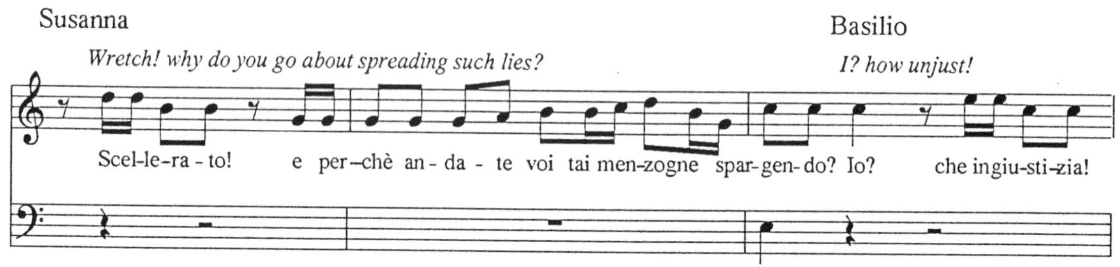

to write interesting music when the words maintain the audience's attention so well, and so the singers' concern is to articulate the words as quickly and clearly as if speaking them.

When, in answer to Susanna's protestations, Basilio points out that he is only relaying what everyone is saying, the Count is unable to contain himself any longer and jumps up from his place of hiding. The recitative only has time for very brief reactions from the other two before the orchestra bursts in with the short introduction to the Trio, which begins as if it were to be an aria for the Count. The two final comments in the recitative are arpeggiac, Basilio's delight leading up to Susanna's horror. The two singers may feel the need to slow the pace a little in order adequately to convey their respective feelings, probably singing in a very intense *piano*, but this must not be overdone, or the momentum of the move into the aria will be lost. Really though it is the Count who controls this passage. His stentorian tones as he emerges from

hiding must lead through to the orchestral introduction which is expressing his own feelings, and through to his entry in bar 4 which is itself a sequential continuation of his outburst in the recitative.

The pace of the transition will be helped by the orchestra's crashing in immediately after Susanna's 'O cielo' without waiting to observe the conventional crotchet rest. That the Count is dominant is made clear in the Glyndebourne production. He draws the audience's attention to himself by a simple movement forwards through the last bar of the recitative and the three bars of the orchestral introduction. This further cements the musical join and gives him a more commanding stage position for the start of the Trio. There is a tradition in some performances of foreshortening the ending of the recitative even further by bringing the orchestra in on the first syllable of Susanna's 'cielo'.[19] This certainly helps the pace and continuity but seems unnecessarily to go outside Mozart's recitative conventions. He was not afraid to break them himself on rare occasions and would no doubt have done so here had he wished.

Example 1.5
Accompanied Recitative 'E Susanna Non Vien?'
from Act III of *The Marriage of Figaro*

The Countess reveals her innermost thoughts in this very beautiful recitative. Little external action is called for, and so the commentary is mostly concerned with the musical interpretation. As explained in the foreword the discussion of this movement owes much to Benjamin Britten.

The still shows the Countess just as she enters looking for Susanna. The key initially is C, the key of the aria to follow, though the movement as a whole centres mostly on an anguished A minor. The first change is to the dominant as soon as the strings enter in the second bar. This is the point where, realising she is alone, the Countess begins to reflect on her own problems. The peak notes C, D, are picked out with arrows: we shall trace the upward motion of these notes (disregarding ornamental notes), to the climactic

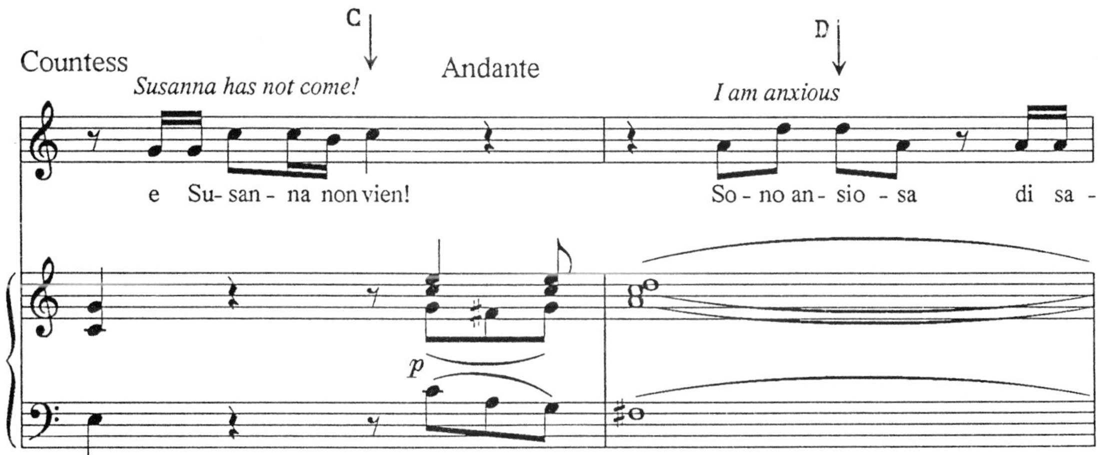

A in bar 24. An interesting feature of this recitative is that up to bar 14 every entry of both voice and orchestra is on an anacrusis. The effect of this is to throw weight on some of the later entries.

The new orchestral figure in bar 4 signals a change of mood as the Countess casts doubt on the wisdom of her plan. She is seen moving forwards a little and turning to register the change. The music intensifies as she thinks of her husband's impetuousness and jealousy, the orchestra supporting her with an assertive dotted figure which will be taken up again later. Then on her cadential word 'geloso' (jealous), the pace quickens for a brief *Allegretto* and the key screws up to A minor. Bar 7 needs to be sung so as to drive towards this moment of musical drama, and with firmness on the strong beats (1 and 3) of bar 8 to act as a springboard for the off-beat orchestral entries.

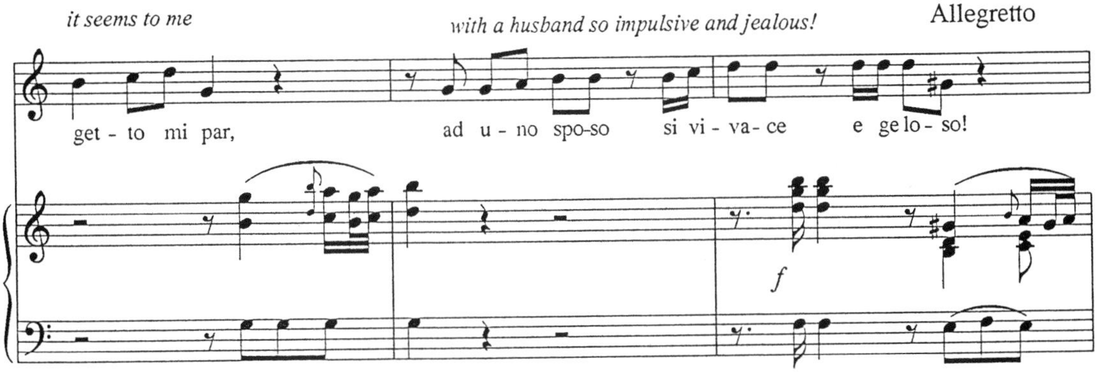

it seems to me
with a husband so impulsive and jealous!
Allegretto
get - to mi par,
ad u - no spo-so si vi - va - ce e ge lo - so!
f

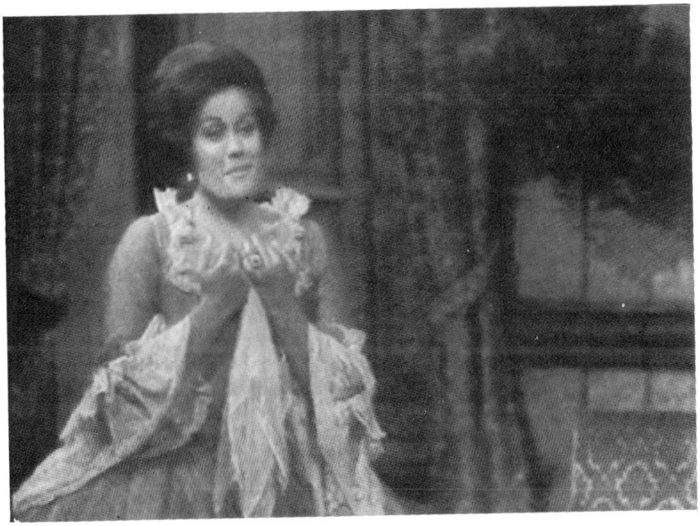

At bar 10 the tempo unexpectedly reverts to *Andante* as she considers that the plan is, after all, harmless. But her involvement in it is not really characteristic, as we can sense from the rather strange harmonic move in bar 12, where, instead of resolving the dominant 7th of bar 10, Mozart slides it down into the sub-dominant, D minor.

But what is the harm?
Andante
changing my clothes with those of Susanna,
Ma che mal c'è? Can-giando i miei ve-sti - ti, con quel-li di Su -
10
p

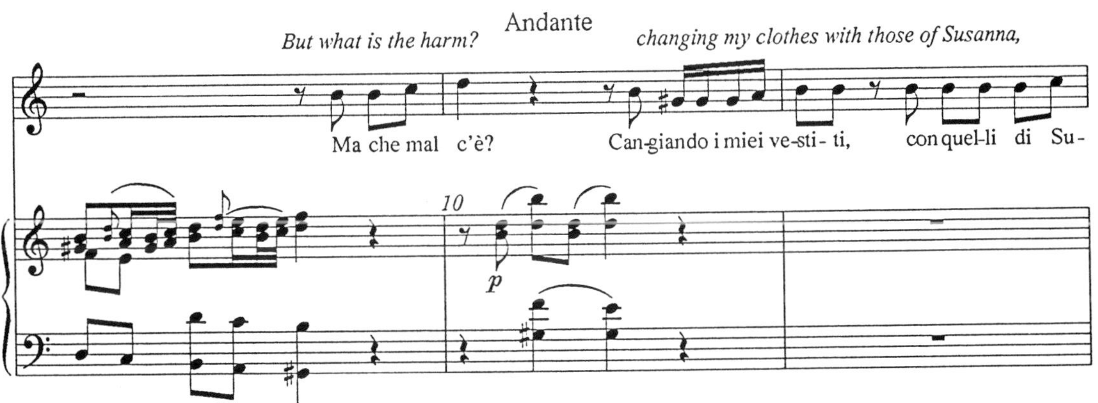

Bar 14 is very dramatic. As the abhorrence of the whole thing forcibly strikes her, both she and the orchestra enter on the beat for the first time in this movement, the vocal peak note having now risen to E. Any freedom of tempo earlier (and there will surely be some) must be gauged so as not to pre-empt the impact of the full crotchet entry on 'Oh', nor indeed the emotive dotted crotchet B flat, expressing her feeling of humiliation in the next bar. From here onwards there is an inexorable forward movement to the end: the tempo, generally, will be firmer and the singer's tone fuller.

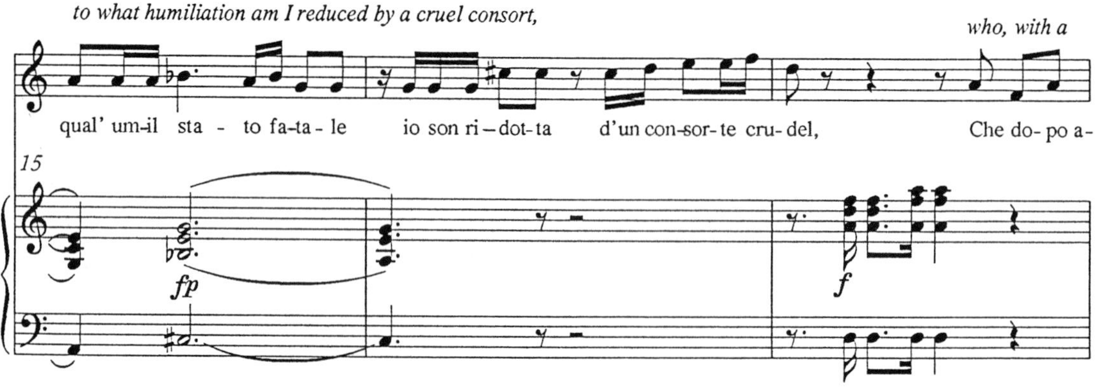

The immediate goal of the music from bar 12 onwards is the cadence in D minor in bar 17, strengthened by the reappearance of the dotted figure from bar 8. Because this cadence is still felt to be within the orbit of A minor, it is reached without any feeling of rest: nor should the singer's demeanour reflect anything but disquiet as she reflects on her husband's cruelty. When the music returns to the anguished A minor in bar 19, the off-beat dotted orchestral chords again call for a firm delineation of the first and third beats by the singer.

strange mixture of unfaithfulness,
of jealousy,
of
ver-mi con un mi - sto in-au- di - to d'in- fe –del - tà,
di ge- lo - si – a
di
disdain,
F
first loved,
then disdained and finally betrayed me,
sde- gni,
Pri - ma a – ma - ta,
in - di of – fe - sa,
e al fin tra-
20
p
f

The Countess rises to high eloquence as the peak notes rise to F and then later to the climactic A. Both these peak notes need to be sung tenuto and given their full notated durations, and indeed they stress important words (literally: first loved me; forces me now to seek help from my servant). In bars 21–2 Mozart keeps up a virtually uninterrupted quaver movement in singer or orchestra, and if that is preserved in performance the forward momentum to bar 24 will be the more effective.

The violins play a crucial role in the articulation of the climax. Beginning on a low A they soar up through two octaves, propelled forward by the last appearance of the dotted rhythm, like a tidal wave on the crest of which the singer's top A can ride. This latter looks forward to a note of the same pitch several minutes later in the concluding Allegro of the aria: the singer's most intense fortissimo will best be saved for that wonderful second appearance of the note.

At the very end, the singer's final B becomes, in both senses of the word, the leading note into the first note of the aria. Although she will probably begin the aria more quietly, the control of the quality of her tone throughout this last line will be concerned to lead as smoothly as possible into the new movement, as indeed will be the aim of her stage action. In the Glyndebourne performance, she is seen at the crucial moment moving slowly towards a chair on which she slowly sits at the very moment the aria starts, remaining in that position for the whole of the first section. Such a slow action suits the music well, though it should be said that there need not necessarily have been any action at this point. The musical move into the aria is so powerful that the singer could simply have remained still to cement the join.

A
now forces me to seek help from my servant!
di - ta,
fam - mi or cer- ca da u - na mia ser- va ai - ta!
25
f
fp
Andantino
Where are the happy moments of sweetness.....
Do - ve so - no i bei mo - men - ti di dol - cez - za e
Ob.
30
Str.
p
Bsn.

The unexpected change of harmony from the dominant of A into C points the formal division of the recitative into the aria, and it has the ultimate logic of being a return to the tonality of the point of departure at the start of the recitative; we can indeed feel we have come home. The sitting position of the

Glyndebourne video is good in that it is expressive of the great intimacy of these memories, and of the deep emotion of the music through which the Countess now confides them. It also enables her to make a good dramatic point of standing to give extra intensity to the aria's concluding *Allegro*, in which her thoughts turn outwards again to express the hope that her constancy will bring about a change of heart in her husband.

Example 1.6
Accompanied Recitative 'Hai già vinta' from Act III of *The Marriage of Figaro*

The Count's anger and tenacity of purpose are depicted in a recitative whose emotional range is greatly enhanced by a notable use of the orchestra, not only in an accompanying role, but also for what are, in effect, ritornelli. The orchestration too is important, particularly in the use of the oboes.

The extract begins with the last line of the preceding secco recitative. The Count is shown standing near the front of the stage overhearing Susanna telling Figaro that they have won their case, and it is his reaction to this which is now explored by his recitative and aria. As he watches the two of them going off he picks up Susanna's phrase and Mozart gives him the identical music. It is important that whatever the exigencies of pace the two phrases should be sung so as to make the musical point clear. That the Count is a completely different personality from the Countess of the previous example is at once evident from the way the orchestra crashes in with dotted rhythms in the very first bar, a strident gesture giving an edge to his character right from the outset of the *Maestoso*.

He turns to register gesturally the emotion implied by the potent augmented sixth beneath his crotchet C (literally, into what trap have I fallen?). The first two phrases of the line could perhaps be softer, as if he hasn't quite taken in the situation, but this third one must have the full force of his exasperation.

In an astonishing outburst of rage (literally Traitors! I intend, I intend so to punish them . . . !) Mozart's music in bar 5 makes a brusque jump from C to the dominant of A. Harshly scored with unison oboes, this is as ungracious an orchestral sound as was possible in his vocabulary. The singer will recognise the extreme force of the gesture and react accordingly: he turns again sharply in a display of temper.

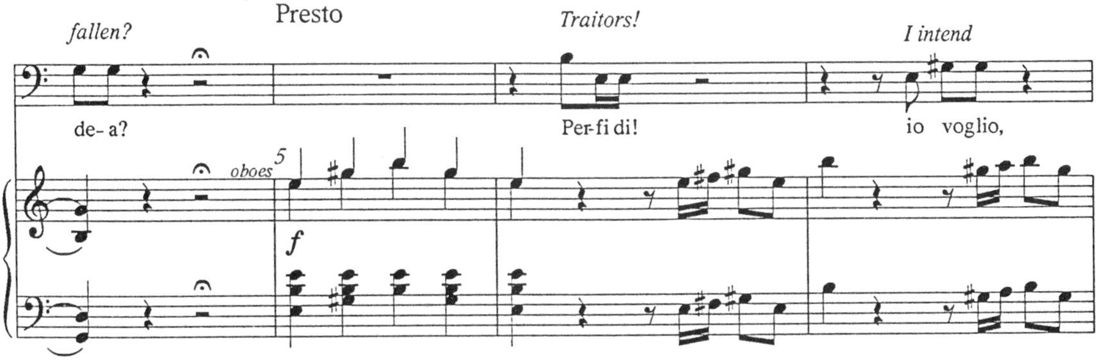

fallen? Presto *Traitors!* *I intend*

de- a? Per-fi di! io voglio,

oboes 5 *f*

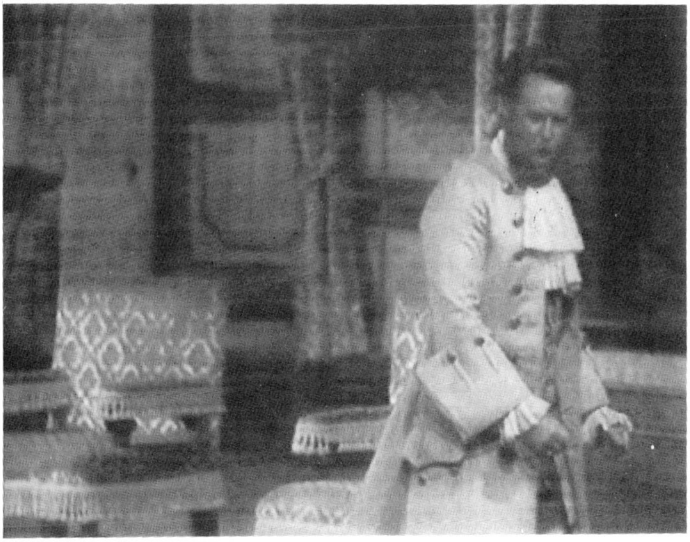

Mozart keeps up the pressure with another unexpected modulation in the orchestra, this time to F sharp minor, an extreme distance from the C major of only five bars back, indicating that he is delineating an anger that is almost out of control. On the video film the Count expresses this gesturally by turning back sharply again, as if he does not know which way to turn.

The orchestra completes the section with the stentorian double dotted chords in bars 12–14, which would seem to call for a stiff aggressive stance from the singer. Now comes a complete change; he calms down as he reflects that the hated Figaro must also be having his difficulties, and the tonality relaxes into D, which is to be the key of the aria to come – his 'home' key. The modulation has an Andante tempo, and is made memorable by a quite different use of the oboes, in mellifluous falling thirds, intensified for a moment with the suspension in bar 16. The singer will hear this and take its character into himself; it is one of those many little touches which make the Count, for all his faults, such a compellingly attractive person. Here in the Glyndebourne production he turns to move much more gently back across the stage, his hand lightly placed on a chair as he turns thoughtfully.

Tempo I
the old woman's claims?
paid her!
gas-se la vecchia preten - den- te?
pa- gar la!
p

in what way?
And then there's Antonio,
in qual ma-nie-ra?
E poiv'èAn to- ni o che'all in-
20
f

who, to an unknown Figaro, will not give his niece in marriage.

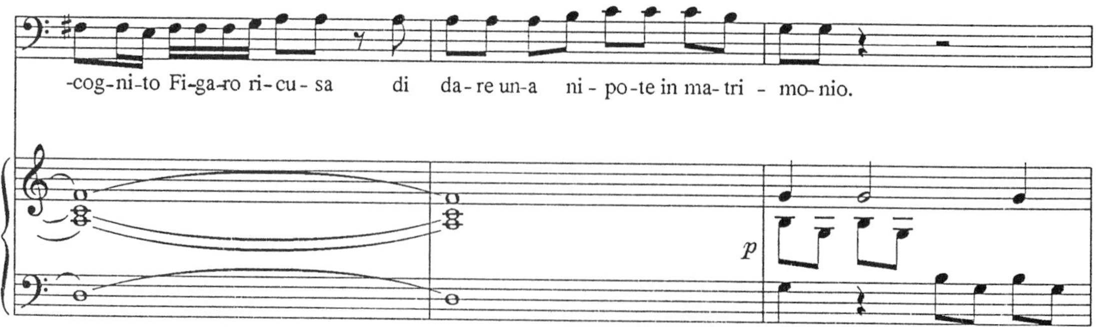
-cog-ni-to Fi-ga-ro ri-cu - sa di da-re un-a ni - po-te in ma-tri - mo-nio.
p

Having reached D, the music approaches the aria via a conventional move into the sub-dominant. What is less conventional is that the main musical interest of this latter part of the movement lies in the orchestral interludes which join up the (in themselves) uninteresting vocal phrases. Thus it is the orchestra which gives the singer the main clues for movement and stances. In particular, because these phrases are all rising, the energy of the character is sustained. Was this perhaps Mozart's brilliant solution to a problem posed by his librettist in not giving him as many words as the weighting of the movement seemed to demand? The Count uses the interludes to move forwards to a more commanding position at the front of the stage ready for the aria.

I will play on that idiot's pride
Col-ti-van-do l'or-go-glio di ques-to mente-
25
p
f
-cat-to.
30
p
cresc
f

All is in my favour.

tut - to gio - va'un rag - gi - ro,

p sf p sf

the die is cast.

il col - po è fat - to.

p cresc. f

The joining of the recitative into the aria is a miracle of characterisation achieved by manipulating one of the traditional recitative conventions. The impetuosity of the Count's character is crystallised in the foreshortening of the usual cadence, so that the final chord is elided with the first chord of the aria. The new orchestral gesture of the opening ritornello is a powerful expression of the man's headlong rage.

At first the singer's entry after the 4-bar orchestral phrase, is in a more lyrical vein – such contrasts were a regular feature of symphonic music in the 1780s. Yet he must feel the cascading orchestral figure as his own and can indeed make it so by a crescendo on the rising scale to the first note of its second statement in bar 48. However he never actually sings it, and indeed couldn't do so on account of its idiomatic instrumental nature: a fine example of an orchestral extension of characterisation. However, even at this quieter moment, his rage is boiling up within him, as can be felt from the impatient foreshortening of the phrase so that it wells up to the return of the orchestral theme in an asymmetric three bars. Singer and audience will feel the very pulse of the man in this impetuous musical gesture. The clenched fist of the video still is an appropriate gesture for the end of the phrase.

Such very human characterisation is the result of the skill of Mozart rather than of Da Ponte, whose words here do not rise above the level of a conventional opera seria rage aria, a convention which Mozart followed more closely in the vocal roulades at the end of the movement; see (*g*) below. That is the climax towards which the singer's interpretation must lead, and some suitable action such as a move nearer to the front of the stage, would be planned to coincide with it.

The range of emotion covered by this aria is even greater than that of the preceding recitative, as the mere listing of the main themes (*a*) to (*h*) helps to show. Clearly, from the sheer diversity of material, the Count is a complex character whose thoughts move quickly from one thing to another; yet his is no butterfly mind. Mozart's symphonic skills enabled him to handle such diverse material with a certainty of purpose which tells us that the Count is a man of enormous determination. Even when his music goes into the minor (*a*) it is not just for a pathetic effect but in order to move with greater certainty to the dominant chord which is the structural root of the passage. Similarly, despite their falling initial figurations, the themes (*c*), based on a diminished 7th chord, and (*e*), on a dominant seventh both lead to assertive cadence figures with two aggressively rising crotchets. At (*f*) he petulently breaks out of the more controlled energy of the rising chromatic scale, to lurch upwards into a majestic cadential figure. A fuller analysis would show how it is that by the time the final clinching of the home key is reached, with its climactic top F sharp (*h*), the Count's purpose seems unassailable. There is a controlled diversity in the way these themes function in the musical structure. The reiteration of the dominant in the passage surrounding (*a*) and the shorter phrase lengths, create a tension out of which the noble line of (*b*) has the greater sense of fulfilment. After this (*c*), accompanied by the orchestra in unison only, has the character of a bridge passage whose thinning of texture makes the coming *Allegro assai* all the more powerful. In such ways the music charts the ebb and flow of a very human anger.

Themes from Vedrò Mentr'io

(a)
60
...who does not return my passion;

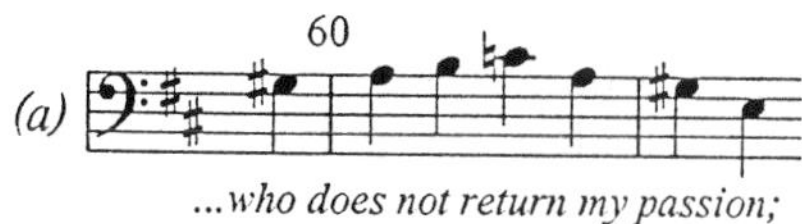

(b)
66
must I see my servant happy while I lament,

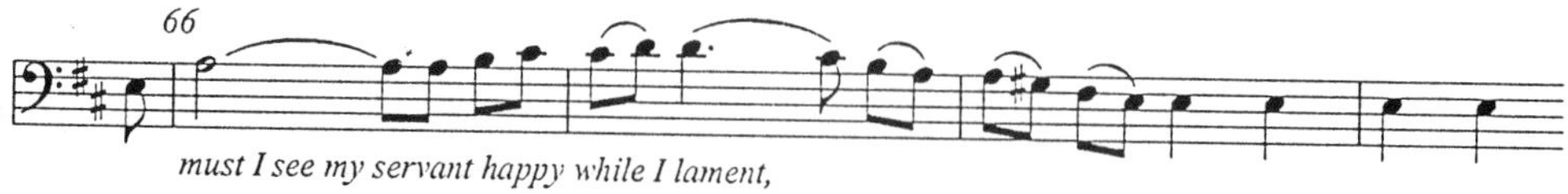

(c)
74
must I see my love united to a contemptible servant?

(d)
Allegro assai
89
Ah no, I will not allow it!

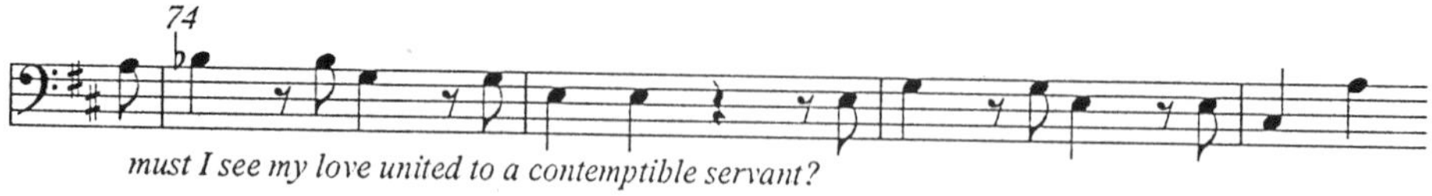

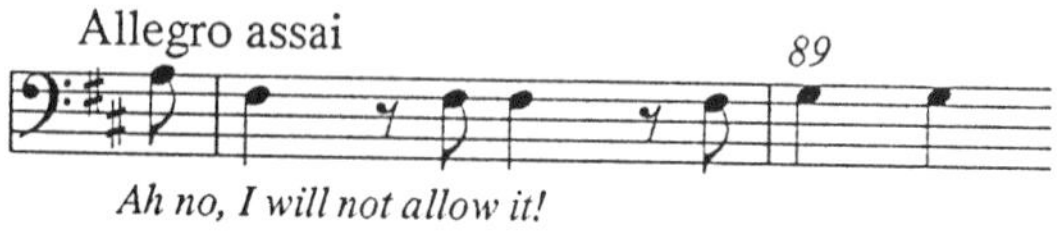

(e)
95
You were not born, impudent man....

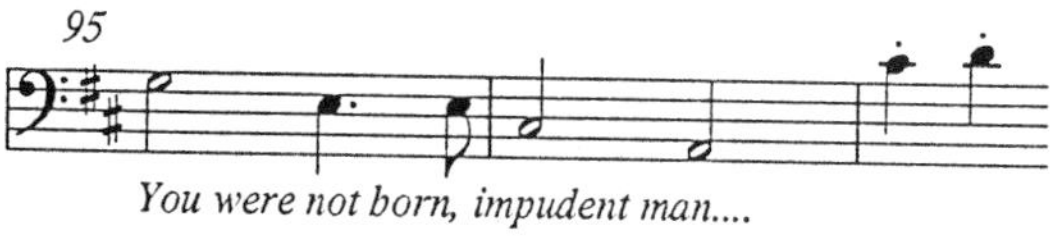

(f)
100
...to cause me torment, and to laugh at my unhappiness.

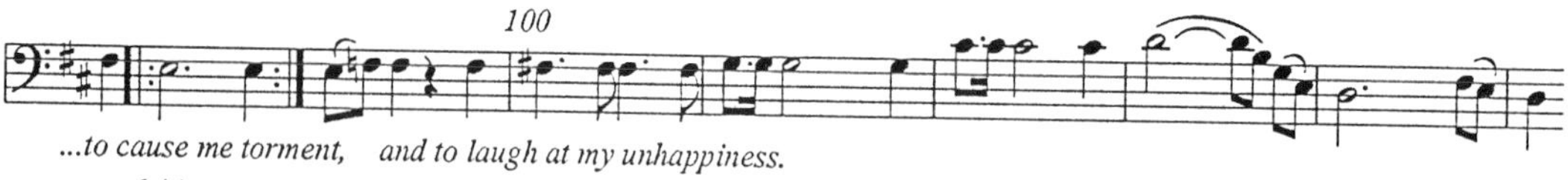

(g)
144
3
3
tr
(hope of vengeance makes me rejoice)

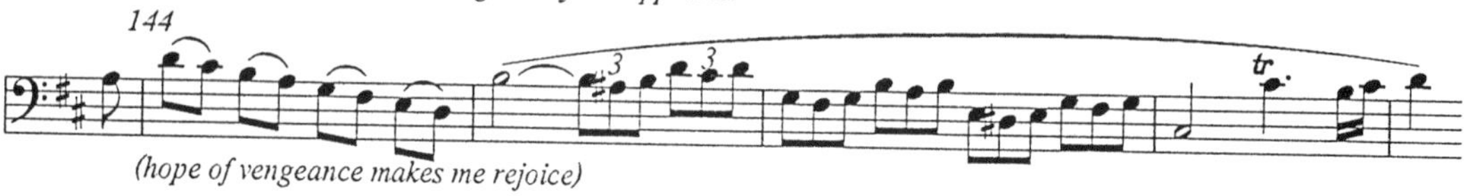

(h)
151

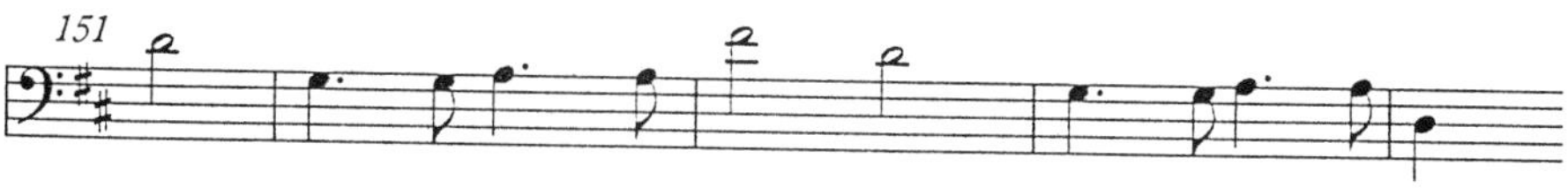

Notes

1 A famous instance is Joseph Addison's writings in the Spectator 1711–12. His amusingly sarcastic review of a production of Handel's *Rinaldo* in 1711 is reprinted in Strunk (1950) pp. 511–17.
2 Grout (1988) p. 215.
3 Dean (1977) p. 389, quotes P.F. Tosi (1723), Telemann (1733) and C.P.E. Bach (1762) to this effect.

4 Mozart prized flexibility sufficiently highly to consent, reluctantly, to shorten two scenes in his opera seria *Idomeneo* because the two singers concerned 'spoil the recitative by singing it . . . so monotonously'. See the letter to his father of 27th December 1780 in Anderson (1938).
5 See Burney (1796), i. 192, quoted in Robinson (1966) p. 111.
6 I feel it is not necessary to go further into the Doctrine of the Affections. Perhaps the best short discussion of the subject is still that in Bukofzer (1947) pp. 388–90, its fullest exposition in Mattheson (1739). Briefly, the aria would be based on a musical figure which signified the emotion being expressed.
7 Eighteenth-century opera house acoustics are discussed in Forsyth (1985). This has illustrations showing orchestra pits in theatres at Turin (p. 81) and Stuttgart (p. 92). Dean 1969 plate 4 reproduces the elevation and plan of the King's Theatre Haymarket, where *Giulio Cesare* was first performed in 1724.
8 Examples of such ornamentation were provided by Handel himself: see Dean (1976). Two important treatises on the subject by P.F. Tosi (1723) and J.A. Hiller (1780), are discussed in section 2(iv) of the article on 'Improvisation' in Sadie (1980). See also Donington (1973).
9 In a later opera tradition the orchestral music can follow a character offstage to a known destination e.g. her death; this will be explored in a later chapter.
10 Metastasio was referring to a production of his *Demofoonte*, the music on this occasion by Hasse, in Dresden in 1748. See Zaslaw (1989).
11 See Drummond (1980) chapter 5, particularly pp. 144–6, for an account of the social background of opera seria.
12 The acting style in Handel's day would have been similar to that of spoken tragedy, the subject of a series of articles: Barnett (1977) ff.
13 See Dean (1977) for a scholarly discussion of this. The delayed cadence is found in the church music of the time, e.g. in Bach, but not in opera, unless the composer specifically prescribes it by placing a rest before the dominant chord.
14 Unfortunately this particular point is not illustrated on the ENO video because Ptolemy's speech is cut. This involves some rewriting of Handel with a sudden modulation to C sharp minor in bar 15 which, although competently done, rather spoils Handel's more gradually sharpening tonal plan.
15 A description and history of opera buffa are given in Grout (1988) chapter 15.
16 Rosen (1971), gives an account of the absorption of the multifarious elements of the symphony into opera, making the point that Mozart's originality lay not in his use of the style, which was in common currency by the 1770s, but in his comprehending its dramatic potential. See also Einstein (1946), pp. 415–9, for an ingenious suggestion as to how, historically, Mozart came to that comprehension through seeing, in 1784, an opera by Paisiello with a lively libretto by Casti.
17 See J. Higgins (1978) pp. 182–3, where John Pritchard enlarges on the problem from the orchestra's point of view.
18 This was the Staatsoper in Dresden. See Forsyth (1985) p. 95.
19 This was done by John Pritchard in the Glyndebourne performance from which these video examples were taken.

Peter Grimes (Jon Vickers) is seen telling Captain Balstrode (Jonathan Summers) about the death of his first boy apprentice. The stage has darkened and Grimes' words are punctuated by orchestral music depicting the approaching storm, whose mood matches his own grim narration. Immediately before the moment here depicted, at the beginning of the monologue, there was a sudden resurgence of the orchestral storm during which, in a corresponding surge of his own emotion, Grimes has walked impetuously over to Balstrode for the words 'Picture what that day was like . . . ' (See p. 77). *Photograph Zoe Dominic*

2 The Solo Voice in the Operas of Other Composers

I Monteverdi's *L'Orfeo*

This first great opera, produced in the Mantuan court in 1607,[1] has proved to be eminently worthy of modern performance despite its very early position in the history of opera. Although, as a sign of its prestigious court première, an unusually detailed printed score of the music was published in 1609, there are still many questions unanswered as to how the piece should be performed; what voices and instruments are to be used, what style of continuo realisation and what vocal ornamentation. In addition there is uncertainty about the staging, the entrances and exits etc. Changing opinions on these matters in the years since Vincent d'Indy's pioneering performing edition of the score in 1904 make a fascinating historical study in themselves, and the controversy is still very much alive.[2] What follows here attempts not so much to address these questions as to look at the music in the light of some of the ideas of the previous chapter and to make some observations which it is hoped will be equally helpful to the understanding of those approaching the work from different standpoints on authenticity.

Monteverdi is often seen as a forward looking composer, the 'Creator of Modern Music',[3] and *L'Orfeo* can indeed be seen as standing at the beginning of a long line of operatic development. Yet to understand the work it must be realised that hardly any element was, in itself, new. There had been a long line of dramatisations of the Orpheus story, invariably using music, going back as far as Poliziano's play *La Favola di Orfeo* of 1480,[4] at least half of which was set to music, though that music is now lost. Striggio's libretto owed much to Poliziano, and much of Monteverdi's music, the choruses, instrumental ritornelli, and even the duets and 'arias', was in the tradition of the music used in the intermedi and pastoral plays stretching back into the sixteenth century: consequently it is to the sources of the past rather than to the future that one should look for clues as to its meaning and interpretation.[5] Certainly the real innovation of *L'Orfeo* was the way in which Monteverdi used and structured the traditional forms so as to give the work a quite new dramatic integrity and power.

There was, however, one comparatively new technique, the recitative style developed from the theories of the Florentine Camerata, and it was this that enabled the dialogue, which could previously only have been spoken, now to be sung and integrated into a fully musical structure. In those early days the recitative was a more flexible form than it became later. It could vary, often in a moment, from what in Handelian terms would almost be secco recitative to passages of aria-like lyrical intensity. Indeed, since the music was structured on a detailed following of the individual words of the libretto, the lyrical level of the music could change from word to word, a concept possibly borrowed from the word painting of the madrigal. As a consequence of this the recitative could be emotionally even more volatile than the later accompanied recitative, where, as we have seen, the contrasts tend to be in longer units from section to section.

One of the ways Monteverdi can 'paint' his words is to give the singer notes which are dissonant with the instrumental bass line; another is to employ ornamentation, though often he is content to set up a framework by elongating important syllables and to leave the singer free to choose whether to add ornamental notes or simply to apply special vocal intensity and colour to the longer notes. He also uses another madrigalian device, syncopation, to stress emotive words, and there are times when the combination of dissonance, syncopation and ornamentation is so acute as almost to give a feeling of the dislocation of the voice from the generally simple continuo accompaniment. The technique has interesting parallels in some twentieth-century opera and it can lead to a certain similarity of characterisation too, though Orfeo's whims and sudden outbursts of passion are perhaps less suggestive of schizophrenia than is the febrile eccentricity of the Doctor in *Wozzeck*. In both cases the apparent dislocation is really no more than a strong rhythmic tension between singer and accompaniment, and it is important in such places that the performers preserve the tactus so that the syncopations are recognisable as such and come to a proper rhythmic resolution (particularly in the case of *Orfeo*) at the following cadence. In other places in *Orfeo* the recitative can be sung more freely, following the feeling of the words and achieving what the contemporary monody composer Caccini referred to as the 'nobile sprezzatura di canto'.[6] Joseph Kerman states the Monteverdian recitative principle very forcefully:

> Music . . . should imitate the accents of passionate speech as best represented by the grand, exaggerated rhetoric of a great actor. Music should follow the cadences and thus the moving implications of the individual word with little heed to the phrase, the sentence or even the total feeling.[7]

Although there is truth in this I believe it overstates its case in suggesting that phrase, sentence and overall feeling can go unheeded, and good recent performances have shown that singers can indeed embrace these dimensions to some extent. The main thing is for the singer to remember to be a musician as well as an actor and to be sensitive to how Monteverdi points the phrasing by crafting together the words and music. An important word may be stressed by being set to a melodic peak note or a syncopated rhythm, or by being ornamented, and the whole phrase can be shaped around it to make both dramatic and musical sense. As for sentences, Monteverdi often relates peak notes of adjacent phrases, or arranges for a new phrase to start on the same note as the previous cadence, so that the singer can relate phrases across the breathing gaps to make bigger entities.

There are larger structures too, like the five verses of La Musica's prologue, held together by repetitions of the framing instrumental ritornello, and, above all, the great aria 'Possente spirto', in Act III, where, exceptionally, Monteverdi suggests all the ornamentation himself. This latter demonstration of Orfeo's musical powers is the very centre of the opera towards which the previous acts have been leading, and although the techniques of elongation and syncopation are similar to those of other music in the opera, the sheer length of the section (partly brought about by the slower word setting), the greater elaboration of the ornamentation and the exceptional employment of instruments to accompany the singer, make its climactic role quite clear. The performers must realise this and scale the previous acts accordingly: to that extent, at least, the total feeling of the opera is, or can be, controlled.

The role of the beautifully placed ritornelli and sinfonie, and how the singers on stage should relate to them is obvious in some cases and a matter for debate in others. When a ritornello is clearly associated with a character, as with La Musica in the prologue, she can surely treat it just like an opera seria aria ritornello and react to it as if it expressed her innermost thoughts.[8] In the preface to *La Dafne*, a court opera produced in Mantua the year after *Orfeo*, the composer Gagliano describes how his own, similarly structured prologue is to be interpreted by the singer:

> At the end of the first verse he must pause for breath, taking a few steps according to the length of the ritornello, and always keeping time with the music. He must start to walk on the penultimate syllable, which must be held slightly, and after the ritornello he must start singing again from his new position. In this way the verses are joined together and display a certain quality of ease and grace.[9]

Of course, a smoother continuity is achieved if the recitative is sung in the same tempo as the ritornello: in addition, the final chord of a cadence can sometimes be shortened so as to lead more immediately into the start of the next section when, as is often the case, they make their joins on the same chord.

To put the last point more generally, a short term harmonic correspondence is invariably a sign that Monteverdi intends a dramatic relationship. By the same token the absence of such a correspondence can be equally significant. Indeed, the high points of the drama are articulated by the arresting harmonic juxtapositions which can be found between consecutive phrases sung by different characters, as in Orfeo's dialogue with the Messenger in Act II, or within a monologue, in the Messenger's subsequent narrative, or between sinfonia and recitative, (see below), and a good performance will give due dramatic weight to such moments of discontinuity.

The tonality of the ritornelli and sinfonie is always worth considering, alongside other factors, in the staging of the opera. For instance the three appearances of the majestic 7-part sinfonia (in G) at the beginning, middle and end of Act III, where the scene has changed to the Underworld, suggest that the ritornello is to be associated with that place. The fact that it is in no sense supporting Orfeo is made quite clear by the composer when Orfeo's first recitative, immediately following the first playing, begins in a different key and on a quite different chord (C minor). The dramatic implication of this could well be that his stage entry is best delayed until near the end of the sinfonia, and that if there is a significant overlap he may need to make it clear (perhaps by looking around him), that the music of the sinfonia represents what he sees rather than what he feels. On the other hand both the Chorus of Spirits and Proserpina, who sing immediately after the two other playings can, as inhabitants of the Underworld, regard the music as theirs, an interpretation confirmed by the fact that they each begin singing over a chord of G.

Example 2.1
Dialogue and Narration from *L'Orfeo*, Act II

The Messenger has arrived at the scene of rejoicing over the marriage of Orfeo and Eurydice and, so far, only disclosed the generally sad nature of her news. At the beginning of the extract she is addressing a shepherd when Orfeo, who has overheard their conversation, breaks in. The first phrase, then, being at the end of a section of dialogue, is very suitable to be ornamented at its cadence. As, in answer to his questions, she painfully reveals that his wife is dead, the tension between them is powerfully expressed in the music by her key being much sharper than his. In Philip Pickett's suggested staging she has conducted her previous conversation from an off-stage left position and now enters to address Orfeo.[10] On the Harnoncourt video film (and in our first sketch) she is still right at the back of the stage, on a higher level than Orfeo and the shepherds. The sudden key change, together with the use of syncopated notes in all three of his little phrases (arrowed in the example), suggest his rather brusque impatience with her. A slight accent on these and a brisker tempo will make this clear.

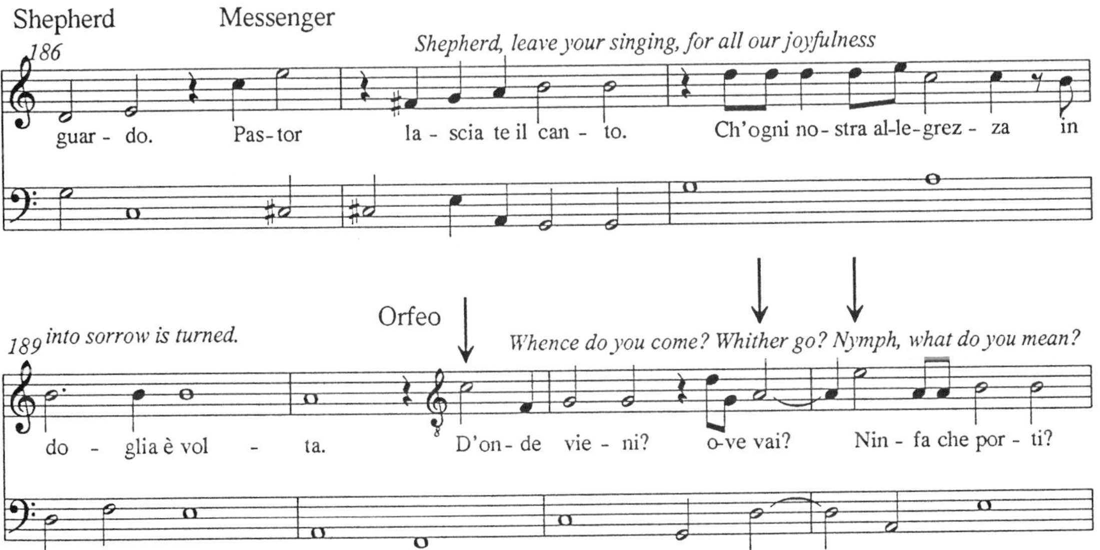

In her reply the syncopated third syllable of the second 'infelice', and even more the aching dissonance on 'bella' will convey great poignancy and suggest a slower tempo. On the video she walks slowly down the steps to a position near to Orfeo, so as to convey her sad tidings with more intimacy. Such a movement seems right and natural despite Gagliano's general injunction to the singer not to move while singing.[11]

There is now an extraordinary harmonic change from this E major to the G minor of Orfeo's reply (the same change will be echoed twice more in the following narrative). There are two interestingly different ways of interpreting it on the currently available CD recordings of the opera. Philip Pickett puts a silence between them, thus highlighting the emotion of Orfeo's response and reinforcing the impact of the change of scoring from organ and lute to harpsichord, cello and lute – this is preserving the scoring given by Monteverdi to the respective characters earlier. John Eliot Gardiner, on the other hand, crashes in immediately with the new chord as if to suggest that Orfeo hasn't yet lost his earlier feeling of impatience. The effect of this is more violent (yet not impossible for Monteverdi on that account) but it also has the effect of keeping up the pace so that later pauses, one of them legislated, have the greater effect. The Messenger continues her sad discourse with much the same music as before, and the same poignant C sharp. On the video she turns away for this phrase as if unable to face him with her news. Again there is a continuity in the instrumental bass line over which a tiny roulade on harpsichord or lute could perhaps prepare us for Orfeo's dispirited reply. And now (bar 201) Monteverdi himself stipulates a silence which, if the performers have put one or more in earlier, must surely be longer than previously.

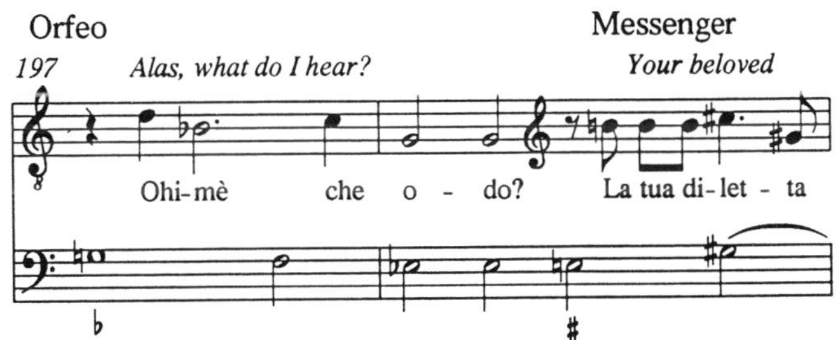

The Messenger now explains to Orfeo the circumstances of Euridice's death. At the start the simplistic lines with much note repetition suggest that some freedom of tempo is expected, a quickening of pace, perhaps, and a more parlando quality of voice. However there are some musical matters which the singer should bear in mind, firstly that the quickening should not obscure Monteverdi's own acceleration of the pace later: in other words the quavers in this passage should definitely be slower than the later notated semiquavers. Nor should the tempo be so free as to lose the force of the syncopations, 'Giva' (walking) in bar 204, and 'angue' (snake) in bar 207, words that he wished to stress in such a way as to spring the music forwards.

The messenger will surely move forwards now to dominate the stage. In the video film she sees on the ground the rope which, in Act I, had been used to tie the lover's knot at the wedding ceremony. She holds it up ironically to represent the snake in her narrative, a moment captured in the sketch, and drops it dramatically for the first reappearance of the E – G minor harmonic change as the account turns to Euridice dying. The dynamic might well change from *forte* to *piano* across this divide. Meanwhile, the music has been rising gradually over a fairly long span: from F in bar 201 to A (bar 204), C (bar 207) and to the first melodic climax on the D of 'punse', (pierced) in bar 208. Later, not included in the extract, there is an even higher rise to the E for 'Orfeo' as she recalls how Euridice called out his name. The music must be felt to move forwards to these climactic points.

The rather unusual chromaticism on 'piè' (foot) in bar 209 is a correct copying from the original editions as transcribed in Bartlett (1993), on which the musical extracts here are based. Some editors, including Malipiero and Stevens, have evidently felt this to be an uncorrected printer's error and have added a sharp to the first G. Although it may seem somewhat wayward to emphasise this particular word there is a case for keeping to the original. The extra splash of emotion which the chromaticism gives to the phrase is certainly consistent with the Messenger's almost uncontrollable emotions as she recounts the sad story.

The very emotional A flat on the last syllable of 'scolorirsi' (draining), suggesting F minor, even flatter than the earlier G minor, needs to make its due point. The steady fall of the line binds these phrases together and suggests the fading life of Euridice.

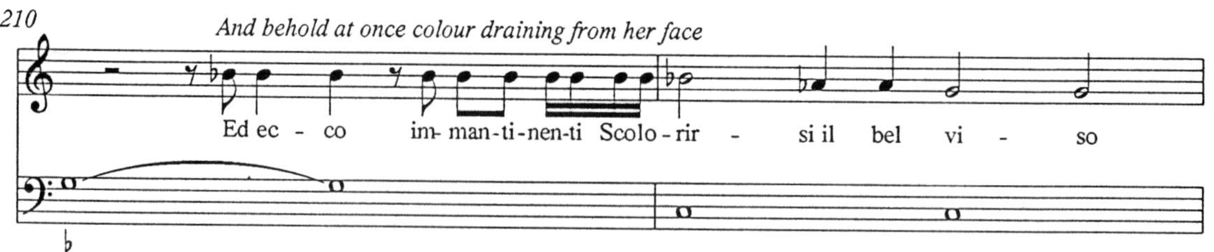

Example 2.2
The Messenger's Lament from *L'Orfeo*, Act II

The messenger, having discharged her sad task of telling Orfeo of his wife's death, sings a lament before leaving the scene. The opening monotonal line cannot, I think, be lightened like the opening of the earlier narrative but is part of a musical phrase which intensifies with the notated quickening rhythm, suddenly to jump to the agonising dissonant B on 'coltello', (blade). The next emotive dissonant note, the D on 'svenate', (bled) is, as so often in Monteverdi, further stressed by syncopation. In short, the passage needs to be sung in virtually strict tempo and, I believe, in full voice.

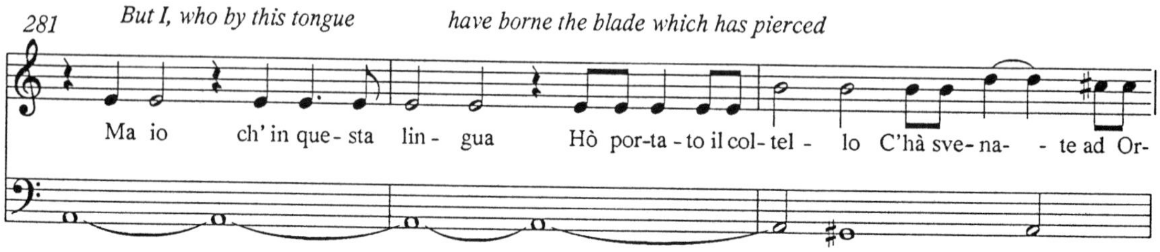

The cadential 'amante', (loving), calls for ornamentation. The unprepared dissonance on the D 'odiosa', (hateful) is a strong one, and then the line suddenly drops to its cadence (it goes down even further in the next phrase) as if she hardly has the courage to continue. At the suggestion of her words here the chorus on the video film withdraw to the sides, leaving her alone in the middle of the stage.

I prefer the second and lower cadence on 'ascondo' (hide), to be unornamented since both the word and the pitch suggest something unostentatious. Then the change of harmony articulates a break to a new musical paragraph. The new phrase is made potent by the syncopation on 'sole', (sun), and the appoggiatura on 'fuggiro', (flee). Then the line drops for the start of a final piece of inspired rhetoric, an inexorable rise to the final word with harsh dissonances against an almost equally inexorable falling bass part. Monteverdi's ability to rise above the monody conventions of his day is evident here. The phrase is very effective if sung with an intense and sustained *piano*.

293 *will lead a life conforming to my sorrow.*

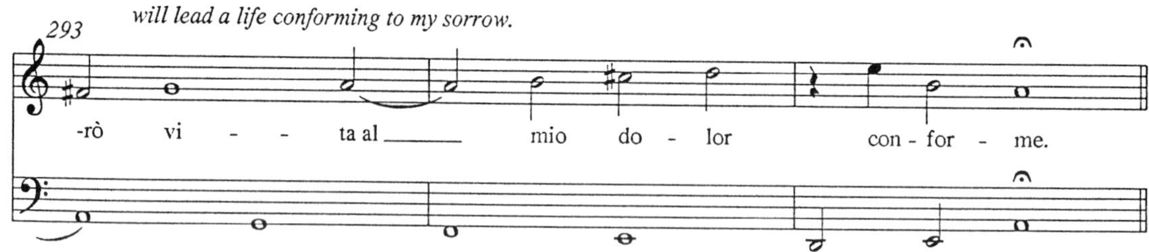

The linear contrary motion of treble and bass in the sinfonia (particularly in the second half where the treble rises and the bass falls) continues and enlarges on the musical substance of the messenger's memorable last line. That is an argument for her feeling the ritornello to be an extension of her aria, and to express her own feelings as she walks slowly off. On the video she goes gravely up the stairs to exit at the back. However, the change of key indicates we are moving on to the next scene (a lament of the shepherds), and on that evidence Monteverdi seems to be suggesting that the music is really theirs, that is to say if they had gone off, as in this production, they could come back in this music as the messenger leaves.

296 Sinfonia

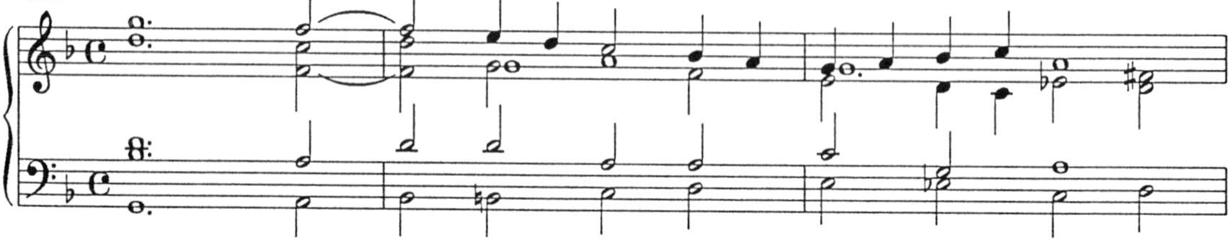

299

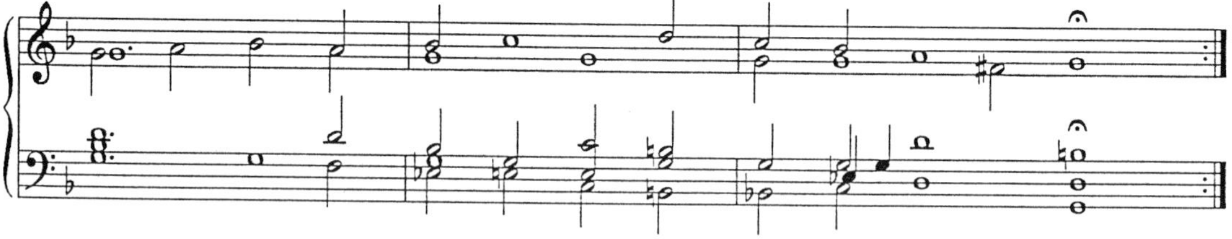

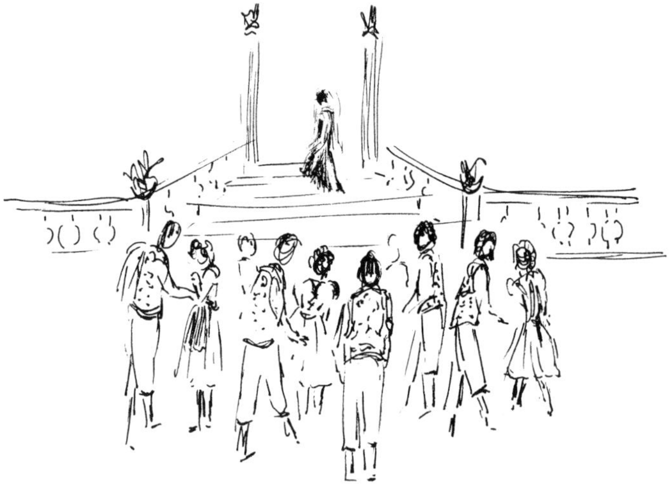

II *L'Incoronazione di Poppea*

The extraordinary change of style between *L'Orfeo* (1607) and *L'Incoronazione di Poppea* (1643) can be attributed in part to the very different social circumstances for which the two works were composed, a fact that performers should bear in mind in deciding on their style of presentation. *Orfeo*, a court opera, appropriately used an elevated myth, whereas *Poppea*, based on an historical subject, had all the realism of character portrayal that would have been enjoyed by the audience in a public opera house: the ambition, anger, lust and hatred of the main protagonists is set off against the humour of some minor characters and the stoic calm of the philosopher Seneca. The projection of this rich and very human characterisation falls almost exclusively to the singers, for the instrumental music, accompaniments and ritornelli, have a very minor role indeed.

The singer who has been looking at *Orfeo* will notice at once the more overtly declamatory nature of the vocal line here. Even when the work seems to revert to long passages of word-centred monody, there is now a more urgent passion, and beauty of phrase will more often be sacrificed to dramatic projection, as for instance in the short separated phrases of Ottavia's Act I monologue which suggest her as almost choking with emotion (her husband has deserted her for Poppea). There can, of course, be some freedom of tempo in such passages, though not to an unnecessary degree because, as in *Orfeo*, Monteverdi does actually write into the score the essential variations of pace and articulating pauses. In general these recitatives can best be sung a little quicker than those of the more staid *Orfeo*, but always so that the words are clearly projected. This should present no problems for the singer because throughout the opera the voice should be accompanied only by the continuo instruments – beguiling as some modern orchestral realisations of the score may sound.[12]

If the freedom of tempo disrupts phrasing and continuity, there is a measure of compensation from time to time in the crystallising out of little 'aria' sections, calling for a more lyrical style and almost certainly to be sung in tempo. In contrast to the prevailing duple time of the recitatives these are mostly in a lilting triple time. They are generally of short duration and seem to reach forward to ultimate fulfilment in the longer closing duet of Act III, where the power of love is finally vindicated. This splendid movement is extended and integrated by being set over a chaconne bass in triple time and even if, as now seems certain, Monteverdi did not himself compose it,[13] he must surely have planned the whole opera with some such lyrical climax in mind.

The balance between recitative and aria in this opera is a balance of equals, for the time had not yet come when the aria was to 'swamp the aesthetics of opera production'. A recitative didn't necessarily lead forwards into an aria as in later opera, but was focussed around its own important words which might or might not come at the end. The form of the aria too would often focus on its important words, wherever they happened to come. It is fascinating to see how Monteverdi rings the changes in his handling of the relationship between the two types of music. One particularly imaginative instance comes in Ottavia's Act I monologue, where the aria is used ironically for the moment when she imagines her husband Nero happy in Poppea's arms, and her tone here must surely reflect her real repugnance. The change back from aria to recitative can be equally dramatic, as when in Act I, Scene 10 Poppea suddenly turns from love-making with Nero (in a seductive 3-time arietta) to a grim recitative in which she urges him to dispose of Seneca, who stands in the way of her ambition to be queen. It is a moment when her character is revealed in its true colours.

The orchestral ritornelli are less important than those of *Orfeo*, lacking both the structural force (e.g. the symmetrical placings) and the more interesting and significant variations of orchestral colour of the earlier opera. The fact that almost all of them are in 3-time, often leading out from or into a 3-time aria, suggests that they are supporting the singer and, for the most part are to be regarded as extensions of the vocal arias, especially so when the harmonies coincide at the joins. It is worth looking at the incidence of the longer arias and ritornelli to see where the lyrical weight of the opera as a whole is to be found. Act III, as we have seen, leads to a lyrical climax at the end, thereby inaugurating a long history of final duets up to *Aida* and beyond. Act II, similarly, climaxes at the end with the appearances of Love (with five ritornelli) to protect Poppea from being murdered. The shape of Act I is rather different. Its climax comes in Scene 11, some three-quarters of the way through, when Ottone's unsuccessful attempts to win back Poppea's love are interspersed with no less than six ritornelli. Later, in the closing scene, his approaches to Drusilla seem less convincing, partly because they are not similarly supported by ritornelli. All this paves the way for the splendid coup de théâtre with which the Act ends, when despite what he has said to Drusilla, he admits that it is really Poppea whom he loves: and so the lyrical climax of Scene 11 is vindicated in retrospect.

Example 2.3
From *L'Incoronazione di Poppea*, Act I, Scene 11

This short example was chosen because it raises interesting points concerning the function of a ritornello and the use of rubato (very little of which is in fact needed). Ottone, Poppea's husband, is trying to win back her love, unsuccessfully because her heart is now set on Nero and on sharing his throne. The passage is the climax of their confrontation, the ritornello being the last of the six in the scene. After it there is no more 3-time music and the ensuing recitative can best be sung in a freer, more declamatory way.

In the Decca video film of the opera, the ritornello music is interpreted as referring to Poppea who is at her toilette, assisted by her nurse. This is right for several reasons; dramatically because its lilting rhythms can be nicely matched by Poppea's seductive movements on her couch, and musically because the tonality always leads into her music so as to confirm the identity. Alan Curtis in his generally admirable edition changes the first chord of this ritornello so as to lead more smoothly from Ottone's preceding phrase, but in so doing arguably misses the dramatic point, that the music doesn't refer to him, except perhaps when he is actually singing of her charms.

Ottone
Is the tomb of my dead hopes.
Di mie mor-te spe- ran- ze, di mie mor-te spe-ran- ze è se - pol - tu - ra.

Ritornello

I have elided the cadence at the end of the ritornello to make the join into Poppea's aria even smoother, the two chords being the same. In the original score the ritornello ends in effect with a dotted minim and a pause.

Monteverdi's own ornamentation of the music is confined to a few significant cadential words, 'rinfacciarmi', 'in pace', 'tendarmi'. It is arguable that no further ornamentation is needed for the moment, the important thing being to hold the mood by preserving the beautifully sprung rhythms of Monteverdi's vocal line. The planning of this scene in the Decca video film is very effective. Earlier in the scene Poppea, concerned with her own charms, took little notice of Ottone. At the start of our extract he comes closer to her and kneels down, to press his suit. In reply, as she builds up to the moment when she finally spurns him, she turns and faces him.

Even the last cadence of the 6/4 section is best sung in strict tempo so as to lead the more directly into the 4/4 section where her thoughts turn to her ambition, a typically quick change of mood also found elsewhere in the depiction of her character. The tactus can be kept constant (old dotted minim equals new minim), and the music will more clearly express the determination behind her aspirations if the new tempo is adhered to strictly. The sketch illustrates the moment in the video performance when she stands up over him, an effective gesture to express her disdain and superior power.

Poppea obeys an imperial command;
now dowse the fire, moderate
cen - no im-pe-rial Pop - pe - a sog- gia - ce; Am-mor-za il fo - co o-mai, tem -
your rage;
I leave you in order to gain kingdoms.
- pra gli sde - gni; Io la- scio te per ar- ri - var, per ar- ri - var

At the last cadence, however, some rubato is clearly called for, and the crucial word 'regni' can be prolonged and ornamented as she reaches the nub of her resolve. After that the purely musical interest wanes, and for the remaining recitative the singing can revert to a declamation nearer to that of the spoken theatre with its less strict adherence to metrical rhythm, but so as to give the most telling articulation to the important words.

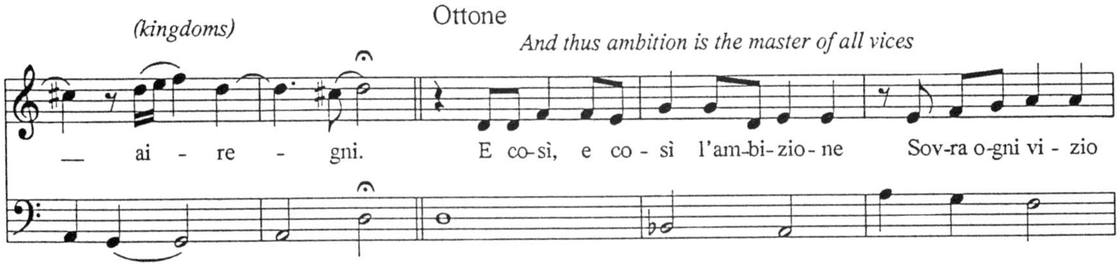

III Verdi's *Rigoletto*

The singer coming to early and middle Verdi from Handel or Mozart would perhaps be struck by the differences of scale even more than substance. Formally the scenes can still often be divided up into units consisting of accompanied recitatives and arias, but these are now more flexibly assembled into larger entities with structural ramifications over a longer span. For example, Gilda's famous aria 'Caro nome', the climax of the second scene of Act I of *Rigoletto*, is the culmination of a whole chain of shorter movements, arias, duets and recitatives, in which Gilda has been participating and increasingly come to dominate the stage over a period of about half an hour. We see her at first as a dutiful daughter to Rigoletto; later, her loneliness is revealed and her exasperation at the way he treats her. But it is only after her duet with the Duke that she is left alone on the stage to sing the aria which shows that her deep love for him is really the strongest motivating force of her character. It is important for the singer so to pace the scene as to make this clear, not only because that is the musical shape of the scene (the prolonged E major of the aria's climactic coloratura overriding her earlier music in flatter keys) but also dramatically because it is this love which is to prove so strong as to lead to her death in the last act.

Although the characterisation could not be said to be clearer than Mozart's, it is stronger in the sense that it focuses more on the simple depiction of extremes (in this case, dutiful innocence, and blind devotion), underlined by Verdi's simple textures, strong melodies and, for the most part, monothematic structures. This, of course, was what he inherited from his immediate Italian forebears, and it was only in works later than *Rigoletto*, that he refined his style with what is in some respects a reversion to a more Mozartian subtlety.

It is evident that 'Caro nome' represents a change of emphasis in Gilda's character, the further meeting with the Duke having enlarged her love for him to such an extent as to dominate her feelings for the remainder of the opera. This is significantly different from the old opera seria idea of an unchanging character revealing distinct facets in successive arias. Another instance of change resulting from an event on the stage is to be seen in Rigoletto's own increasing morbidity after Monterone's curse. However this is not more than a change of emphasis, for there are hints of the morbidity in his music before the curse: and in the case of Gilda too, her radiating love is felt even before her first appearance on the stage, in the passage chosen for Example 2.4.

Verdi's recitatives vary flexibly from near parlando to arioso, and to that extent are nearer to Monteverdi than to Mozart, though he now uses the full resources of the modern orchestra to help the singer. One contemporary critic referred to a later instance of Verdi's word setting as 'dramatic declamation in strict time substituted for classical recitative on the one hand and Wagnerian polyphony on the other'.[14] There are some passages where the voice sings entirely unaccompanied, one of them in Example 2.4, but that is quite different from the old secco recitative, which has virtually disappeared in Verdi (though something quite close to it reappears on occasions in *Falstaff*, right at the end of his life). Generally speaking, Verdi uses the device as a means of laying especial emphasis on emotive words before the fuller music takes over, and so the passages call for expressive vocal colouring rather than pace. Although the tempo need not be absolutely strict, a close approximation to the notated rhythms generally works best in that it will enable the words to be brought out without sacrificing Verdi's intentions as to moving forwards into the next section.

Verdi's most favoured overall shape for his arias was a flexibly treated cavatina – cabaletta form, where the cavatina (or sometimes cavatinas) might be surrounded by recitative involving other characters or the chorus, and the final cabaletta became a powerful climax to the whole scene.[15]

Example 2.4
Verdi *Rigoletto*, Act I, recitative 'Pari siamo'

This fine example of the form is cast in a number of short sections varying from near secco recitative to what are virtually little arias. It explores the whole gamut of Rigoletto's character as Verdi wishes it to be understood at this stage of the opera. The mastery of the musical form is evident in the way that the diverse tapestry of emotions is nevertheless made to drive forwards to the end, where it is taken up into the duet 'Deh non palare'. The momentum to the end must also be a concern of the performers, especially in preserving the continuity at the cadences where one section leads into the next.

In the earlier part of the movement before the start of our extract, Rigoletto has been roaming quickly across his present life, reflecting that in his way he is just as destructive as the assassin Sparafucile with whom he has recently been in conversation. He remembers the curse, and rails against his fellow human beings and against his own tortured role as cripple and fool. Verdi paints every one of these aspects with precision. Then, as a short orchestral ritornello leads into the beginning of our extract, the sombre mood changes momentarily. The light pizzicato bass line suggests an echo of one of the court dances from the opening scene of the opera and Rigoletto can preen himself so as to impersonate the Duke. Because the accompaniment is so light (staccato clarinet with pizzicato violas and basses), a correspondingly light singing tone is enough, but of course to be kept in strict tempo to fit the rhythmic accompaniment.

The first sketch shows Rigoletto (as on the video film) extending a mock gracious hand in impersonation of the Duke beckoning to his jester. The stopping of the accompaniment in bars 11 and 12 is a hint that the tempo can have an element of freedom again. The phrase 'forzar mi daggio' in bar 12 heralds a sudden change of mood but is best kept soft both because of its register and also in order to highlight the sudden and venomous *forte* at the outburst of his real feelings, 'Oh dannazione!', when the full orchestra crashes in with a savage tonal lurch, E major from B flat minor.

The volume, but not the aggression can be reduced in the passage which now follows, bearing in mind that it must lead forwards to its climax in bars 23–4. There is a strong argument for singing 'per cagion . . .' in tempo so that the long E on 'solo' is heard as its notated four beats: then the three orchestral chords will be heard as an extension of the vocal phrase and will lead forward to give the greatest dramatic impact to the further complete change of mood which now follows.

The new Andante section looks ahead to Gilda's 'Caro nome', having the same key and a very similar melody. The short orchestral ritornello gives Rigoletto the chance to establish the identity with Gilda and his home – the sketch shows him looking over in their direction. Rigoletto's 'Ma in altr'uomo qui mi cangio!', must match the flute's gentleness and lyrical warmth. It is a sound which will recur not only in 'Caro nome', but also in the tragic duet at the very end of the opera.

After this Verdi gives an articulating pause before a reappearance, this time softly, of the 'curse' motive, a memorably simple figure on a reiterated note. It is heard at various points in the opera, beginning with the Prelude, but its dramatic significance is first made clear when Monterone pronounces his curse in the scene before this one. Rigoletto's fatalistic feelings are now well reflected in its ominous double dotted rhythms (to be sung in tempo to make their effect), and in the dark woodwind chord underpinning his long C on 'maledivami!'. His tone should be coloured to match this chord.

But here I change into another man!
Andante ♩ = 76
Ma in al - tr'uo - mo qui mi cang - io!
25
Fl.
p dolce
Str.
pp

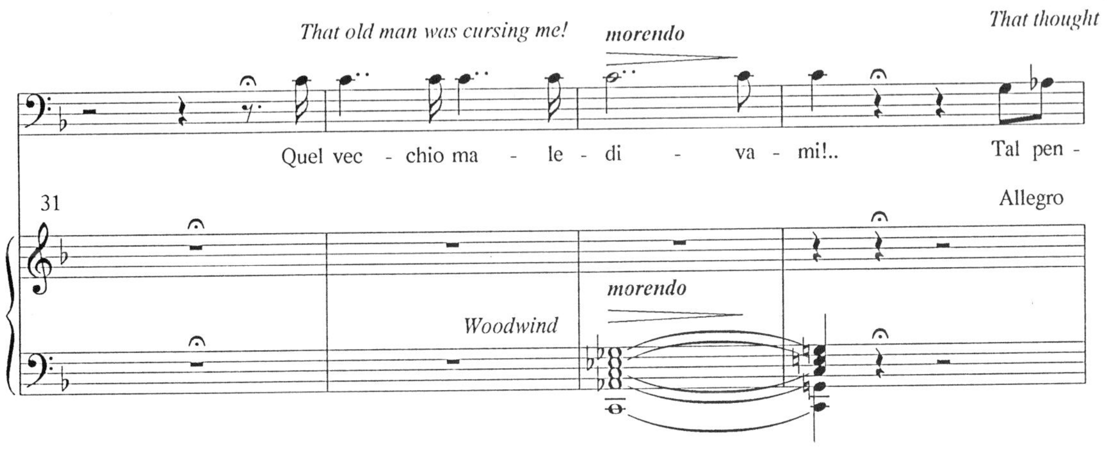
That old man was cursing me!
morendo
That thought
Quel vec - chio ma - le - di - va - mi!..
Tal pen -
31
Allegro
morendo
Woodwind

The pause in bar 34 is bridged if the following phrase 'Tal pensiero . . .' starts off at the same dynamic and tone as the curse phrase, but now at the new Allegro tempo and with rising urgency to lead into the Allegro vivo for Gilda's entry. Verdi marks no change of dynamics along here, and so the whole passage is technically *piano*. However, it does seem to need to drive forwards to a *forte* for the big cadence in bar 41 and is invariably so performed. The continuity will be strengthened if the last notes of both vocal and orchestral phrases in bars 38–40 are given full values so as to leave no gaps except where rests are notated. Then, at 'è follia!', when the tempo can be relaxed, the singer's sustained tone propels the cadence into the Allegro vivo. That is his exit music: as soon as the new music starts Rigoletto turns and enters the courtyard of his home.[16]

IV Puccini's *La Bohème*

Puccini's operas are in many respects within the same tradition as those of Verdi, with the singer generally dominant, both in the textures and also in the articulation of the musical forms.[17] There are, however, characteristic devices which he made his own: one is to have the voice singing on a monotone while the essence of the expression is conveyed by the orchestral music.[18] The device can appear in an aria when the orchestra takes over the main melody, leaving the singer to enunciate words which, in earlier opera, could well have been set as recitative. These words are, in a formal sense, taken up into the lyrical continuity of the aria, but they don't need to be sung in the same way as aria. Generally speaking their performance calls for a parlando style with rather more tone than secco recitative but the same priority of clear enunciation of the words; and of course they must be performed more or less strictly in tempo, so as to be synchronised with the musically dominant orchestral tune. Dramatically the technique is very useful for prosaic conversation which is consonant with (or resulting from) the high emotion of the main aria. It is to be understood, then, that although their surface levels may for the moment be different, the orchestra is in fact fully expressing the real underlying emotion of the singer, and the following example shows a similar technique used in a well known passage of recitative.

Example 2.5
Puccini *La Bohème*, recitative from Act I

Rodolfo, the others having gone out, is trying to get on with his writing, but has run out of inspiration. The bright little flute passage with wind accompaniment suggests perhaps that he has some ideas but they aren't quite right, and the dispirited bit of unaccompanied recitative indicates a lack of creative energy too. The video still shows him at his desk.

Then there is a knock at the door and Mimi is heard. The two of them engage in polite conversation, set in vocal phrases of no melodic interest, to be sung so that the words are clearly articulated. However the orchestral part is no mere secco recitative accompaniment, but tells us, in a hushed *pianissimo*, that Mimi is a young lady of considerable personal charisma (the music is in fact a preview of her aria to come) and that Rodolfo, underneath his actual words, has instantly become attracted to her offstage voice.[19] This orchestral music is actually a more beautiful and extended version of the Mimi theme than what she actually sings later in her aria, where she soon abandons it for other material. Puccini picks out the melody in a haunting way on two clarinets an octave apart, against a hushed string background: it is as if he is suggesting that the unique thrill of this first encounter is never quite recaptured later. It is the more important, then, that her monotonal 'scusi' should be sung with an arresting *mezza voce*. It brings about love at first sound! With such an orchestral presence buoying them up the singers can concentrate on their words and to this end small deviations from a rigidly strict tempo will be acceptable. However the monotonal phrases must be absolutely true in pitch, to blend with the orchestral harmonies. It is a rather nice touch in the video film that the door is at a higher level than the studio, so that Rodolfo has to walk up some stairs (after straightening his tie), as if going up to a new experience with the rising orchestral phrases of bars 14–17.

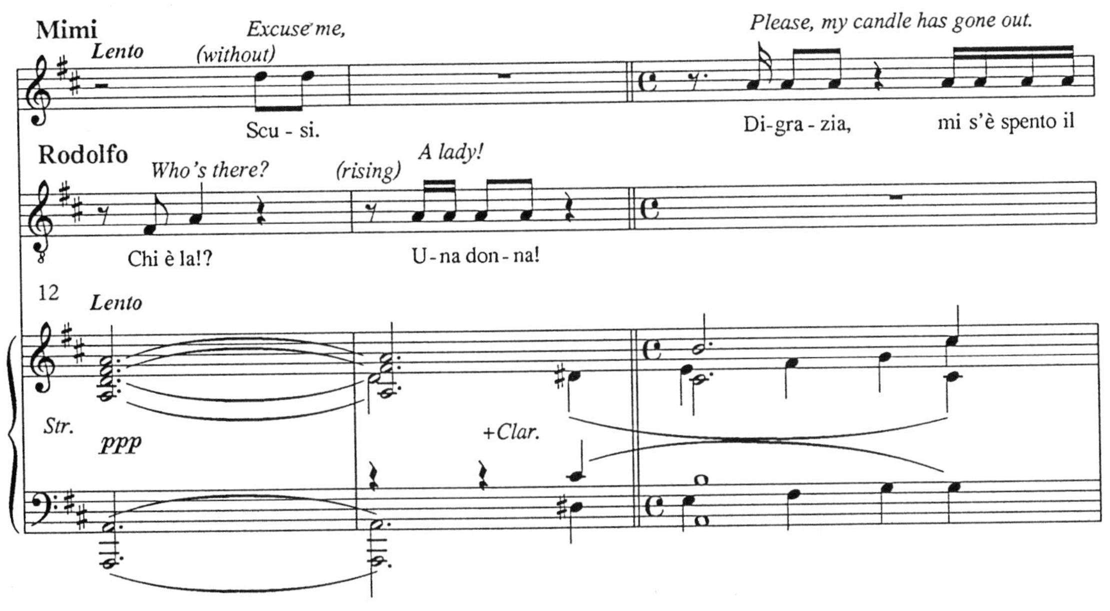
Mimi
Lento
Excuse me,
(without)
Please, my candle has gone out.
Scu - si.
Di-gra - zia,
mi s'è spento il
Rodolfo
Who's there?
(rising)
A lady!
Chi è la!?
U-na don - na!
12
Lento
Str.
ppp
+Clar.

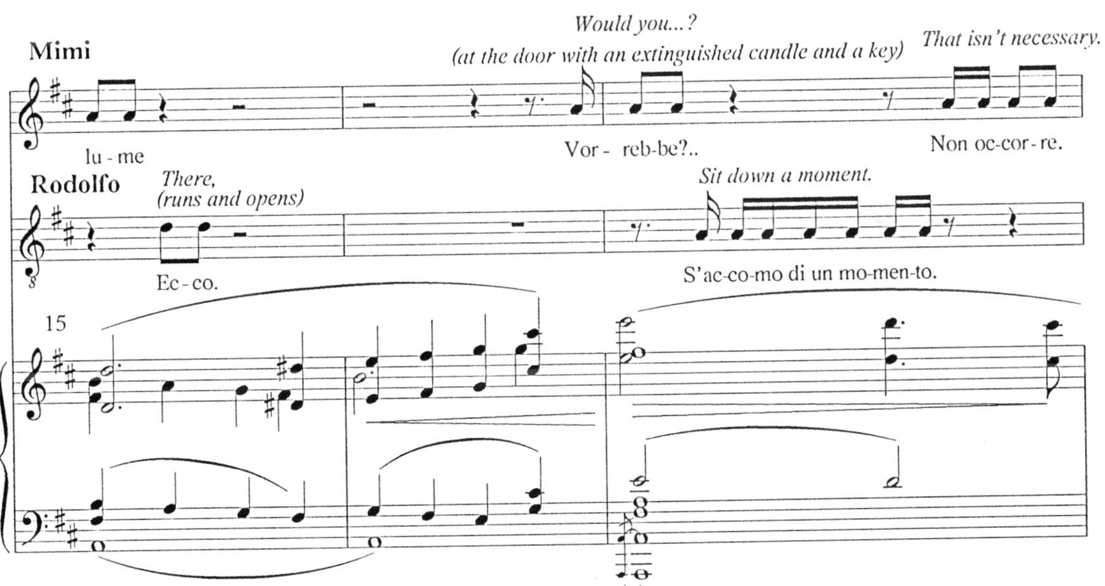
Mimi
Would you...?
(at the door with an extinguished candle and a key)
That isn't necessary.
lu - me
Vor - reb-be?..
Non oc-cor - re.
Rodolfo
There,
(runs and opens)
Sit down a moment.
Ec - co.
S'ac-co-mo di un mo-men-to.
15

The orchestral C natural to which we have now come in bar 18 is particularly emotional and calls for a poignant colouring of Rodolfo's *mezza voce* to harmonise with it. The depth of his sudden concern at her coughing is again expressed in the passionate orchestral phrase rather than in his monotonal and restrained vocal line. The orchestra gets softer but tells us of his continuing concern while she attempts to reassure him in her reply.

In bars 23–4 the orchestra swoops down through three octaves to accompany Mimi's self-pitying little phrase, which is melodic enough to be sung with as much feeling as is compatible with the fact that she is fainting. In other words the music becomes more like conventional accompanied recitative for a moment with the orchestra supporting the singer in the traditional way. The action of her fainting and his coming to her aid takes over our attention so fully that Puccini only thinks it necessary to suggest Rodolfo's continuing concern with a simple unsupported falling semitone on the violins. The still shows their positions at this moment. Rodolfo's next phrase is unaccompanied and back to secco tone again. Puccini is taking his time here (as can the singer) in preparation for a more formal duet.

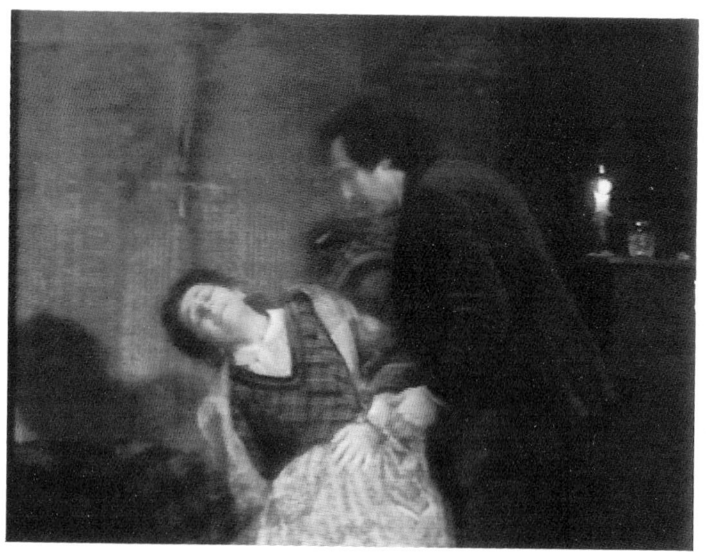

The performers must decide what is the meaning of the phrase in bar 34 high up on solo violins pizzicato. Clearly it is concerned with some kind of stage movement involving water, perhaps dampening the kerchief to wipe her face, as on the video still or even, as suggested by Newman,[20] the sprinkling of it on her face. Whichever is chosen, the action and the music must coincide, or the music will be made to seem pointless, for it has no other raison d'être.

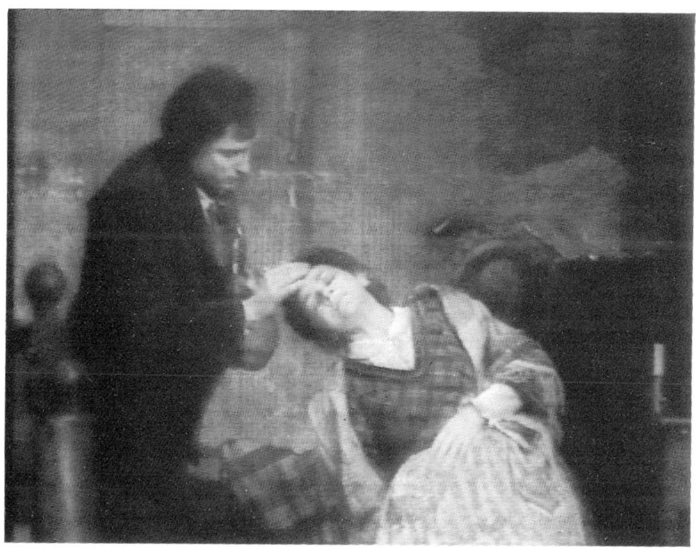

V Britten's *Peter Grimes*

In many respects the opera techniques used by Britten in *Peter Grimes* are essentially the same as those of Mozart and Verdi. Britten himself referred to his adoption of 'the classical practice of separate numbers that crystallise and hold the emotion of a dramatic situation at chosen moments'.[21] Certainly Verdi's technique of building up scenes with a flexible assembly of accompanied recitative, arioso and full-blown aria, is mirrored in almost every scene of *Grimes*. It would even seem, on occasions, that Britten used a particular Verdi scene as a model.[22]

Of course the musical style is different, as is the writing for the voice, which often made use of Peter Pears' characteristic ability to 'float' a phrase across wide musical intervals: and Britten makes much more widespread use of thematicism than did the earlier composers. An important aspect of this is his use in the orchestral accompaniments of a motif whose significance can be traced back to an earlier appearance in a voice part. This gives the motif a meaning, because it is understood as a reference to the words used at that first appearance. Example 2.6 illustrates this device when, at the end, the brass instruments enter with the theme to which Grimes had earlier sung 'Picture what that day was like'. It is as if he is still trying to share his experience with Balstrode. In interpreting Britten's operas, it is always worth looking at the accompaniments from this point of view in case they have any such specific connotations.

Britten may perhaps have got the idea from Wagner, a few of whose leitmotifs first appear in the voice (e.g. the Renunciation motive in *Rheingold*), or even from Janàček, who uses the idea extensively in *Jenufa*, often building up the accompaniment over a short section (a page or two of music) from varied repetitions of a vocal phrase heard at the outset. The effect of the technique is to convey the impression that the words of the phrase continue to dominate the character's mind over the whole section, even though other words are subsequently sung. Curiously (for it was a most effective new opera technique) Janàček used it much less after *Jenufa*. The music still tends to divide into sections each dominated by a speechsong-like motif in the orchestra, but the motif has no longer a specific reference through having been sung first.[23]

The origin and processes of the creation of *Peter Grimes* have been the subject of much interesting scholarly work, notably by Philip Brett.[24] The character of Grimes himself was transformed from the coarse ruffian of Crabbe's poem to the more sympathetic visionary outsider of the opera, but still retaining a harsh streak. His demise is ultimately brought about by his own stubbornness in only accepting Ellen on his own terms rather than on hers. This complexity of character is most fully explored in the Act II, Scene 2 soliloquy.[25]

Example 2.6 is from earlier in the opera, the first (and almost self-contained) part of the Act I scene with Balstrode, where Grimes recounts the death of his first apprentice, the circumstances of which continue to haunt him. To that extent the passage shows the more sensitive side of his character, but the tough independence of the man is evident in the setting of the aria; for instead of joining the other villagers in the shelter of 'The Boar', Grimes has stayed outside in the teeth of the oncoming storm. Indeed he virtually identifies himself with the storm, whose harsh power is so inimical to the Borough: the musical dimension of this is that his melody in the aria is a close transformation of the orchestral storm motif.[26]

The musical identification of man and storm gives Britten a successful way of solving the old operatic problem of the narrative aria, the recounting on the stage of an event which took place on another occasion. Such an aria was often necessary near the beginning of an opera in order to give the audience the background knowledge crucial to their understanding of the plot. Even when musically interesting it could easily become dramatically tedious: Ferrando's aria at the beginning of *Il Trovatore* is notoriously hard to bring off because it is referring to a string of events which can hardly be related to anything seen on the stage, and whose musical depiction is consequently without significant points of reference. Loge's narration in Scene 2 of *Rheingold*, where he recounts to the assembled gods and giants the story of Alberich's theft of the Rhinegold, has two big advantages over the Verdi. One of these is musical: since we in the audience have already witnessed the event in Scene 1, the music can be built around motifs which have already been given a visual/dramatic meaning and so their modified re-use adds a powerful new interpretation to the story. There is a dramatic advantage too in the way Wagner exploits an already tense stage situation in which the main group of gods is in conflict with both Wotan and the giants. The different reactions of all these characters as Loge's story is cunningly unfolded, the astonishment of the gods and the awakening interest shown by the giants in obtaining the gold for themselves, can be reflected in the changing stances on the stage, and thus give to Loge's story a new dimension of visual interest. The scene is the subject of further study in Chapter 5.

But Britten was working in this case on a smaller scale and needed no such artefacts, because the earlier event also took place in a storm. Thus the orchestral music, representing not only the present storm and the storm which killed the apprentice but also the turbulence of Grimes' soul, so encompasses the whole situation that very little action apart from the freezing of appropriate stances will be necessary to hold the atmosphere on the stage.

Example 2.6
Britten *Peter Grimes*, scene from Act I, Scene 1

Grimes and Balstrode are alone on the stage, the other inhabitants of the Borough having gone off to shelter from the approaching storm. The short opening orchestral ritornello uses material from the storm music as if depicting a sudden resurgence of the gale, and echoes of this continue to pervade the orchestral writing throughout the scene. But because of the motivic correspondences between this music and Grimes' melodic lines, an identity is established between him and the storm such that we can feel the orchestra to be fully supporting the singer, expressing his every change of mood. This opening ritornello, then, can be interpreted as a sudden surge in Grimes' emotions as he recalls the boy's death. In the video film at this point he moves impetuously across to Balstrode. The very light accompaniment (two flutes and solo cello) means that there is no danger of the singer's *mezzo piano* not being heard. The immediate musical problem for him is to achieve the composer's phrasing, and particularly to take the opening minor ninth into the phrase by employing, as suggested, a modest portamento.

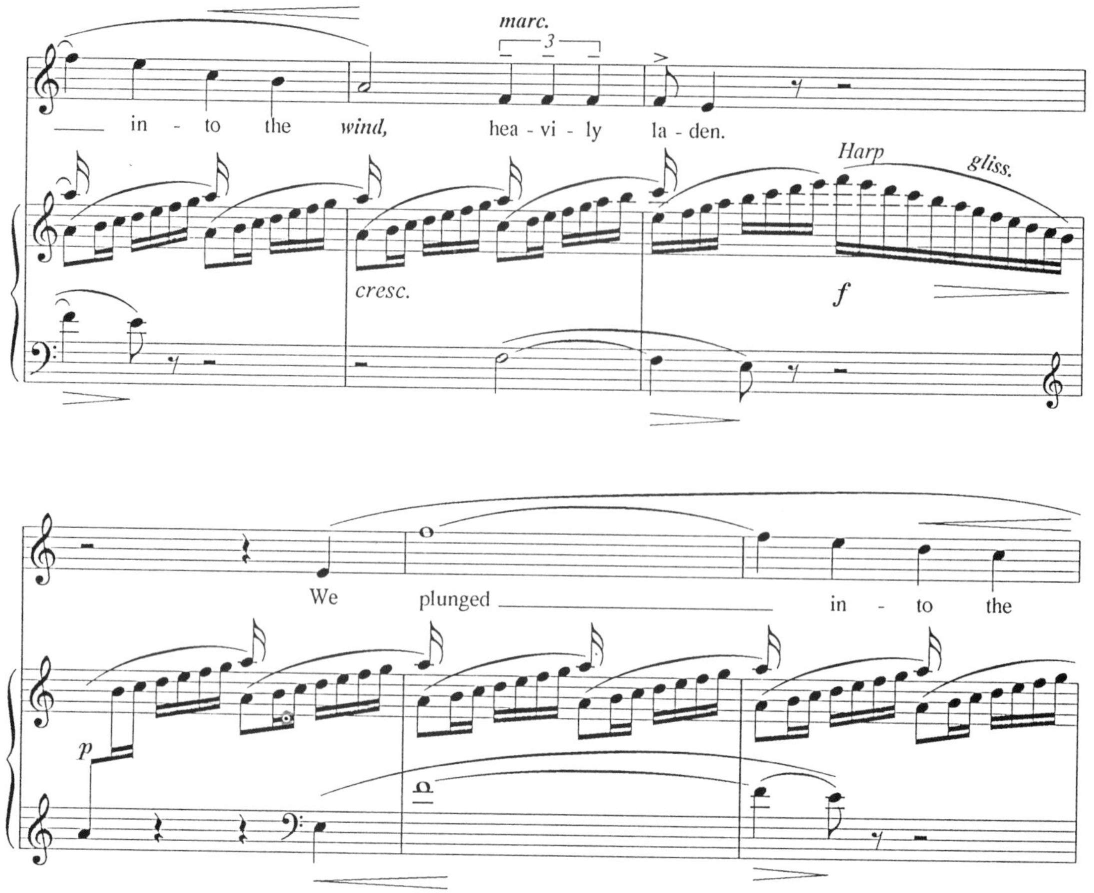

marc.
3
— in - to the *wind,* hea - vi - ly la - den.
Harp gliss.
cresc.
f

We plunged ——— in - to the
p

The semitonal inflections of the vocal phrase (F–E, D–C#), are taken up to G–F# by the muted violins, and it is at this new pitch that the voice takes it over *con più voce*. In other words, as the intensity of the paragraph grows, the orchestra and singer can be felt to be sharing a rising melodic line with its associated crescendo. Grimes' growing preoccupation with his memories is expressed by turning away from Balstrode here.

The climax point comes at the word 'illness' where the key fatalistically returns to the tonic, A minor, and oboes strengthen the violins. On the video film Grimes marks this musical watershed with an appropriately heartfelt gesture, turning back to clutch Balstrode's arm. The music quickly falls away to an intense *piano* for a recapitulation in the home key as Grimes remembers the actual death of the boy, the original flute accompaniment being now transposed down to a more hollow, even softer clarinet sound. He turns away again for this.

ill-ness.

+ob. gliss. gliss. Clar.

ff f mf pp

p

Then home a-mong fish-ing nets,

più p

pp

It is a nice touch of madrigalian word-painting that on the word 'alone' the singer should be left unaccompanied for the last vocal phrase of the section, a floating line which suddenly dips down into an orchestral ritornello where the full force of the storm, and by implication Grimes' feelings, are suddenly revealed. The brass recapitulates the motif of the singer's opening phrase, strongly underlining his obsession with the memory of 'that evil day'. The sudden musical violence calls for a big gesture or a powerful stance.

Notes

1 Where exactly the performance took place is still uncertain. There is an intriguing suggestion in Pickett (1992) pp. 1–3 that it was in the Galleria dei Fiumi, on the first floor of the Palazzo Ducale. If so, it was in a very small room by the standards of later opera houses, about 2000 m^3 (cf. Bayreuth Markgräfliches Opernhaus of 1748, 5500 m^3).
2 See Nigel Fortune, 'The Rediscovery of Orfeo', in Whenham (1986). Two differing views are to be found in Jane Glover, 'Solving the Musical Problems' in Whenham op.cit. pp. 138–55, and in Pickett (1992).
3 The title of Schrade (1950).
4 See Sternfeld, 'The Orpheus Myth and the Libretto of Orfeo', in Whenham, op.cit. pp. 28–30.
5 See Whenham, op.cit. and Pickett, op.cit. for summaries of recent scholarly opinion.
6 The word 'sprezzatura' refers to the expressiveness and use of rubato in this style of singing: see article by Nigel Fortune in Sadie (ed.) (1980), vol. 18, p. 27. Caccini's full and important exposition of the art of singing in his day is to be found in the foreword to his collection of solo songs, *Le nuove musiche*, published in Florence in 1601–2. A translation is given in Strunk (1950), pp. 377–92.
7 Quoted from Kerman (1956), p. 30.
8 The later appearances of this ritornello are discussed in Chapter 4.
9 Quoted from Pickett (1992), p. 39.
10 See Pickett, op. cit., p. 39.
11 See Erber (1978).
12 See Curtis (1989), preface, p. xii.
13 This movement is almost certainly not by Monteverdi but by Francesco Sacrati (1605–50): see Curtis (1989), pp. vii–viii. Whoever wrote it, it is a splendid and fitting ending to the opera.
14 From a review of the first performance of *Otello* in 1887, quoted in Toye (1931).
15 There is confusion and widespread inconsistency in the use of these terms. 'Cabaletta' may mean the final quick section of a bipartite movement or there may be implications of internal structuring, e.g. strophic form. The matter is well sorted out in Noske (1977), p. 273.
16 Further comments on performing the opera are to be found in Chusid (1980).
17 See Carner (1974) for a survey of Puccini's whole technique and style.
18 Puccini did not invent the device, which can be found even in Mozart, e.g. towards the end of 'Non più andrai' in *The Marriage of Figaro*.
19 Newman (1934) p. 57, perhaps goes too far in suggesting that this use of the Mimi theme 'tells us who is without'. Strictly speaking we have had no reason in the opera as yet even to have heard of Mimi.
20 Newman, op. cit. p. 57.
21 From the introduction to Crozier, Eric (ed.) (1945), *Benjamin Britten, Peter Grimes*, Sadlers Wells Opera Book No. 3, London (1945), reprinted in Brett (ed.), (1983).
22 See Brett (ed.) (1983), pp. 137–9, where David Matthews shows Ellen's aria from *Peter Grimes* Act I and the ensuing ensemble to be based on Desdemona's scene in *Otello* Act III. In Chapter 4 we shall consider the storm in Act I, Scene 2 of *Peter Grimes* as a creative re-thinking of Verdi's storm in the last act of *Rigoletto*.
23 Janacek's 'speech melodies' (though not their transference to the orchestra), are discussed in Tyrrell (1982), in the introduction, pp. 9–21.
24 See Brett (ed.) (1983), Chapter 3.
25 See Peter Pears 'On Playing Peter Grimes', in Palmer (ed.), (1984), Chapter 8.
26 See Evans (1979) for an excellent musical analysis of the whole opera.

This photograph, from the 1971 Royal Opera House production of *The Marriage of Figaro*, shows the scene at bar 45 of the Trio No. 7 (see p. 116). The Count (Victor Braun) and Basilio (Alexander Oliver) have just rushed over to support the troubled Susanna (Reri Grist), who is playing for time by acting out a fainting fit. The slightly comic imitative style in which the two men sing almost identical phrases throws some doubt on their sincerity in coming to her aid. The positions here can be compared with those on the video still used on p. 116, showing the same moment in a different production in which Susanna, taking the hint more literally from Mozart's cascading descending scales in the previous bars (38–42), has actually slumped right down on the floor. What is important is that she should be in a good position to spring away from them for her dramatic return to consciousness in bar 65, p. 117. *Photograph Zoe Dominic*

3 The Duet/Ensemble

I The Equal Duet

The idea that two or more characters on stage could sing at the same time seems to have been an unquestioned assumption by even the very earliest opera composers, who not only incorporated into the new genre the older ensemble forms of madrigal and balletto, but were also quick to see the dramatic possibilities of the new chamber duet.[1] At first the two singers expressed identical sentiments by singing the same words in textures which were either homophonic (generally moving in parallel thirds), or imitative of each other. It was only later, notably in Monteverdi's *L'Incoronazione di Poppea* in 1643, that the possibility was realised of setting up a dramatic tension between the singers by giving them different words at the same time.

The ensembles at the beginning of Monteverdi's *L'Orfeo* all arise from the chorus of nymphs and shepherds, whose stanzas are variously set to be sung by one, two, three or all of them. There is a hymn to Hymen, an invitation to dance in the fields, to put aside earlier sorrows and to be joyful, it being understood that all these sentiments are shared by the whole company however many of them are actually singing. In the duet for two shepherds, 'In questo prato' near the beginning of Act II, both the voices and the two violins in the interspersed ritornelli move in parallel thirds, in such a way that the two groups can take over from each other at the ends of the phrases to make a seamless whole. The close identity of vocal and instrumental sections means that the actions or gestures on the stage (dancing, perhaps?[2]), can be planned as a continuity throughout the whole scene. The two shepherds themselves, being conceptually 'chorus', do not need to be individually characterised, for that would transcend the music and the pastorale genre. But to say that their actions must be felt to arise from identical emotions does not mean that the actions themselves should be identical since this, unless very discreetly stylised, could have an undesirably comic effect.[3]

Example 3.1
Monteverdi *L'Orfeo*, Act V, final duet

This duet is of a rather different nature from those referred to above, and much closer to the duets of later operas in that each of the two characters concerned has a distinct dramatic role, Apollo having descended from heaven to take Orfeo back with him. Although the two vocal lines are musically equal, moving mostly in parallel thirds or with imitation at the same pitch, it is quite proper to look for signs of characterisation in the music which will suggest stage action, and Monteverdi does not fail to supply these. At the beginning of the duet it is Apollo who initiates each new musical idea, and who is evidently either physically leading Orfeo or perhaps showing him the way.

(Apollo and Orfeo ascend to heaven, singing)

Apollo

Let us ascend

Sa - liam, Sa - liam

Orfeo

Let us ascend

Sa - liam

However at the end of the duet the two voices sing the final two phrases together in thirds, sometimes with Apollo, sometimes Orfeo taking the upper line, and with the implication of equality for the two singers. A staging sensitive to the music could well reflect this with the two of them alongside each other as they ascend together into the higher realm of the gods.

The example illustrates in a very simple way a very common feature of later opera, that many ostensibly 'equal' duets turn out not to be exactly equal for the two voices all the way. One that certainly does get very close to equality is the celebrated duet for Poppea and Nero at the end of *L'Incoronazione di Poppea.*[4] It should be stressed that the equality here isn't only a matter of the equal sharing of musical material, with close imitation and mostly parallel homophony, but also an equality of pitch, since the role of Nero was written for a male soprano singer. As the result of this, the two miscreant but triumphant lovers can consort musically in close harmony throughout the duet, sometimes one, sometimes the other having the upper part, and their musical efforts can be directed towards obtaining a perfection of blend and balance. Some commentators[5] have drawn attention to the fact that contemporary audiences may well have been aware of the full story in which, later, Poppea was to be kicked to death by Nero. However, that could only have meant that for them the beautiful ending of the opera would have had an ironic twist, not that it could have been played with that possibility in mind.

Example 3.2
***L'Incoronazione di Poppea*, Act III, Scene 8**

The short passage was partly chosen to show that casting Nero as a baritone does violence to the music. This is particularly so from the fourth bar onwards, where the transposition of the part down an octave creates ungracious sonorities with the voice below the continuo line and as much as two octaves below Poppea. The staging of the duet is probably best left as static as the nerve of the producer will allow. All the subterfuge and plottings are over, and those who opposed their union are murdered or banished. If they adopt a good tableau position, the sensuality of the music will speak for itself. In the Harnoncourt video film of the opera the two of them lie down towards the end of the duet as if about to engage in sexual love when the curtain falls. This interpretation, although not inconsistent with what we know of their characters, is arguably wrong for the music, which is in a strict ternary form whose reprise, even when as beautifully ornamented as in this performance, does not seem to lead to more than a closure of the overall stasis.

Poppea
No more do I die,
O my life,
o my treasure,
no. Più non mo - - ro, non mo - ro, O mia vi - ta, o mio te-so - ro, –
Nerone
No more do I suffer,
O my life,
ro. Più non pe - - - no. O mia vi - ta, o mio te-so - ro, -
— o — mia vi - ta, o — mio te so - - ro, —
— o — mia vi - ta, o mio te - so - ro, —

'Equal' duets can pose interesting interpretative problems for the performers when the two characters concerned may be understood to have different understandings of the common sentiments (or actions) of the common music. In the duet 'Bei Männern' from *The Magic Flute*, when Pamina and Papageno sing in almost equal musical terms of their desire for fulfilled love we know that the quality of that love in the two cases will not be equal. The bigger problem here is for Papageno who, because the nature of the music is entirely serious, must suspend his clownish humour for the duration of the duet, and this will seem inconsistent if he is too much of a buffoon elsewhere. It must be said, though, that the simple triadic nature of the music of the duet is not in itself inconsistent with his other music and so should not present insuperable difficulties for a singer who works out his whole interpretation from the music.

Example 3.3
Mozart *The Magic Flute*, Act I, Duet No. 7

For most of the duet the two parts are strictly equal, first one singer and then the other taking the lead. However our extract comes from towards the end of the duet when Mozart does differentiate between them by giving to Pamina the most elaborate melodic decoration of the movement. While her part soars, as it were, into the higher realms of the spirit, Papageno simply provides the bass part to the harmonies; that is to say he is consonant with her and supportive, but simpler and quite distinct. We might, perhaps, compare two of the currently available video recordings at this point. In the Sawallisch interpretation (not illustrated here) the musical distinction is nicely realised by Papageno's turning away from her, as if to go off, at the moment of her highest roulade; but she pulls him back (their hands are still tied to the rope earlier used by Monostatos to imprison her, and from which Papageno has been freeing her) so that they complete the cadence side by side. This is not so amusing as to detract from the seriousness of the duet, and it does have the virtue of arising from the music. In the Haitink video illustrated here the smaller gestures are to the same general effect: Papageno turns to look at Pamina in bar 46 as she scales the heights and turns back to sing the cadence in an equal relationship again.

Pamina
(reach) to divinity.
an die Gott heit an,
an die Gott-heit an.
Papageno
an die Gott - heit an,
an die Gott-heit an.
fp
f
p

An equally lovely, but quite different, treatment of the same musical genre is in 'Sull'aria', from Act III of *The Marriage of Figaro*: of especial interest here is the ingenious role of the orchestra in supporting the singers. The music is in effect an arietta, with a continuous melody taken over in turn by each singer and the orchestra. The sharing of the melody between the two singers negates any differentiation of character between them,[6] and is quite acceptable here because they are both completely absorbed in a joint activity, the Countess dictating a letter to Susanna, who writes it down, taking a little time to do so. This causes some gaps in the singing which are filled in by the orchestral oboe and bassoon to keep the melody going, with the dramatic consequence that the orchestral melody is understood to represent the actual writing of each clause until the moment when Susanna repeats the last word(s) to indicate that she has finished.

The idea is varied in delightful ways, as when Susanna queries the ending of a phrase she hasn't quite finished. Later, when the two of them read the letter back, they are, of course, able to sing the whole melody themselves without needing the support of the woodwind instruments: and at the end they both ornament their concluding cadences 'the rest he'll understand' in such a way as to indicate their almost childlike excitement (the Countess, now, as well as Susanna) at the trick they are playing on the Count. The scene is a brilliantly imaginative re-creation of a fairly conventional type of eighteenth-century aria, usually involving a lawyer dictating a marriage contract in Latin.

Example 3.4
Mozart *The Marriage of Figaro*, Act III, Duet No. 20

The Glyndebourne video shows the scene played in what has become the traditional way: in the short opening ritornello the Countess walks over to a good position for dictating while Susanna sits at the desk. At bar 7 we see them, the Countess watching while Susanna writes, at a moment when neither of them is actually singing, the musical intensity being held by the continuity of the melody on the oboe and bassoon (doubling at the octave below) in the orchestra.

In bar 12 there is a subtle shift in tonality for the second phrase of the letter. The Countess moves off to the dominant key as if to a new region of delight, and on the video she makes the point visually by looking away for the moment. Susanna, of course, duly copies her by cadencing in the new key. The video picture catches the moment between the two while Susanna is still writing and again neither of them is singing. The stance of the Countess might seem a little exaggerated here were it not for the ecstatic intensity of the supporting melody which continues in the oboe and bassoon.

Bar 22 and its picture show the moment when Susanna queries the words and turns to the Countess accordingly. Mozart's humour is delightfully subtle here. He makes nothing at all of the point in the music, for the key is back in the tonic and the orchestral melody floats on serenely without regard to Susanna's little phrase, which is only an unostentatious counterpoint to it.

At a later moment in the duet, bars 39–43, when Susanna has finished the letter, she moves over to the Countess and the two of them are seen reading it over together. They can now sing the entire melody themselves and so don't need the same level of contribution from the orchestral oboe and bassoon, which simply provide occasional accompanying sonorities.

The equal duet is a condition to which many operatic ensembles revert after using other techniques, and it is often used as a climactic device, as in the opening duet of *The Marriage of Figaro* where the two singers at first have different music for doing different things: Figaro measuring the floor and Susanna trying on a hat. But when she calls him over to admire the hat he takes over her melody which they then share for the remainder of the movement. A particularly beautiful and moving instance of a somewhat similar idea occurs right at the end of the opera when the humiliated Count asks for forgiveness and the Countess grants this musically by continuing his incomplete vocal phrase so as to make a single melody – the first sign of musical unity between the two of them in the whole opera. This scene is to be discussed further in Chapter 7.

In the nineteenth century the equal duet was popular as a device for bringing a scene or act to a forceful conclusion, reaching its climax at the very moment of the fall of the curtain. To express the strong emotions of the characters on the stage there was generally a big tune which they shared, and this could lead to a temporary neglect of characterisation, as our next example shows.

Example 3.5
Verdi *Rigoletto*, Duet at the end of Act II

This is a problematical instance of the employment of the technique because the two very different characters are also experiencing quite different (though equally strong) emotions at the time when they have to sing, in effect, the same music. It must be understood that the passage in question (the final Allegro vivo) is the climax of a long duet scene in which the characterisation of the two has been sharply delineated. At the beginning of the scene, Gilda joins her father immediately after her abduction and seduction by the Duke, and she tells him how she had fallen in love with the him, not knowing his real identity, but nevertheless trusting him. Then, just as the remorseful Rigoletto begins to vow vengeance on the Duke (the key is A flat for this), the conversation is interrupted by a group of men leading Monterone through the palace to a place of execution. Monterone stops for a moment before a portrait of the Duke and admits that his earlier curse on him has failed. His dispirited exit rekindles Rigoletto's zeal for vengeance and (the key returning to A flat), he vows to fulfil the curse himself, as he sings the first stanza of the cabaletta.[7] The quiet orchestral accompaniment means that for the moment he can sing softly, though with as much venom as in any loud passage. Only the first four bars are shown here and the sketch suggests a common positioning for the verse with Rigoletto near the centre of the stage and Gilda behind him.

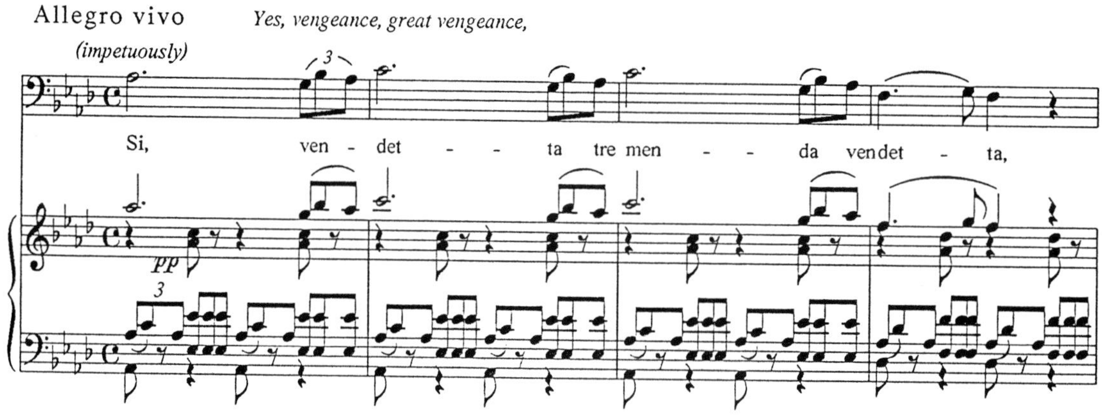

Allegro vivo
Yes, vengeance, great vengeance,
(impetuously)
Si, ven - det - - ta tre men - - da vendet - ta,
pp

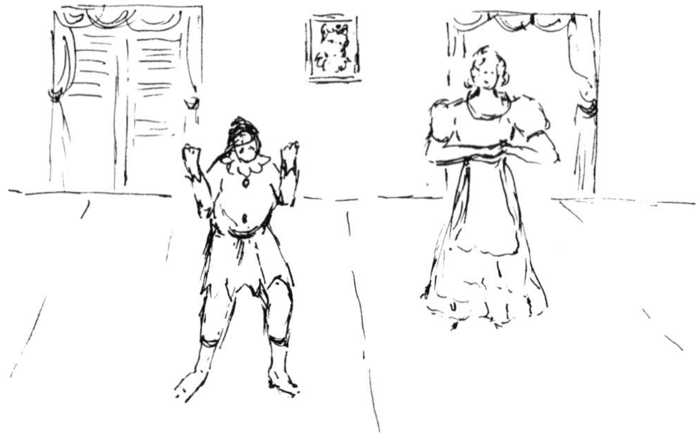

The second stanza is sung by Gilda and consists of the same music transposed up to D flat to suit her vocal range (rather than for any dramatic reason), and obviously to be sung with equal force, though her feelings are quite different from his. She refers to the fierce look in her father's eyes and entreats him to forgive her lover, a plea which he brusquely rejects with outbursts 'No!', unfortunately more often shouted than sung in performance. Gilda could move downstage nearer to Rigoletto for her verse, perhaps actually looking into her father's eyes to make the point. Again, just the first few bars are given.

Gilda
O my father,
what a fierce glint (in your eye)
O mi-o pa - - - dre, qual gio - - ia fe-
Ob.,V.1.
p

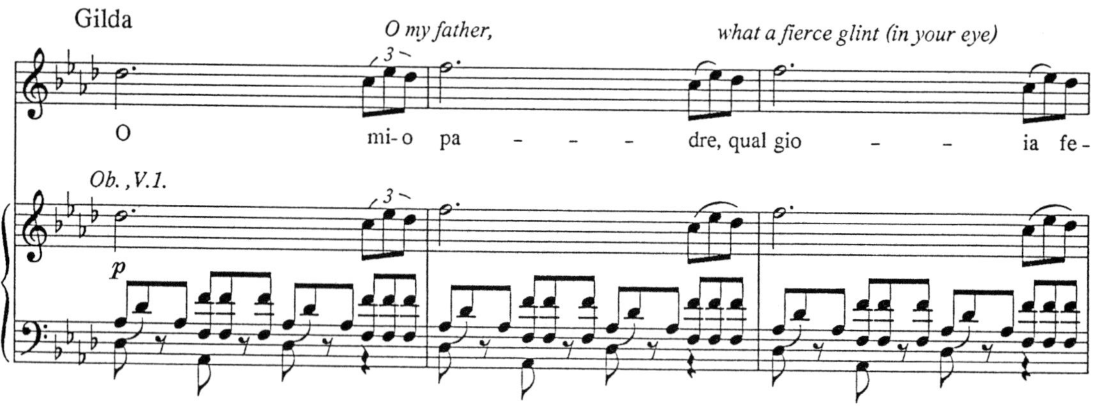

Then, in a final più mosso they each sing the last lines of their respective stanzas in tense homophony, perhaps side by side and facing resolutely forwards so as most naturally to let the music make its powerful effect.

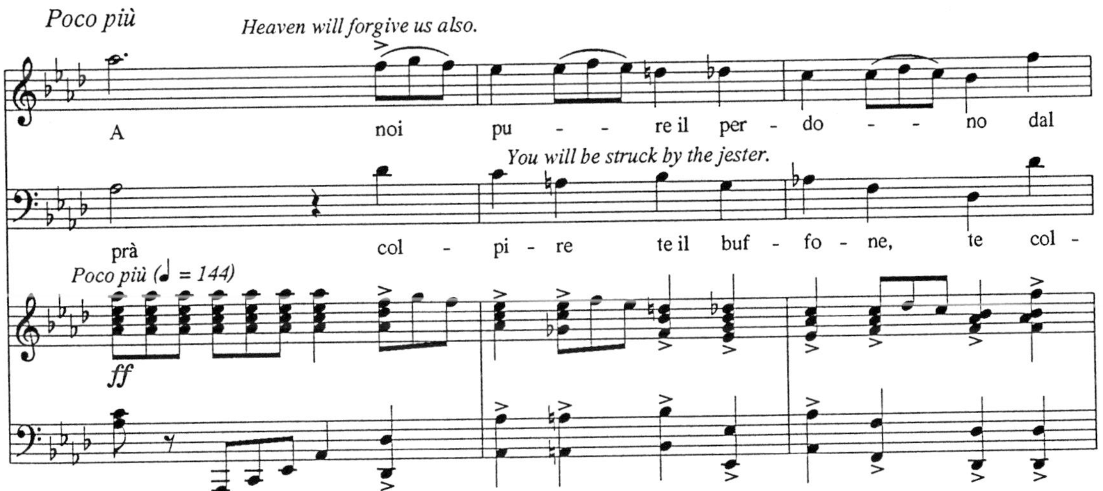

It certainly makes an impressive musical culmination to the scene and the whole act, a veritable 'cabaletta sfarzoso' as Verdi described it in a letter to his librettist Piave.[8] Verdi went on to justify the use of the same music for Rigoletto and Gilda, 'I find it ineffective to have two characters singing about their separate affairs, one on one side, the other on the other, especially in quick movements'.[9] Needless to say, such an argument, involving a rough compromise for the character of Gilda, does not satisfy operatic idealists. Noske comments, 'Although quite capable of strong feelings, Gilda remains throughout the drama an ingenuous young girl who has no affinity with the violent contradictions in her father's nature. The cabaletta is therefore fundamentally inconsistent with her character.'[10]

Performers having to come to grips with the problems of interpreting Verdi's masterpiece may perhaps opt for one of the following approaches for Gilda in this passage: she can take her opening words literally: 'O mio padre, qual gioia feroce Balenarvi negl'occhi vegg'io!' (*O my father, what a fierce glint burns in your eyes!*), look into his eyes and understand her music, at least for these first two lines, as referring to his torment. Or, as in the ENO video production, she can use the music simply to transfer the tension and urgency of Rigoletto's desire for vengeance to her own fearful pleas for forgiveness for her lover.

In the same video performance, as if to affirm that the music she sings is really his, Rigoletto draws attention to himself by loading his pistol as she sings. Such an action could not be said to be wrong, though it does to an extent have the unfortunate effect of upstaging her. This in turn gives rise to further action in the final orchestral curtain music after they have finished singing, and for which the only Verdi/Piave stage direction is to exit through the centre door. She attempts, unsuccessfully, to grab his pistol and he thrusts her away offstage. Again, we can hardly feel that this action does any violence to the fierce orchestral coda, but we may question whether it is truly consistent with her character, or indeed with his, in that it involves a gesture of violence towards her.

II The Unequal Ensemble

All the duets considered so far have had it in common that the two voices have shared the same, or largely similar melodic material. When, as we shall now investigate, they sing different material, the problematical compromises of characterisation noted above are immediately avoided, but new problems of musical cohesion and continuity may be created, of which the performers should be aware. The opera seria composers tended to avoid the problem altogether by having very few ensemble movements at all, so that the confrontations between characters came only in the recitatives where the musical interest is minimal and the responsibility for the expression of tension is largely taken by the words which are declaimed with something of the pace and nuance of a spoken play. When, a century earlier in *L'Incoronazione di Poppea*, Monteverdi forcefully expressed his dramatic conflicts in his own type of recitative (which had elements of aria incorporated into it), he met the problem head on, as the two following examples show.

Example 3.6
Monteverdi *L'Incoronazione di Poppea*, Act III, Scene 3

This is part of the scene in which Nero accuses the innocent Drusilla of the attempted murder of Poppea (it was in fact Otho, dressed in Drusilla's clothes, who had intruded into Poppea's room). The characterisation in the music is quite clear. Nero is very aggressive: his questions are in a major key, each phrase revealing pent-up energy by finishing on a high note, and he bursts in on her second denial with a change of metre for the command to torture her. She, on the other hand, sings in a minor key and pleads innocence with gentle descending melodies, the gentleness accentuated by the fact that her second phrase is a rather meek repetition of the first. The tension and discontinuity are accentuated by the unexpected harmonic moves at each turn in the conversation.

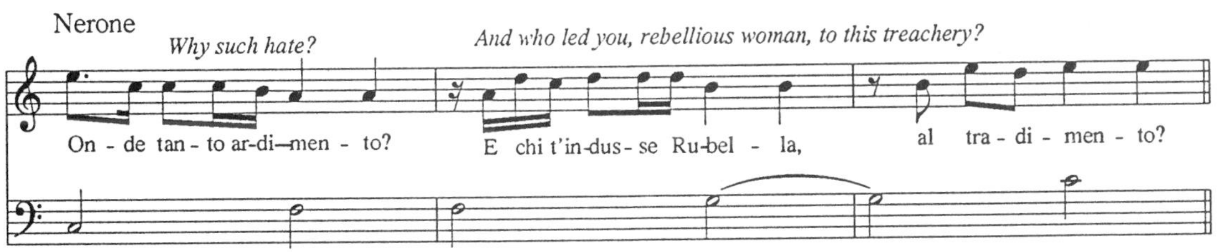

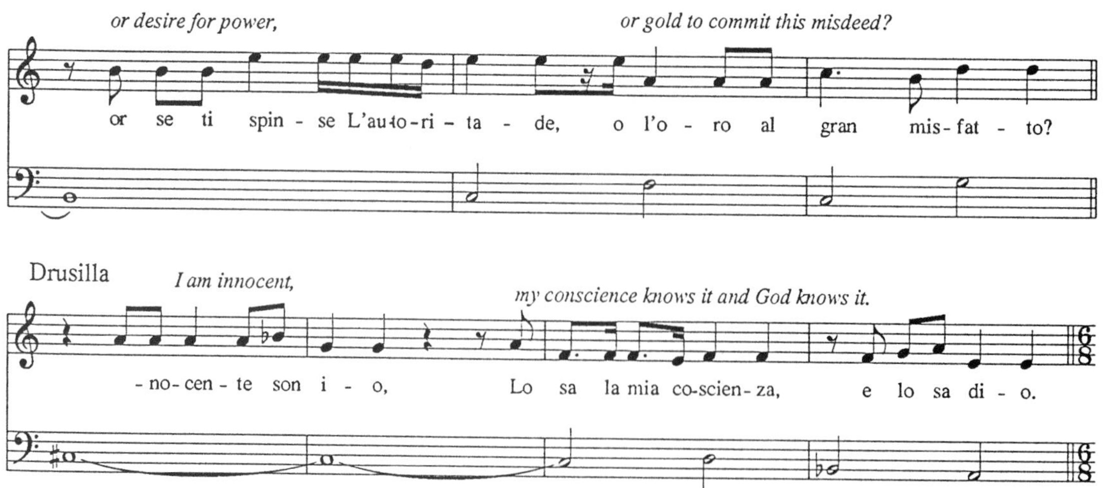

The absence of detailed dynamic and other expression markings in the score makes it the responsibility of the performers to decide how the balance between characterisation and continuity is to be pitched: is Drusilla, for instance, to emphasise her feminine weakness by singing her phrases at a slower tempo (as Malipiero suggests in his edition), or should she sing her line in such a way that it is heard to be a continuation of Nero's, allowing the music to drive forwards to his climactic torture outburst? If this were an entire scene and the outburst a major climax point one would perhaps choose the second option. As it is, though, it is only part of a bigger unit whose climax is of a different nature: Drusilla is about to change her mind and confess guilt in order to save Otho, whom she loves (this happens just after the end of this extract). Her quiet protestation of love as she is led off to execution is dramatically more powerful than anything the blustering Nero has to say. Seen in that perspective the overall pace of this earlier part of the scene is less important than the clear delineation of her character: the forward momentum can be left until later. To return to our extract, after her second denial Nero evidently loses his temper and immediately orders the most violent torture, to extract the truth from her. On the Harnoncourt video film, and suggested in the sketch, he beckons for his armed guard to surround her and threaten her with their spears.

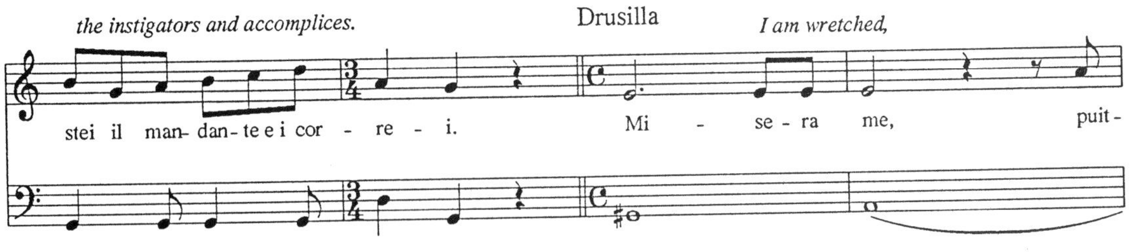

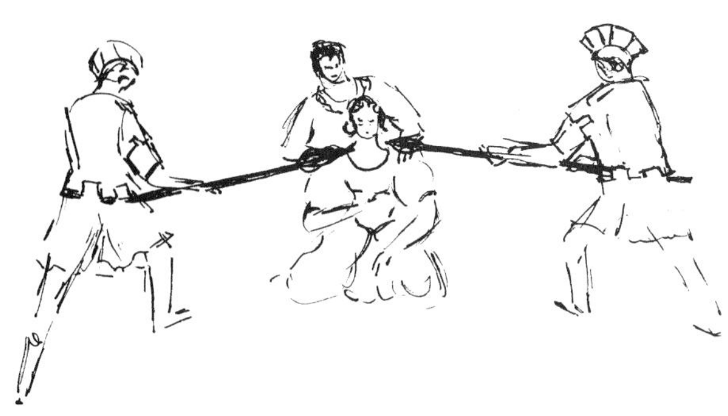

That, of course, is strictly dialogue rather than duet. But Monteverdi was a master, too, of devices to give characterisation within genuine duet writing. One of these is simply to make one of the voices dominant and the other subsidiary, a procedure of which he was so fond that he converted some 'arias' (as they appeared in the libretto) into duets by interpolating comments from a second character. Since, in baroque music, the customary drive is towards the cadences, these places become the favoured moments for the adding of a second part.

Example 3.7
Monteverdi *L'Incoronatione di Poppea*, Act II, Scene 5

This section is built on a ground bass. As Nero's servant Lucan sings of Poppea's physical charms, Monteverdi gives to the infatuated Nero gasps of ecstasy at each cadence point, the longer phrases for the more important cadences in his design. It is to be noted that the music is virtually in the same key as 'Pur ti miro' (see Example 3.2), and is strikingly similar in some figurations too. Nero's three little phrases in bars 2–6 are not as disjunct as they might look: despite the gaps between them they can be sung as components of a single phrase leading forwards to the cadence in bar 6, where the climax of the syncopated G/C sharp dissonance between the voices confirms the reading. In this way it is possible for Lucan's words to come over clearly without sacrificing the forward drive of the music to the cadence: in other words to obtain characterisation plus continuity. Moreover, although Nero sings less than Lucan we know from the way he seals the cadences that he is really the dominant character and that his passion is our real centre of interest. In the Harnoncourt video film they are side by side at this point.

Nero
Lucan
ahi,
ahi,
(her) mouth which, when it speaks or laughs,
boc-ca, che se ra - - gio-na, se ra-gio-na, o ri - - - de,
ahi, ahi, des-tin,
Con in-vi-si-bil ar-me pun-ge, e all' al - - - ma -
brings joy,
ahi,
while it kills.
ahi, des tin,
O mouth,
Do-na fe-li-ci-tà men-tre l'uc-ci - - de. Boc-ca,

Later on in the duet Lucan moves round behind Nero, suggesting something almost insidious in the way he is inflaming Nero's infatuation: it is, after all, shocking that they should be celebrating in this way so soon after hearing of the death of Seneca. This action matches very well the elongation of the melisma in bars 12 and 13, which will quicken up into semiquavers a few bars after the end of this extract.

The concept of 'aria with additions' reaches its apogee in the celebrated quartet from Act III of *Rigoletto*. This is the movement which caused Victor Hugo, when he saw the opera, to comment on the advantages of opera over spoken drama: he asked, 'what would the ordinary dramatist not give to be able to make four people animated by different sentiments speak all at the same time, each in character, and each fully intelligible to the audience!'[11] However, the fact that the singers are equally characterised does not mean they are equally important throughout, and up to the coda, when Gilda takes over the dominant role, the movement is essentially an aria for the Duke, to which the others add their melodies in counterpoint.

Example 3.8
Verdi *Rigoletto*, Act III, Scenes 1 and 2

Before discussing the quartet itself, a word must be said about how Verdi leads up to it. At the beginning of Act III we see Rigoletto bringing Gilda to a place on a roadway from which she can look into a nearby inn and witness the Duke's infidelity to her. A short quiet orchestral introduction leads into a recitative whose beginning is quoted below. Verdi refers in a letter to Patti's performance of this passage:

> I was struck dumb not only by her marvellous technique but by certain dramatic traits in which she revealed herself as a great actress . . . I remember (her) . . . above all in the recitative preceding the quartet in *Rigoletto*, when her father points out her lover in the tavern and says 'And you still love him?', and she replies 'I love him'. I cannot describe the sublime effect of those words as she sang them.[12]

It would be good to know just what Patti did to those three unaccompanied notes to move the composer so greatly. One fairly safe surmise is that she relied on the tone quality of the appoggiatura on the first syllable of l'amo: the note B is dissonant in relation to the preceding A minor chord and she could pace and colour it so that it is more poignant than the same note sung by Rigoletto immediately beforehand (which doesn't yet have the emotional force given to it by the string chord). Rigoletto, when he sings the same notes for a third time in his next phrase will make less of them because they are now part of a longer phrase leading forwards to his condemnation of the Duke, 'vile infame!'. Another surmise is that Patti's reading of the phrase was such as to set up an interpretation of a scene which has dozens more such appoggiaturas to come.

Soon after this the Duke appears inside the house and launches into his famous 'La donna è mobile' denouncing all women as fickle, and this in turn leads to the beginning of the quartet proper, a short Allegro in E, in which the characters are mostly heard singly. Only now do we come to the main part of the movement, an Andante in D flat with the form A B A′ coda, and in which we have to accept the convention that those inside the inn are unaware of the two onlookers. The A section is sung by the Duke alone to the famous melody given below: he sings flamboyantly of female beauty, with a nice touch of swagger in the grace notes on the second syllable of 'amore', usually most effective with a little accent sung on the beat. The diagram overleaf shows a typical set position for this verse, based on the ENO video. The front section of the wall is cut away to reveal the interior of the inn.

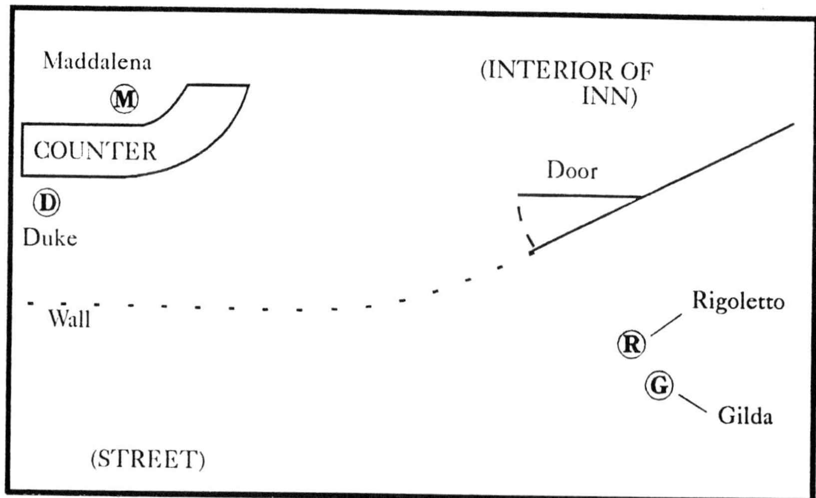

We jump now to the B section where characteristic passages for each of the others are introduced, singly at first. Maddalena has evidently lured the Duke here in order that her brother can assassinate him, and her coquettish manner is aptly characterised with a staccato semiquaver figure, which stands out well with an appoggiatura (but not of an expressive nature) on every strong beat. Gilda expresses her impassioned reaction to the Duke's infidelity in phrases whose very intense appoggiaturas veritably weep, while Rigoletto's grim mood is etched in a line with many repeated notes. If there is a purely musical problem it is for Rigoletto, whose part sometimes merges with the harmonic bass line and sometimes acts as a sort of harmonic 'tenor' part. Ideally it should be sung so as to give a firm foundation to the harmonies, or a good harmonic blend if not the bass, without his losing the sense of his dramatic situation which by now is desperate.

The next excerpt shows the beginning of the shortened reprise A′, and it is here that the Duke's aria is counterpointed by the other three parts in the way that Victor Hugo so much admired. The counterpoint is so good that, provided the singers are faithful to the pitches and rhythms of the notes, the more distinct their characterisation of their individual lines (particularly the phrasing) the better. That Verdi intended the Duke still to be dominant here is obvious from the fact that he starts alone and sings his aria melody intact, with the others coming in to give continuity at the cadences (just as in the previous Monteverdi extract). No change of stage positions from those of the A section is necessary.

However in the extended coda section Gilda takes over the musical dominance, and that is only right because it is her reaction to the Duke's behaviour that is really the main focus of our interest in the drama at this point.[13] Verdi highlights her line by giving her a positive stretto of heart-rending appoggiaturas, at first on the 2nd, 3rd and 4th beats of each bar, later, in the second line below, even more intensely on the half beats, soaring above the others. It could well be, on the stage, that she would turn away from the others to clarify this change of emphasis, as in the ENO production and in the sketch.

Don't burst,
-piar, no, no, no, no, no, no, no, non scop-
I'm quite used to such jokes, fine sir.
-zar, si, si, so no av-vez-za, bel sig-no-re, ad un si - mi-le scher -
tar ah! si, vie - - - - - - -
I shall strike him down
ta - - le, io sa - - prol-lo ful-mi-nar, io sa-prol-lo ful-mi -

III A Mozart Trio

None of the examples so far considered has embraced a developing dramatic situation with action, and most of them have either to some extent compromised full characterisation in the interests of an overriding musical idea or, as in the Nero – Drusilla duet (and in recitatives), avoided a closed musical form altogether. There is of course, for the composer, a purely musical problem in the assembling of diverse, strongly characterised material into a convincing overall structure and this was one of the preoccupations of the writers of the classical symphony. It was Mozart's achievement not only to perfect that art but also to transfer its achievements to the opera house,[14] and our last example shows his incomparable art in moulding sharp characterisation and a developing drama into a closed symphonic form.

There still had to be a certain structuring of the drama, for there were probably limits to the extent to which even Mozart could have made a beautiful musical form out of an open-ended section of dialogue. But he made the constraints seem perfectly natural, and the incorporation of action into the musical form enabled him to pace the drama much more flexibly than would have been possible in baroque opera with its action sandwiched between the dramatically static set pieces. One of Mozart's constraints was the need for places of recapitulation, when there could be a return of the principal theme and key, and these are always places of which the performers should be aware, since the whole musical structure rests on them. In the following trio they coincide with the renewal of the Count's anger at each successive turn of events, and that is enough to give Mozart the chance of using a type of rondo form: the Count can highlight these moments by the way he dominates the stage at each of them. There are other recurrent ideas too, giving the movement elements of sonata form, the whole structure being uniquely and perfectly moulded to the drama.

Example 3.9
***The Marriage of Figaro*, Act I, Trio No. 7**

The trio arises from the recitative already studied in Chapter 1 (Examples 1.3 and 1.4). It begins as the Count emerges angrily from behind a chair to confront Basilio whom he has overheard gossiping about him. He is as yet unaware that Cherubino is hiding in the front of the same chair, covered over with a dress of Susanna's. Basilio, retreating immediately from the Count's wrath, feigns a half-hearted apology and Susanna pretends to faint, though she recovers quickly enough when the two men come to her aid and start handling her. She now has to deny Basilio's rumours concerning Cherubino, but this leads to another angry outburst from the Count, who goes on to relate how, only the previous day, he had found the young man hiding under a tablecloth in Barbarina's room. As if to illustrate that disclosure he lifts the dress and to his astonishment finds him again. The Trio finishes with an ensemble showing the reactions of all three of them to the latest turn of events, the Count angrier than ever, Susanna near to despair after being compromised in this way and Basilio continuing to relish every new twist of the developing scandal.

In the following discussion the complete libretto is given but, for reasons of space, only extracts from the music: ideally, the reader should refer to a musical score. The main themes are shown below.

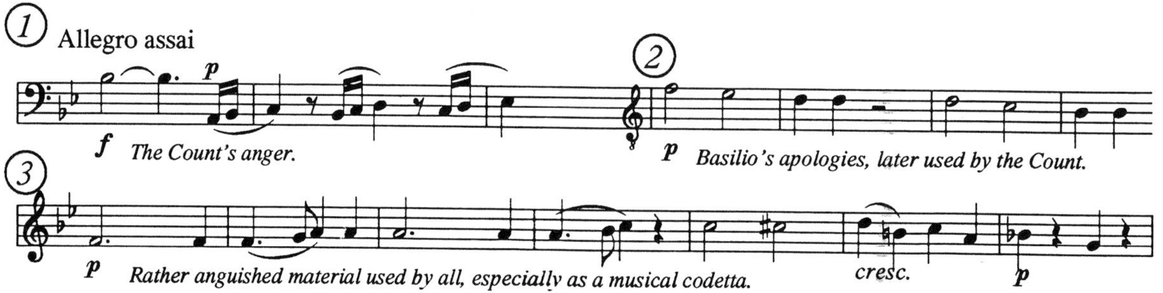

The theme with which the trio opens expresses the Count's anger and it reappears on two further occasions. These three moments are musical landmarks in that they define the beginnings of each of the three main formal divisions of the movement; the exposition, the first recapitulation (line 20 of the libretto), where he rejects the pleadings of the others for Cherubino, and the second recapitulation (line 33), where his anger turns on Susanna. The structural force of these reappearances of the theme is underlined by their each marking a return to the tonic key, B flat.

Basilio's patently insincere apologies (lines 3–4 of the libretto) call for a different theme (theme 2). This starts off in the Count's tonic key, for Basilio is intending to sound subservient to him, but it very soon modulates, acting as a bridge passage to the dominant minor key for Susanna's fainting. It recurs for lines 16 and 17, again in a modulating role, bringing the tonal excursions of the development section back to the tonic key for the Count's next outburst. The effect of these modulations is to emphasise Basilio's shiftiness of character. Mozart also inserts those same lines to complete his design in the coda – this was not shown in Da Ponte's libretto – and, as Kerman has observed, Basilio has by now moved from unctuousness to sheer impertinence.[15] Theme 2 is also sung by the Count for his innocent (in the libretto) lifting of the dress. Such a use by the Count of Basilio's theme seems to suggest that Mozart felt the action to be not entirely innocent; perhaps he has seen the dress move!

If themes 1 and 2 are clear and unitary, theme 3, as often in Mozart, is in fact a little group of themes associated in lines 7–8 and 14–15 with the 'concern' of the two men for Susanna, but providing material at the end for a general ensemble of perplexity. The three themes dominate the whole movement, and the only significant passage not related to one of them occurs near the start, when Susanna panics and faints (lines 5–6). This turns out to be only a minor bridge passage and it does not recur: after all it is only a simulated faint and doesn't last long.

It would seem from all this that perhaps the most interesting characterisation is given to the Count, who not only has his own angry theme 1 but also takes over Basilio's to show another facet of his personality. Those two themes initiate the main musical argument but always eventually lead into theme 3 for musical fulfilment and climax. Theme 3 serves a common role for all three characters of expressing the general tension on the stage. It is theme 3 which ultimately has the most weight (its prolongation in the coda amounts to about a fifth of the whole movement) and its accumulating force at the end drives the crisis on the stage to boiling point.

One of the factors contributing to dramatic pace is the rate of the word setting. The chart on p. 112 isolates this feature by plotting lines of the libretto against bars of the music: the steeper the slope the faster the pace. This crude but useful approach shows that the quickest passages are associated with Susanna, her fainting (lines 5–6), and her shaking off her comforters (lines 9–12). This certainly concurs with her vivacious character and with the fact that she has to think very quickly indeed to extricate herself from a succession of embarrassing situations. The Count's narrative is shown as quick too: allowance has been made for it being partly in recitative, at about half the musical speed of the main movement.

The chart also shows, as horizontal lines, the slowest passages (in this sense), where no new verbal ideas or dramatic twists appear, leaving the music to explore the situation in its own way. One of these prolongs the opening situation (bars 27–43) keeping us waiting for Susanna's fainting and so drawing more attention to that action. The passage also has the tonal function of consolidating the new key for what is in effect the formal second subject when the two men go over to pick up Susanna. However, the main horizontal line of the graph comes right at the end, showing a tradition of final musical consolidation stretching back as far as Monteverdi. It must be stressed that slowness in this sense does not involve any slowing of the pace of the music itself or any lack of tension – quite the reverse. Indeed, far more than merely prolonging the conflicts on the stage, Mozart's verbal repetitions positively enlarge and intensify them.

The first section of the libretto, up to line 11, is the basis of the exposition of the movement (bars 1–69), where Mozart sets up the main areas of dramatic tension: the angry and suspicious Count, the unctuous Basilio, and Susanna, trying desperately by simulating fainting to give herself time to find a way out of her embarrassments.

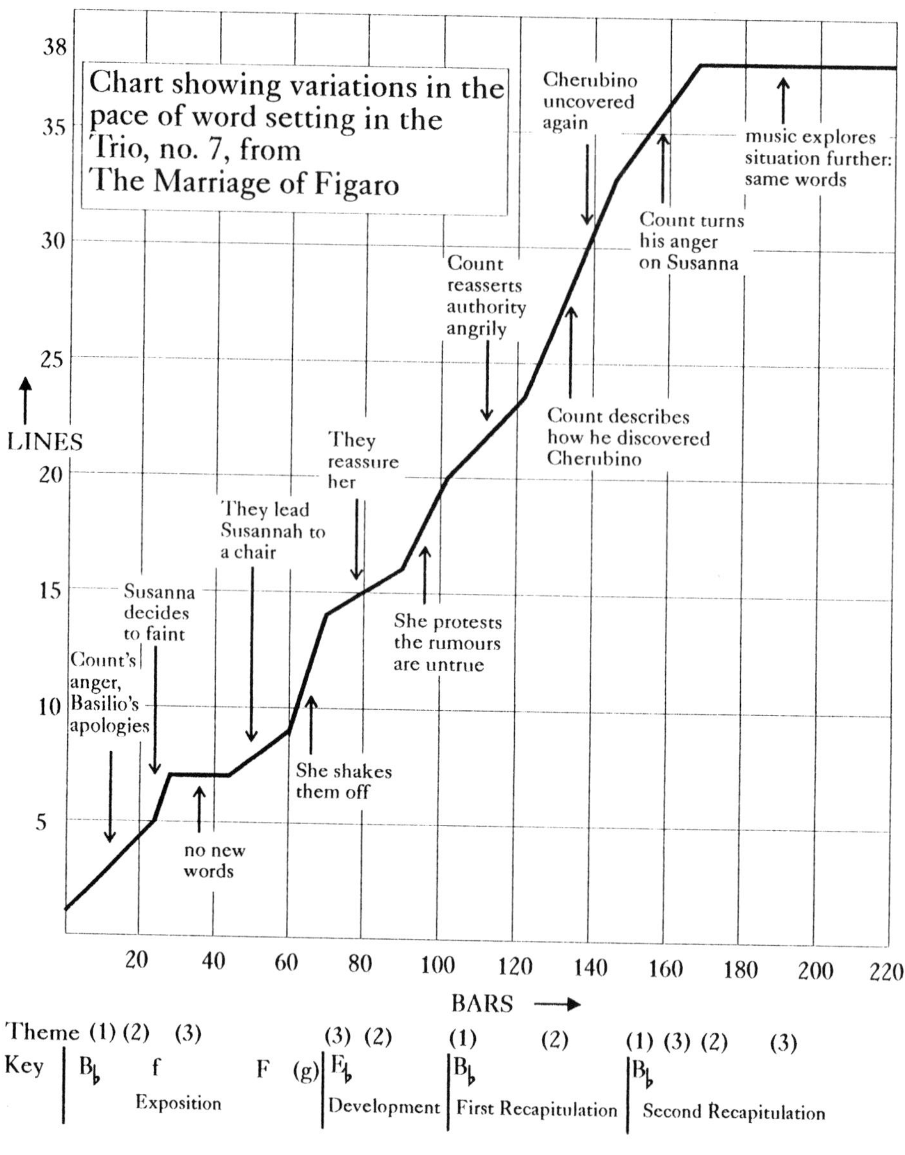

Key	Theme		Line
		COUNT (*to Basilio*)	
B flat	(1)	Cosa sento! Tosto andate	1
		E scacciate il seduttor.	
		What do I hear? Go at once	
		and send the seducer away.	
		BASILIO	
	(2)	In mal punto son qui giunto!	3
		Perdonate, O mio signor.	
		My presence is badly timed!	
		Forgive me, O my lord.	

SUSANNA (*half fainting*)
f Che ruina, me meschina! 5
Son oppressa dal dolor.
I'm ruined, wretched me!
I'm overcome with misery.
COUNT and BASILIO (*supporting her*)
F (3) Ah, già svien la poverina! 7
Come, oh Dio, le batte il cor.
Ah, the poor girl has fainted!
O God, how her heart is beating.
BASILIO (*leading her to the chair*)
Pian', pianin, su questo seggio
Gently, gently onto this chair.
SUSANNA
Dove sono? Cosa veggio? 10
Che insolenza! Andate fuor!
Where am I? What do I see?
What insolence! Go away!

As discussed in Example 1.4 the Count could well walk forwards at the opening of the movement to give visual expression to his powerful control of the stage, implied by the music, and there could be a similarly strong gesture at each recurrence of the first theme. Basilio's bogus contrition is caught in the video still, as the music goes its rather circuitous way through G minor and C minor to the dominant, F. The Count in the Glyndebourne video swings round to face him.

Basilio
My presence is ill-timed,
Forgive me,
- tor
In mal pun-to, son qui giun-to;
Per - do - na- te, o
20
p

The next picture gives a view from the side of the stage at the moment when Susanna first sings, in nervous little phrases, a nervousness also to be heard in the restless quaver movement of the second violins. She feels very much on her own and away from her friends and so her action here in having moved away from the others to the side of the stage has a symbolic force, mirrored in the move of the music away to the minor of the dominant key. We have come now to the passage marked on the chart as a horizontal line. For the moment the two men take no notice of her: the Count is continuing his diatribe as at the start, and Mozart cleverly gives Basilio a close variation of his theme 2 for the repetition of his words. Thus the melodies of this passage fit all the characters as sharply as those of the *Rigoletto* quartet.

O my Lord. Susanna *I'm ruined! wretched me! I'm overcome with misery,*

mio si - gnor. Che ru - i - na! me me - schi - na! Son' op - pres - sa dal ter -

25

- ror! Susanna *I'm ruined*

Che ru -

Basilio *My presence is badly timed*

In mal pun - to son qui

Count *Go at once*

Tos - to an - da - te, an - da - te, e scac -

f *p*

30

When Susanna in a momentary panic decides to faint, the first violins take over the continuous quavers from the seconds, transforming them into long cascading downward scales, which quite graphically depict her collapse to the floor. The two men now hurry over to her and are seen in the picture kneeling by her as they sing theme 3, the 'second subject' in F major.

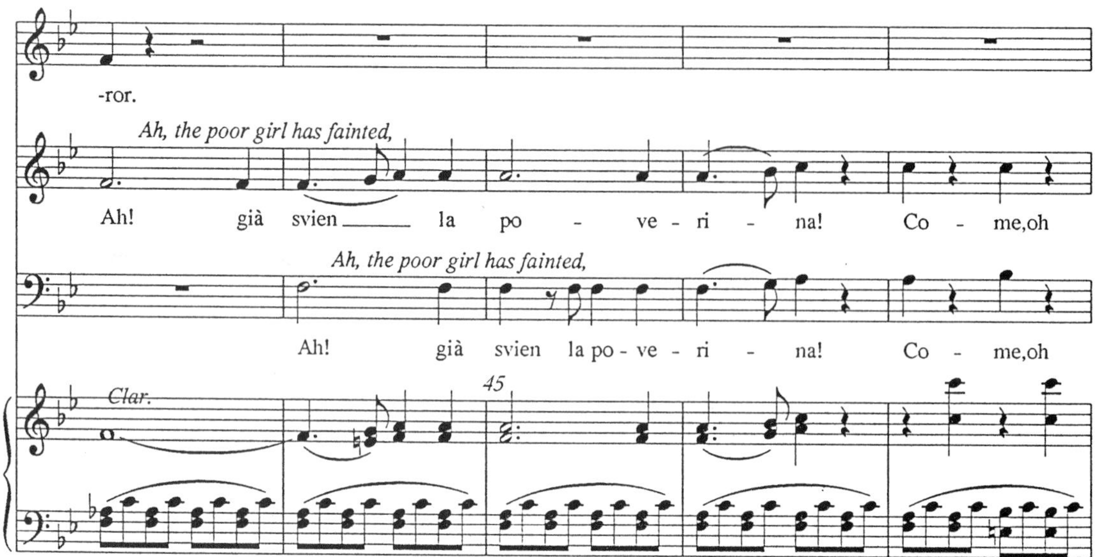

Basilio
O God, how her heart is beating!
Di - o! le bat - te il cor, co - me oh Di - o! le
Count
50
cresc.

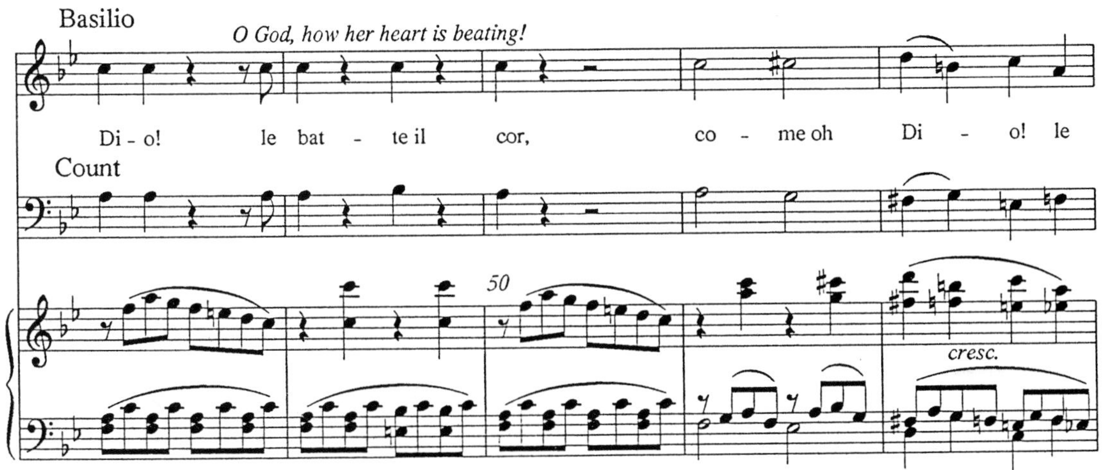

Later, at the end of the section, Susanna recovers and her sudden movement as she breaks away from the two men is as clearly depicted in the music as was her fainting earlier. There is a sudden and almost violent lurch into the unexpected key of G minor, with violence too in the dynamics (*fp* with crescendo to *f*) further to stress the tension she feels.

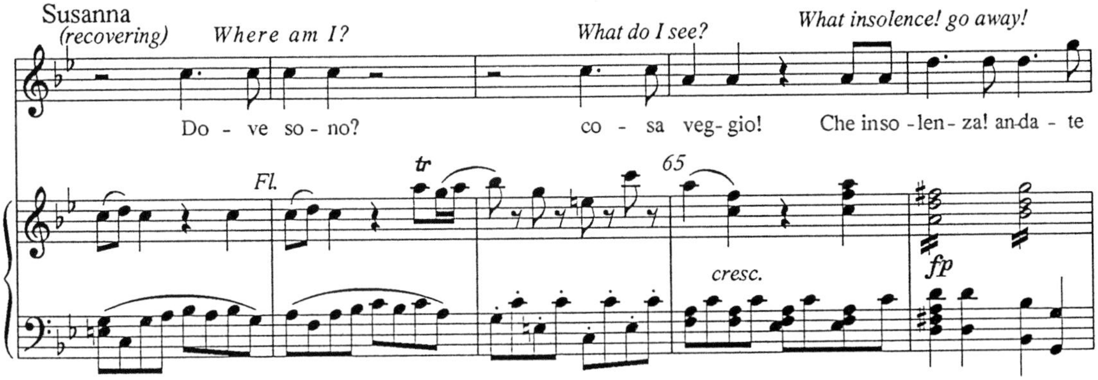

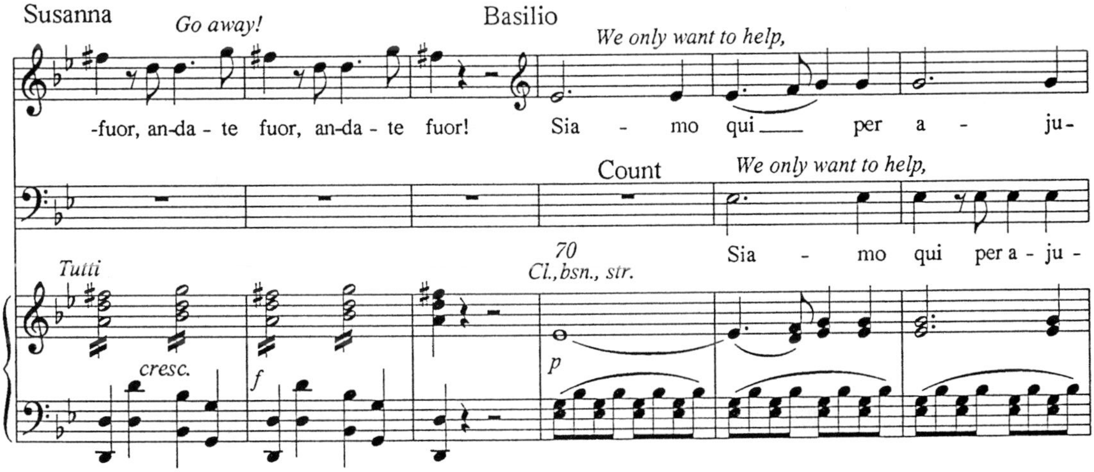

Susanna
(recovering) Where am I?
What do I see?
What insolence! go away!
Do - ve so - no? co - sa veg- gio! Che inso - len- za! an-da - te
Fl.
tr
65
cresc.
fp

Susanna
Go away!
Basilio
We only want to help,
-fuor, an-da - te fuor, an-da - te fuor! Sia - mo qui per a - ju-
Count
We only want to help,
Sia - mo qui per a - ju -
70
Tutti
Cl., bsn., str.
cresc.
f
p

Susanna's strident cadence chord in bar 69 is on the dominant of G minor, and the rests which follow it throw considerable weight on what is to follow. Presumably the two men can move a little or make a small gesture in the rest, since it is their next phrase which attempts a resolution of the musical impasse. But in this context the E flat key in which the development section now begins sounds decidedly unstable. It is as if they have little real hope of convincing Susanna of their honourable intentions. Nor will Susanna's later protests of innocence really convince the Count, for the music has a clear, almost fatalistic, direction back to his home key of B flat, ready for his next outburst of anger at the first recapitulation. The whole passage gives a good example of how Mozart shapes the drama through his key structures.

Key	Theme		Line
		COUNT	
E flat	(3)	Siamo qui per aiutarvi,	12
		Non turbati, o mio tesor.	
		We only want to help,	
		Don't be distressed, my treasure	
		BASILIO	
		Siamo qui per aiutarvi,	14
		E sicuro il vostro onor.	
		We only want to help,	
		Your honour is secure.	
		(to the Count)	
	(2)	Ah, del paggio, quel ch'ho detto	16
		Era solo un mio sospetto!	
		What I said about the page	
		Was only a suspicion of mine!	
Dominant		SUSANNA	
of B flat		E un'insidia, una perfidia:	18
		Non credete all'impostor.	
		It is a plot, a lie:	
		Don't believe the imposter.	

The first recapitulation of theme 1 in the tonic key brings us back exactly to the tensions of the opening, but this time when the conversation touches on the subject of Cherubino, it goes on to take a quite different turn, even less welcome to Susanna.

Key	Theme		Line
		COUNT	
B flat	(1)	Parta! Parta, il damerino!	20
		Away! Away with the young fop!	
		BASILIO and SUSANNA	
		Poverino!	
		Poor boy!	
		COUNT (*sarcastically*)	
		Poverino!	
		Poor boy!	
		Ma da me sorpreso ancor.	22
		I have caught him out again.	
		SUSANNA BASILIO	
		Come? Che!	
		How? What!	
		COUNT	
(Recit)		Da tua cugina	
		L'uscio ier trovai rinchiuso	24
		Picchio, m'apre Barbarina	25
		Paurosa fuor dell'uso.	
		Io dal muso insospettito,	
		Guardo, cerco in ogni sito,	
	(2)	Ed alzando pian, pianino	
		Il tappeto al tavolino	30
		Vedo il paggio!	
		(*he imitates the action with the dress and sees the page*)	
		Ah, cosa veggio!	
		At your cousin's house	
		Yesterday I found the door shut	
		I knock, Barbarina opens to me	
		Looking more than usually alarmed	
		I, made suspicious by her face,	
		Take a look all round	
		And lifting gently, gently	
		The cloth from the little table	
		I see the page!	
		Ah what do I see!	
		SUSANNA	
		Ah, crude stelle!	
		Ah cruel heavens!	
		BASILIO	
		Ah, meglio ancora!	
		Ah, even better!	

The next musical extract shows the passage at the beginning of the section when the Count (almost like a cat playing with a mouse), plays sarcastically with the 'Poverino!' phrase of the other two, and Mozart plays with the phrase too, taking it momentarily away from the tonic key through G minor and F. The Glyndebourne production matches this idea when the Count, now very much in command of the stage, paces around the others, eventually stopping at the chair where the next revelation is to be made; and this is nicely timed to coincide with the return of the music to the home key (dominant chord) at bar 115, an admirably musical piece of production.

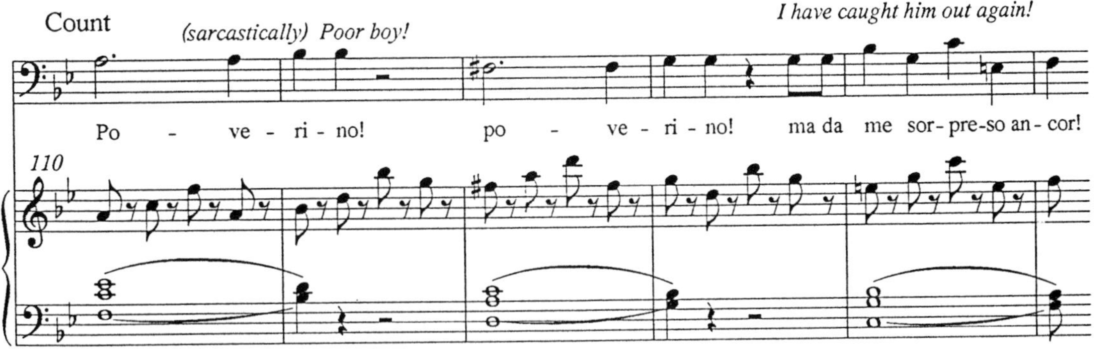

Mozart's use of a half-solemn accompanied recitative for the narration is witty[16] and the Count can surely smile a little to indicate his satisfaction as he recalls the events leading up to his earlier trouncing of the page. His taking over Basilio's theme for the uncovering is very clever: it is as if he is inviting Basilio to add this further incident to his repertoire of gossip and scandal. However the music of the recitative itself is of no distinction, for the interest is in the words here, and the paused rest before it starts in bar 121 gives the Count every opportunity to focus attention on this change of level and purpose. The video picture catches the very moment he lifts the dress: his looking the other way at the time gives him the better opportunity of dramatising shortly afterwards his reaction to the untimely disclosure of the page, saving this for the short pause immediately prior to the return of his main theme. This gives his reaction a strong musical dimension.

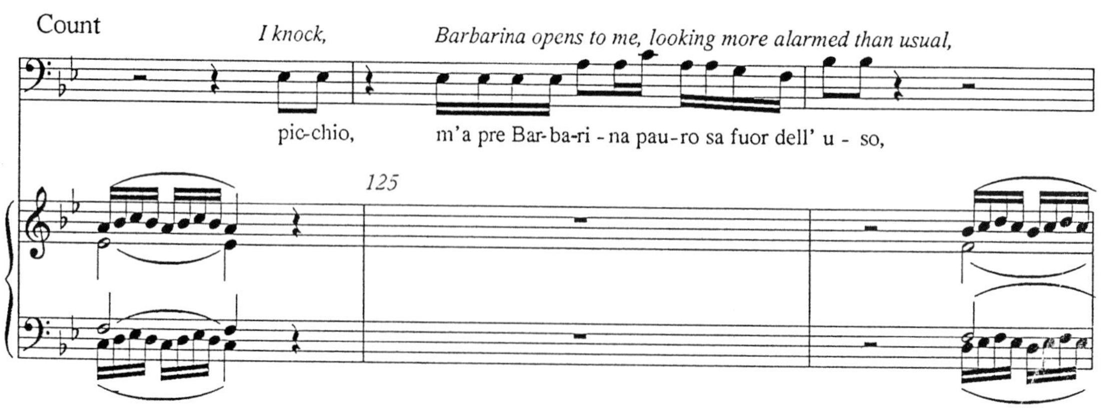
Count
I knock,
Barbarina opens to me, looking more alarmed than usual,
pic-chio,
m'a pre Bar-ba-ri - na pau-ro sa fuor dell' u - so,
125

Count
I, made suspicious by her face, take a look all round,
and lifting,
Io, dal mu-so in-so-spet-ti - to,
guar- do, cer-co in o- gni si - to,
ed al - zan- do,
f
p a tempo
130

Count
gently, gently,
the cloth from the little table,
I see the page,
pian', pia - ni - no,
Il tap - pe- to al ta - vo - li - no,
ve - do il paggio
135

The second and final recapitulation contains no further action but simply allows the music to explore the situation at some length. The six lines of the libretto are repeated many times, causing the section on the chart to contain the longest horizontal line of the whole movement. Nor, for the most part, is the music itself new: it is its sheer weight rather than any new invention which gives such force to the reiteration of the tonic key.

Key	Theme		Line
	(1,3)	COUNT	
B flat		Onestissima signora!	33
		Or capisco come va.	
		Most honest lady!	
		Now I understand how things are.	
	(3)	SUSANNA	
"		Accader non puo di peggio;	35
		Giusti Dei! che mai sarà?	
		Nothing worse could happen;	
		Just God! What will become of me?	
	(2,3)	BASILIO	
"		Così fan tutte le belle!	37
		Non c'è alcuna novità.	
		All pretty women behave thus!	
		There's nothing new in this.	

In this final section the main themes all return in the tonic key, including Basilio's 'Ah del paggio . . .' (line 16), not reprinted here because not part of the received libretto. William Mann[17] first quoted this theme with the addition of an appoggiatura to the third note. This is not incorrect, of course, and it could indeed be sung in this way from the start, in which case the Count, too, would have similarly to ornament his singing of it. That would certainly give a little emotional luxuriance to Basilio's patently insincere apologies at the start. An even better idea might be to save the ornamentation for this very last appearance of the theme, thereby compounding the impertinence.

Basilio should be aware of the significance of his phrase in bars 161 and 165, 'Così fan tutte . . .' which will pierce through the musical texture quite easily on account of its register. It was to be exactly quoted, some four years later, in the overture to the synonymous opera. Basilio has relished every moment of the trio, but this enunciation of his most cherished philosophy will call for especial ecstasy, reflected in the following video still from the Glyndebourne production. However despite all this interest for Basilio, it is really Susanna who takes the dominant role in the final ensemble and it is obviously her feelings that Mozart is most anxious to convey in the closing bars of the movement. The picture opposite shows her position for this in the same production. The Count is glowering at her from behind and Cherubino still doesn't know which way to turn. Awkwardly thrust forwards to the front of the stage, it is her voice which is ringing out above the others. There is little call for further stage movement in such a scene and with such music.

Notes

1 See Whenham (1978).
2 Strictly speaking only two movements, the balletto 'Lasciate i monti' and the final moresca, are specifically designated as dance movements. However it is clear from the writings of the time that dancing was an integral part of the performance tradition. See, for example, an anonymous treatise of 1592 attributed to Bardi, summarised in Pickett (1992) p. 37. Certainly the Harnoncourt film production has much dancing.
3 Both Gagliano in his preface to *La Dafne* of 1608, tr. Erber (1978), and Rinuccini in the treatise *Il Corago* of 1628–37, summarised in Pickett (1992) pp. 40–1, stress the desirability of uniformity and synchronisation in the movements of the chorus. To find humour in this is perhaps a modern reaction stemming from the experience of such later comic opera traditions as in the works of Gilbert and Sullivan.
4 See Chapter 2, note 12, for a note on the authorship of this movement.
5 See, for example, Iain Fenlon and Peter Miller's chapter 'Public Vice, Private Virtue' in John (ed.) 1992.
6 The Countess is in a socially disorientating situation. Noske (1977) p. 25, discusses the social implications of her having to sing an 'equal' duet with her servant, an embarrassment which Mozart makes clear by setting the duet in a 'low' 6/8 metre. No doubt the eighteenth-century audience would have appreciated this and felt her self-humiliation more acutely than we would today.
7 On the use of this term see Chapter 2, note 3 where reference is made to Noske op. cit. p. 273.
8 See F. Abbiati (1959), vol 2, pp. 98–9.
9 Quoted in Roger Parker 'The Music of Rigoletto' in John (ed.) *Rigoletto* (1982), p. 22.
10 Noske, op.cit. pp. 288–9.
11 Quoted in Newman (1954), p. 611.
12 From a letter to Giulio Ricordi dated 6 October 1877 quoted from Osborne (ed.) (1971), p. 201.
13 Mozart does the same for Susanna in the coda sections of several of the big ensemble movements in *The Marriage of Figaro*, and arguably for the same reason.
14 This idea is worked out in Charles Rosen (1971), Chapter 5.
15 See Kerman (1956) p. 87. These harsh judgements on his character do not prevent Basilio from being

played as an extremely likeable gossip and rogue, as John Fryatt shows in the Glyndebourne video recording.

16 The idea is not, however, new. There is some fine dramatic interspersing of recitative and aria in several of Handel's operas. Mozart probably would not have known these, but would have met the same thing in the work of the reform writers, Traetta and Gluck.

17 Mann (1977), p. 386.

Part II
The Orchestra Enlarges the Stage

This is a moment from the pub scene of *Peter Grimes*, Act I, Scene 2, shortly after the passage discussed in Example 4.8. The landlady's two 'nieces' have appeared (Catherine Benson and Meryl Drower) and are seen singing a tiny duet 'Oo! We'll all be drowned', to which Balstrode (Jonathan Summers) appends a caustic 'Perhaps in gin!' Holding it all together musically is the continuing presence of the storm outside, lightly suggested at this point by a sustained soft cymbal roll from the orchestra. *Photograph Zoe Dominic*

4 Dance and Atmospheric Background

I Early Instances of Orchestral Independence

Although the main concern of this chapter is with the nineteenth and twentieth centuries, it is tempting to look back earlier to see where the drift of the orchestra away from the singer may have started. The quest takes us right back to the beginnings of opera, for already in Monteverdi's *Orfeo* there is a tantalising uncertainty as to the precise role of the instrumental ritornelli, and it is worth looking at them not only for themselves, but also to focus our thinking on some of the later issues.

The *Orfeo* ritornelli are independent of the vocal sections and have no obvious musical connections with them except, usually, a common key or mode. It is not known for certain what their dramatic function was originally conceived to be, and it is unfortunate that the most interesting source of information about contemporary production, the preface to Gagliano's *La Dafne,*[1] written in 1608, the year following the first production of *Orfeo*, does not specifically help in this regard. This is because the ritornelli in *Dafne* are shorter than those in *Orfeo*, and are obviously conceived simply as small punctuating codettas to the vocal sections. However, the staging advice given in the preface links the ritornelli so exclusively with practical matters like the entrances and exits of singers, evidently felt to be supported by the instrumental music, that one feels the technique would probably apply to other operas of the same tradition. This concurs with our musical feeling, given the common key shared by recitative and ritornello, that there is no hint in *Orfeo* of the tension that was later to develop between singers and orchestra. Almost invariably the last chord of each vocal passage is the same as the first chord of the ensuing ritornello, and when, in a recent production,[2] the cadential chords were appropriately foreshortened to enable each section to lead more immediately into the next, a smooth continuity was obtained. Indeed, in these sequences of movements, the opera seemed so homogeneous as to belie the fact that the ritornelli have no overt thematic connections with the vocal recitatives, nor, apart from one instance, do the obbligato instruments ever actually accompany the solo singers. The fact that it worked so well in this way was due in no small measure to the acting of the singers who felt it to be so, simulating with their movements the continuation from recitative to ritornello and back. I do not think that a concert performance of *Orfeo*, sung with no actions, would achieve such a feeling of integrity; it is an example of how the theatre can modify purely musical considerations.

Example 4.1
Monteverdi *L'Orfeo*, Prologue

The extract shows the fourth of La Musica's stanzas, the one in which she first mentions the name of Orfeo. The singer takes her starting note from the end of the orchestral ritornello and the same D harmony too, though this is probably now in the minor. At the end of the section her passage cadences on A to lead in a similar way into the abridged ritornello. It may be felt that the vocal line needs ornamenting. This would not affect the point being made about the continuity from the ritornello but it would be an anachronism to emphasise that continuity any further by incorporating into the ornamentation any motivic figures from the ritornello.

Ritornello

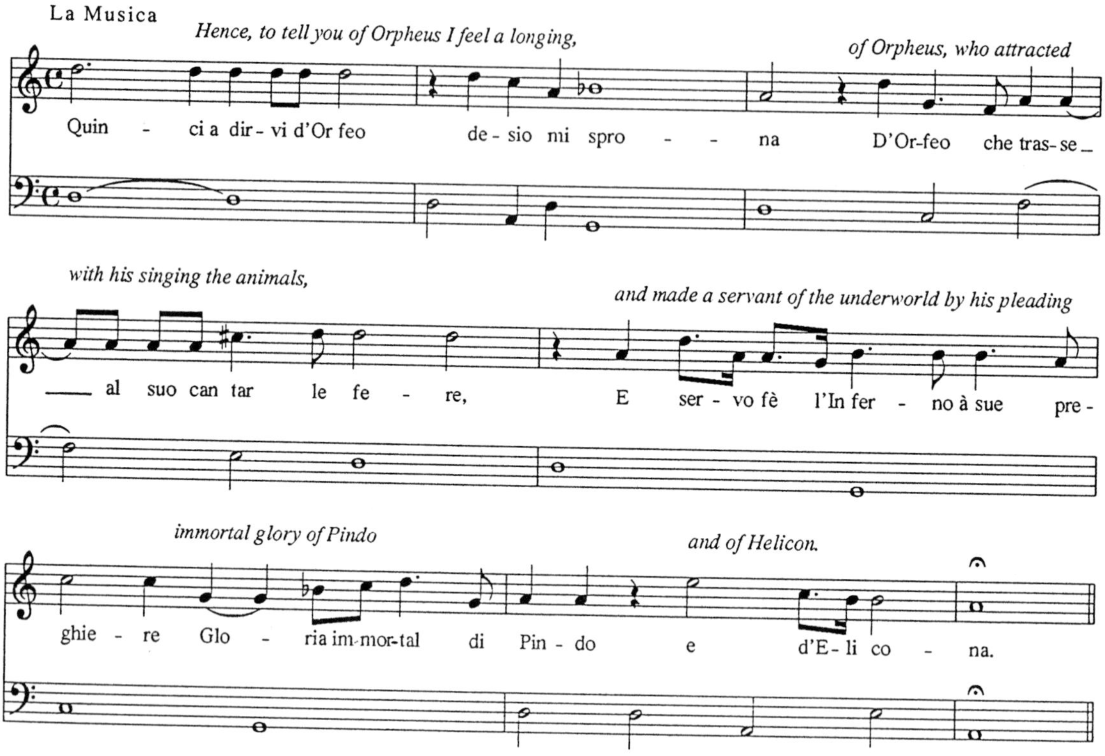

La Musica

Hence, to tell you of Orpheus I feel a longing, *of Orpheus, who attracted*

Quin - ci a dir- vi d'Or feo de- sio mi spro - - na D'Or-feo che tras-se_

with his singing the animals, *and made a servant of the underworld by his pleading*

_ al suo can tar le fe - re, E ser - vo fè l'In fer - no à sue pre -

immortal glory of Pindo *and of Helicon.*

ghie - re Glo - ria im-mor-tal di Pin - do e d'E- li co - na.

Ritornello

It was even possible, in the same Norrington production, to integrate into the opera the toccata with which it opens and which, with its brilliant style and unique scoring for five trumpets, is quite unlike anything heard later. Monteverdi marked it to be played three times 'before the curtain is raised'. Accounts of the treatment of similar instrumental introductions[3] suggest that they functioned as a general call to attention, or even possibly to announce the arrival of the aristocratic members of the audience. In this particular case it was used as a processional to bring the cast into the theatre, and thereby it affirmed the almost unchanging role of the orchestra in this opera of supporting the singers.

There is, however, a tantalising moment when a recapitulation of the ritornello of the prologue later in the opera seems to open up a new dimension for the orchestra. In the prologue itself the five verses of La Musica's strophic aria are enfolded in six playings of the ritornello, the first and the last, presumably, covering her entrance and exit. The grave beauty of the music can be felt by La Musica (and of course by the audience) as expressing her own innermost thoughts. Bearing in mind the number of playings and that this is the very first ritornello of the opera, we can only conclude that Monteverdi wanted to imprint it on our memory: he was too careful a composer for all this preparation to have been accidental.

The ritornello returns at just two later points in the opera, and it is with the first of these, at the end of Act 2, that the difficulty arises. Orfeo has by then left the stage to go down to Hades to seek Euridice, and the Messenger too has departed in sorrow, leaving only the chorus of nymphs and shepherds to comment on the cruelty of fate and finally to go off to mourn over Euridice's grave, presumably using this ritornello as their exit music: it has a certain sadness of mood which makes it very suitable for this. Although it might be argued that it is not strictly in the same key as the chorus, it leads on from it reasonably smoothly and indeed, in the context, its second bar reverts to the key, A, of the chorus. John Whenham is surely right to say that it suggests 'the power that music has to provide consolation in grief',[4] and this thought could well be dominant in the minds of the singers as they identify with the music in their exit.

But why this particular music? Monteverdi seems to be positing another dimension, reaching over the heads of the singers on the stage (who were presumably not present at the earlier playings in the prologue), to enable the audience to make the connection with the wider visions of La Musica. Whenham goes even further: since La Musica's prologue referred specifically to Orfeo captivating Hades, an event which for Act 2 is still in the future, he goes on to say that this ritornello 'shows the power that music will have to move the spirits of the underworld'. If this is not reading too much into the intentions of the music, then we have at least a hint of that looking backwards and forwards in time (backwards to La Musica's prologue, forwards to Orfeo's triumph in the underworld), independently of the singers on the stage, as was to be such a notable development in opera two centuries later. In this case, however, it was achieved without the orchestral music abrogating its primary function of supporting the singers, who can at least identify with the expressive gestures of the music if not its referential implications.

Some of these concepts do seem to come across in performance. The Harnoncourt video film clarifies the reference of the music by bringing La Musica herself back to the stage for it, as though to remind us that the story is still in a sense under her control. This is an excellent idea because it is indeed her music, but it may well be felt that the effect on the film is spoilt by her weeping, an ingenuous action from one who has shown herself earlier to be outside the time and space of the narrative, and has already predicted that Orfeo will triumph over the underworld.

If Monteverdi himself appreciated anything of these implications then it must be said that so far as we know he seems never to have thought the idea worth repeating; certainly the final appearance of the same ritornello at the beginning of Act 5 is more easily explained. Its function then is to bring Orfeo back to the stage on his return to earth, having finally lost Euridice. We can readily accept Monteverdi's use of the La Musica ritornello now, because he has proved himself to be the very embodiment of music's power.[5]

The idea behind the recapitulation of this one ritornello in *Orfeo* was not, to my knowledge, used by any other composer later in the seventeenth century. It was a time when an important new compositional preoccupation was the development of much stronger motivic bonding between the contiguous vocal and instrumental sections, tying each ritornello more firmly to its immediate location in the opera. In *Dido and Aeneas* this bonding was also strengthened sometimes by a common compositional device such as an ostinato continuo line or, for the witches, an echo effect. When a dance is joined to an aria in this way it can be the occasion for a ballet whose dancers could remain on the stage for the aria, presumably without moving. The singer, similarly, would not move significantly during the dance, but there would be a continuity of stance from or into the aria so as to make clear the bonding.

As for the overture to *Dido*, its emotional weight suggests that it can only refer to Dido herself: there is even a certain similarity of harmony as well as key[6] between its slow opening section and Dido's final recitative. The use of the same key enables it to lead directly into Belinda's first aria, as though the two movements were part of the one musical gesture. This, of course, suggests a dramatic continuity, with the strong implication that Belinda's reassuring aria is a response to a situation in which Dido has been telling her of her premonitions during the playing of the overture. Certainly at the moment the curtain rises the two singers can act as if this had indeed been the case. The closeness of the relationship of this overture to the beginning of the opera was exceptional at a time when such pieces were often simply a call to attention. Although it has its own integrity as a self contained French overture it can be compared with the openings of much later operas (Gounod's *Faust* and Debussy's *Pelléas et Mélisande* come to mind) which dispense with a formal overture and have instead a short orchestral prelude leading straight into the first scene.

II Orchestral March and Choral Dance

Possibly the first big break-through in the discovery of a new role for the orchestra came, it would seem, by accident rather than design. It arose from the fact that in writing the libretto for *The Marriage of Figaro*, Da Ponte was, unusually, adapting a play. It had long been a convention of the spoken theatre that music could be used as a background for dialogue, and Beaumarchais uses this idea twice (for a processional and a Fandango dance) in the passage which was adapted for the finale of Act III of the opera. Da Ponte's (or Mozart's) only conceptual advance was to have the dialogue sung, rather than spoken, over the background orchestral music. It seems likely that they thought of this as so obvious a way of adapting the play as to be quite unremarkable: no mention is made of it in their letters or memoirs. Yet this apparently tiny innovation carries the revolutionary implication for opera that the orchestra, being entirely concerned with the background march or dance, is not now necessarily supporting the solo singers, who may pursue their drama independently of it.

Although it is clear from the libretto that the lines marked (x) in the following passage were to be sung during the march and (y) during the Fandango dance, it is not obvious from the words what kind of vocal level, e.g. recitative or aria, Da Ponte expected Mozart to use: he seems to have hedged his bets by using a rather prosaic verse form. Mozart, for his part, avoids any recognition of the poetic qualities of these words, setting them to irregular rhythmic patterns sometimes on a monotone giving a parlando style not unlike recitative, and sometimes in a more melodic way, but never so as to detract from the fact that the main melodic interest and musical continuity are in the orchestra. The solo singers, relying on this, and of course keeping strictly in time with the orchestra (musically, that is, not gesturally) will primarily be concerned to sing their lines so as to enunciate the words as clearly as possible. They must understand that the orchestral music does not now necessarily express their innermost feelings.

Perhaps something should be said about the use of the chorus here. Auden described the function of the opera chorus with characteristic concision: 'The chorus can play two roles in opera and two only, that of the mob and that of the faithful, sorrowing or rejoicing community.'[7] In those terms there is no doubt that the members of this chorus, for all their gentleness and decorum, are mob, supporting Susanna and Figaro's quest for emancipation from aspects of serfdom: nor can there be any doubt that the orchestra is supporting them in this. Figaro's own tussle with the Count is sometimes interpreted as coming to a head in the recitative immediately preceding the Finale, and it is here that our extract begins.

Example 4.2
Mozart *The Marriage of Figaro*, Act III, Finale

The libretto is given first in its entirety, and then some passages are selected for comment with the music.

FIGARO Che diamin canta?	*What's his story?*
COUNT Non canta, no, ma dice, ch'egli saltò stamane in sui garofani.	*No story, but he says it was him who jumped on the carnations this morning.*
FIGARO Ei lo dice! sarà se ho saltato io, si può dare ch'anch'esso abbia fatto lo stesso	*He says that! Well, if I jumped, he could have done the same.*
COUNT Anch'esso?	*Him too?*
FIGARO Perchè no? io non impugno mai quel che non so.	*Why not? I never dispute what I don't know.*
No. 22 Finale (x) Ecco la marcia, andiamo! A'vostri posti o belle, a'vostri posti. Susanna, dammi il braccio.	*There's the march, let's go! Take your places, you beauties, Susanna, give me your arm!*
SUSANNA Eccolo!	*Here it is!*
COUNT Temerari!	*What temerity!*
COUNTESS Io son di ghiaccio.	*I feel like ice!*
COUNT Contessa!	*Countess!*
COUNTESS Or non parliamo. Ecco qui le due nozze: Riceverle dobbiam; alfin si tratta d'una vostra protetta. Seggiamo.	*Let us say no more now. Here are the two couples: We must receive them; one in particular has your protection. Let us be seated.*
COUNT Seggiamo, (e meditiam vendetta).	*Let us be seated, (and plan revenge).*

(*they take their seats*)

(*Enter the huntsmen shouldering their guns, lawyers, peasant men and women, two young girls carrying a bridal cap with white feathers, two more with a veil, two more with gloves and a bouquet of flowers, two more with a bridal cap and veil for Susanna etc. Bartolo leads Susanna up to the Count and she kneels before him to receive the cap etc. Figaro leads Marcellina up to the Countess for the same.*)

TWO PEASANT WOMEN Amanti, constanti, Seguaci d'onor, Cantate, lodate Si saggio signor. A un dritto cedendo Che oltraggia, che offende, Ei caste vi rende Ai vostri amator.	*Faithful, honorable girls* *Sing the praises of such a wise Lord.* *By renouncing a right which outrages and offends,* *he leaves you pure for your lovers.*
CHORUS Cantiamo, lodiamo, Si saggio signor.	*Let us sing the praises of our wise Lord.*

(y)

(*A fandango is danced. Susanna, kneeling before the Count, tugs his coat and shows him the note. She points to her head and the Count, as if adjusting her cap, takes the note, hiding it quickly in his breast. She rises and curtsies; Figaro comes forward to receive her. Marcellina soon rises and is received by Bartolo from the hand of the Countess.*)

COUNT (*taking the note and pricking his finger with the pin*)

Eh, già, si sa; solita usanza:	*Ah, yes, the usual custom.*
Le donne ficcan gli aghi in ogni loco.	*Women stick needles everywhere.*
Ah ah! Capisco il gioco.	*Ha ha! I understand the game.*
FIGARO (to Susanna)	
Un biglietto amoroso	*Some passing flirt has slipped him a billet doux*
Che gli diè nel passar qualche galante;	*sealed with a pin on which he's pricked a finger.*
Ed era sigillato d'una spilla	*Narcissus is looking for it. Oh what a sensation!*
Ond'egli si punse il dito.	
Il narciso or la cerca. Oh che stordito!	

(*The Count reads the letter, looks for the pin, finds it and puts it in his pocket.*)

Recitative
COUNT

Andate amici! e sia per questa sera disposto l'apparato nuziale colla più ricca pompa, . . .	*Now you can go, friends, and let the wedding celebration be arranged for this evening with the richest ceremony . . .*

Before the start of the extract, when Figaro entered, he was anxious to get the wedding festivities under way, but he had to parry awkward questions from the Count and Antonio. Confronted by the apparent inconsistency that both he and Cherubino had now admitted to jumping out of the Countess' window, his reply, 'Why not, I never dispute what I don't know', is taken exactly from the Beaumarchais play, where it is often interpreted as a point of crisis in the drama, with Figaro defiantly looking the Count straight in the eye. This reading has spilled over into the opera too, notably in the justly famous interpretation of the role by Geraint Evans.[8] If something big is made of this in the opera, it is certainly consistent with the implied threat to the Count of the ensuing wedding march and indeed, it might be said to enhance our awareness of that threat. The case against it is that Mozart doesn't call for it in the music, as he could easily have done had he so wished. Mozart's concern seems only to be to lead smoothly forwards into the following march. Tonally speaking, the phrase simply consolidates the modulation to G which is established six bars before. It is true that Figaro's melody for the crucial words is exactly the same as that used by the Count at the corresponding place six bars back, but the phrase is a recitative cliché used regularly by all the characters and at that distance could hardly be interpreted in itself as even mildly impertinent. If there is any threat to the Count in the music it can only be in the march itself, announcing the arrival of the whole court to celebrate the weddings he has tried to frustrate. So, strictly speaking, the only musically justifiable moment when Figaro could look defiant or smile triumphantly is when he hears the orchestra strike up, which is after he has finished singing. In the video picture from the Glyndebourne production he is seen at this moment looking firm but not arrogant.

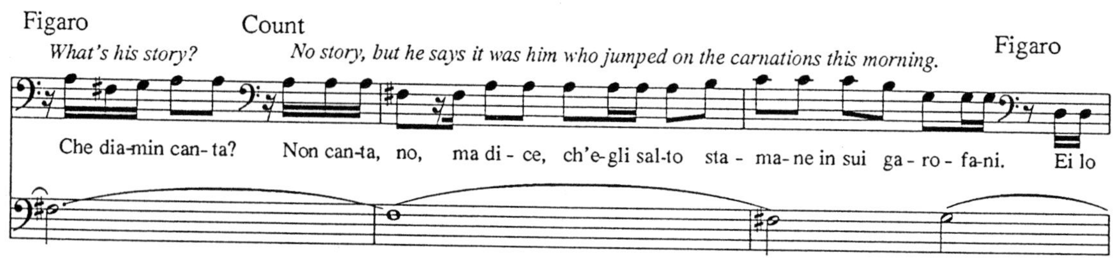

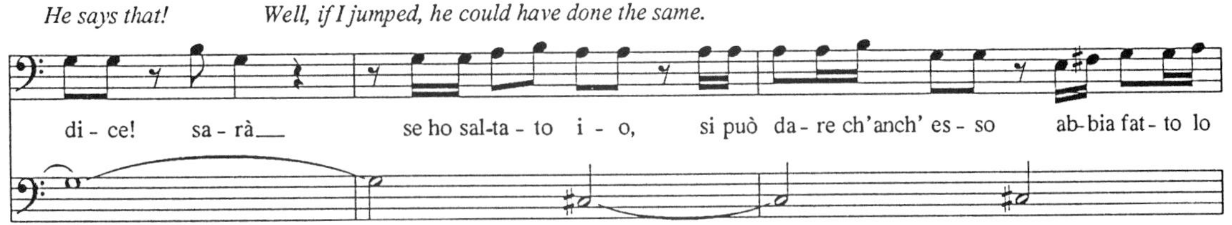
He says that!
Well, if I jumped, he could have done the same.
di - ce! sa - rà
se ho sal-ta - to i - o, si può da - re ch'anch' es - so ab-bia fat - to lo

Count
Him too?
Figaro
Why not? I never dispute what I don't know.
stes - so. An - ch'es-so? Per-chè nò? io no im-pu - gno mai quel che non

Marcia
Figaro
There's the march, let's go!
Take your
so. Ec-co la mar-cia, an - dia - mo! Ai vos-tri
Fl, Ho, Str.
pp

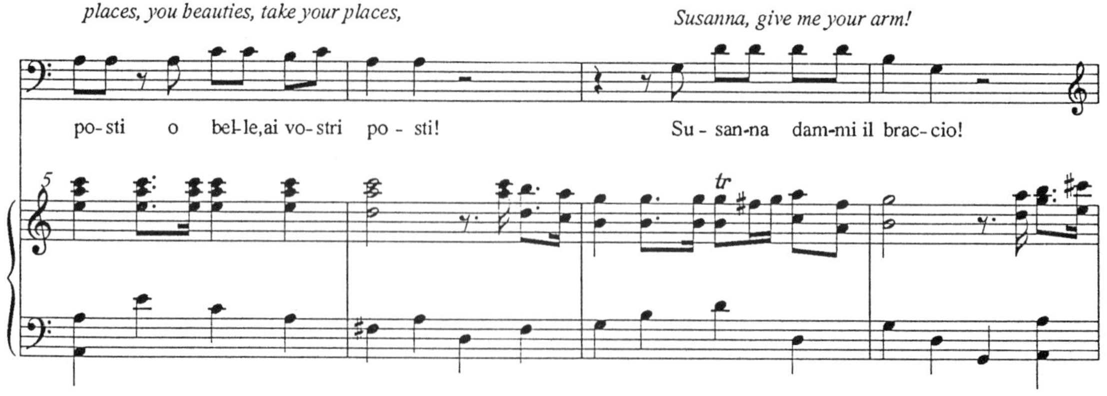
places, you beauties, take your places,
Susanna, give me your arm!
po-sti o bel-le, ai vo-stri po - sti!
Su - san-na dam-mi il brac-cio!
tr

The rather odd tonality of the march itself can possibly be explained by the fact that, as its *pianissimo* beginning helps to make clear, it is to be understood to have begun earlier and only just come within earshot, another original orchestral extension of the stage. The march, as it stands, is cast in 4 sections which are motivically identical:

Section	B	A	A	B
Bars	1–14	15–28	29–42	43–end
Key	G–d–C	C–a–G	C–a–G	G–d–C

We might assume that the 'complete' march would have started in the home key with an A section, perhaps repeated to balance the middle repeat, but yet if it were played like that it would have more repetition than the material can really stand. Indeed, it already has more repetition than would be desirable in a concert piece, but in the context of the opera, where there is (and must be) interesting stage movement throughout[9] we accept it as just right: Mozart was an impeccable judge of these things. The unusual stressing of the supertonic before each cadence with dissonant turns on the woodwind adds to the popular Spanish flavour a certain tension which, in the context, can be understood as further threat to the Count. Figaro's part causes no interpretative problems for the singer here since he is announcing the march and organising those going off to take part in the procession: in other words he can sing as if the orchestra were supporting his every word, and the same applies to Susanna. But for the Count and Countess it is quite different. He views the approaching procession with anger and frustration, she with foreboding, and they have to colour their voices so as to sing against the orchestral music, showing little relish for its seductive rhythm. In her stiff reply to his address she is seen raising her hand as if not only against him, but also to shut her off from the music.

There is a nice touch on the video film when at 'Seggiamo' he shows her to her seat. This is evidently reluctant because it is she who first suggests it, and he does it with a little bow which is ironically related to the music: but he turns quickly away from her for the following aside.

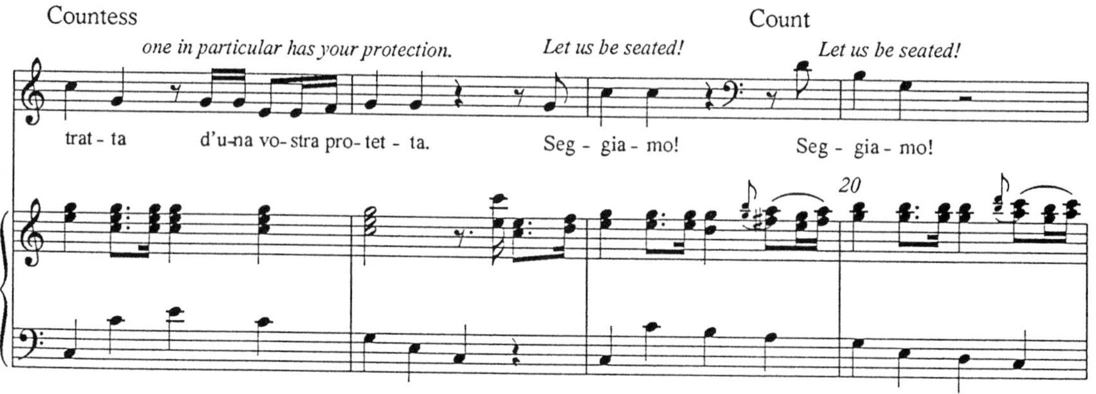

The music, meanwhile, pursues its own sweet course quite independently of the Count and his feelings: even the intriguing patterns of its rather unusual modulations have nothing at all to do with him. He is now seated, but his stance can still show his unease at the approaching procession and its associated music.

Count
and plan revenge.
(the Count and Countess sit. Enter huntsmen with guns....)
e me-di-tiam ven- det ta.
tr
tr
25
un poco cresc.

The marriage ceremonies set out in the libretto are to take place during the song and chorus and give rise to no specifically operatic problems for the performers. Traditionally Basilio, as the court musician, is credited with the composition of the piece and 'conducts' it from the side, but this must not be done in such a way as to divert attention too much from the main stage business. In fact the action is not consistent with Beaumarchais (not that that matters), since in the play Basilio is not yet present but will shortly make his entrance and ask for Marcellina's hand, an episode cut out by Da Ponte and Mozart. The choir may be seen to be enjoying the occasion, the music allows that, but there is nothing in the music to suggest that they should overtly show in their actions that they are antagonistic towards the Count.

The movement leads straight into the Fandango. This was a Spanish dance of popular origin,[10] also cultivated by the upper classes in a more restrained form, as is probably appropriate here. Certainly Mozart's contrapuntal bass line gives his dance an aristocratic elegance but, as in the march, the dissonant ornamental notes in the oboe and bassoon (appoggiaturas in this case), generate a degree of tension to match the dramatic tension simmering just below the surface.

As in the march it is the Count whose part gives a problem of interpretation. As he turns away and reads Susanna's note, actions nothing to do with the occasion or the spirit of the dance, he again has to adopt a cold tone which synchronises with the orchestral music but is not expressively a part of it. This is difficult because this time his vocal line does actually double the dance melody for the first phrase. It goes without saying that any bodily movement suggested by the dance, however small, would be quite wrong. Figaro, on the other hand, is enjoying both the dance and what he sees of the Count's actions.

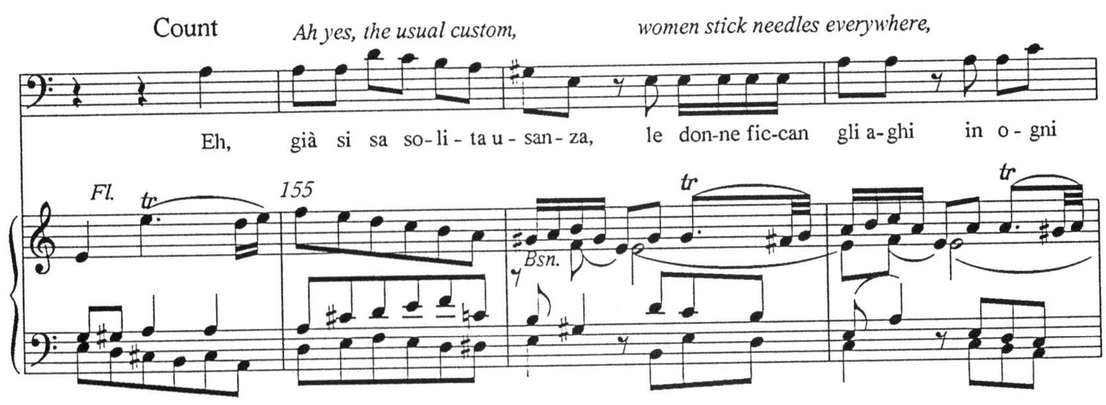
Count
Ah yes, the usual custom,
women stick needles everywhere,
Eh, già si sa so-li-ta u-san-za, le don-ne fic-can gli a-ghi in o-gni
Fl.
tr
155
tr
Bsn.
tr

Count
Ha ha! I understand the game!
Figaro
Some passing flirt has slipped him a billet-doux,
lo-co, ah! ah! ca-pi-sco il gio-co! Un big-liet-to a-mo-ro-so che gli diè nel pas-sar qual-che ga-lan-te,
tr
160

As became the custom in many later examples of such dance sequences, a moment of drama recalls us all, including the orchestra, back to the normal opera conventions. The Count calls a halt to the dancing by announcing (in accompanied recitative) the further celebrations for the evening. As suggested by the video picture he will probably stand up and walk forwards for this, to indicate his resumption of command of the stage. The finale is then brought to an end by a reprise of the chorus, and in the Glyndebourne production this music is used to get the chorus off stage, though the *forte* finish suggests rather that Mozart intended the curtain to fall on a full stage.

When in the following year Mozart returned to the idea in Act 1 of *Don Giovanni*, he developed it in several ways. In place of the one pit orchestra he simultaneously used three bands actually on stage in different rooms, to give a musical space to the Don's seduction strategies. Although later composers did not, in general, copy this virtuosic combination of bands, the idea of a small on-stage ensemble has often been used to add authenticity to dance scenes. Later composers also emulated Mozart's theatrical flair in realising that the return of the main pit orchestra could be very effective if it coincided with a dramatic coup on the stage. In this case Zerlina, in one of the rooms with Don Giovanni, suddenly calls out for help and at once the main orchestra interrupts the dancing with an unexpected and very dramatic move from the prevailing key of G into E flat. The orchestra is now back to its customary role, fully supporting Zerlina. It is a nice practical point that the new situation gives the on-stage musicians a good pretext for making a quick exit.

What is so innovatory in this technique is that it provides a credible musical continuity (in the orchestra) against which vocal dialogue can take place and the action can move forwards. It was this which appealed so much to the Romantic opera composer. If the librettist gave him a social environment where music was appropriate, for example a court ball or village fete, then by stringing together suitable dances he could give musical coherence over quite a big span to 'realistic' dialogue which in earlier times could only have been set as recitative. There is a fine example of a string of such dances in the very first scene of Rigoletto, the overall scheme of which is shown below.

Example 4.3
Verdi *Rigoletto*, Act I, opening dance sequence

	DANCE MOVEMENT	DRAMATIC SYNOPSIS
(a)	Allegro con brio (off-stage band)	The Duke tells Borsa of a new amorous adventure.
(b)	Allegretto (pit orchestra)	The Duke's solo ballata reveals his general attitude to women.
(c)	Minuet (on-stage band)	He flirts with the Countess Ceprano and goes off with her.
(d)	Tempo I (off-stage band)	Rigoletto taunts Ceprano.
(e)	Perigordino dance (on-stage band)	Dancing on-stage while seduction is taking place off-stage.
(f)	Tempo I (off-stage band, joined later by pit orchestra)	Marillo enters with news of Rigoletto's alleged mistress.
(g)	Più vivo (off-stage band plus pit orchestra)	All the dancers from the inner rooms come forward to swell the chorus for the climax.

Clearly the structuring here is more complex than that of the scene from *Figaro*, and the scale is bigger. However the relationship between singer and orchestra varies from moment to moment in a rather similar way, and just as Mozart used the device to articulate an important feature of the plot (the opposition of the court servants to the Count), so Verdi's skill in superimposing action on the musical continuity of the dances makes for a highly effective and original[11] exposition of the opera's main dramatic situation. In fact, as in a Mozart finale, the main actions come at the joins between the movements.

There is constant variation in the source of the dances (pit orchestra, on-stage and off-stage groups) helping to create the atmosphere of a big court reception: certainly the superficial quality of much of the dance music itself is appropriate for this hedonistic court. Although we are to understand that most of the actual dancing is centred on the off-stage 'inner rooms', it can spill over onto the main stage to give movement there too. However, the Minuet (c) and Perigordino (e), accompanied by the on-stage band, are presumably danced on the main stage. Over the dance background the vocal writing can move quickly and flexibly from prosaic dialogue to lyrical effusion, enabling Verdi to establish his characters very clearly. A particular achievement is the integration of the Duke's ballata (b) into the sequence, by giving it the qualities at once of dance and aria.

There are several general principles to be drawn as to how such a sequence works in the theatre. Once the dance is under way its music carries the momentum and the singer can, as appropriate, vary from dry parlando to 'aria' singing without the momentum being disrupted. In this respect the singer enjoys a greater freedom than would normally be possible in an aria.

Whether the dancing can be seen or not doesn't seem to matter, so long as it is established that it is to this that the orchestral music is referring. When the dancing is unseen but is nevertheless affirmed by the music, we can think of the orchestra as enlarging the stage in an almost literal sense. The Duke's ballata (b) shows how this idea can be manipulated by the composer. It begins as if it is to be another dance, with what sounds like a conventional musical invitation to take up positions for the dance. But the producer who interprets the music in this way will almost certainly want to get the dancers off the stage quite soon in order not to distract attention from what is in effect the Duke's first aria. There is also the practical consideration that the Duke will want to treat the section as an aria with rubato at some of the later cadences, and dancing at such moments would be impossible. What actually happens during the movement is that the role of the orchestra changes almost imperceptibly from providing a dance to supporting an aria. It is a fact of operatic life that such a change, or its reverse, can be made easily and is readily accepted without question in the theatre.

When dancing does take place on the stage the producer must decide how involved in the main drama of the opera the dancers should be. Arguably when they are dancing they are in a different category from when they are the chorus (whose nature it is to be articulate in participation or comment), and on the whole it is better for them to be detached from the drama. Certainly in the Perigordino, there is good dramatic irony in their dancing purely for the pleasure of the dance, as if unaware (or at least uncaring) of the seduction taking place off-stage. Verdi's bland, rather vacuous dance music supports them admirably in this, providing a good foil to the passions about to be unleashed. The dancers may, of course, revert to being chorus later.

In the ENO production on video, this scene is set in a San Gennaro cocktail party in Little Italy, New York in the 1950s. There is very little dancing at all except in the Perigordino, and we have to accept the orchestral music somewhat in the spirit of modern taped background music: it seems to work well enough on that level. It is important, however, that there is sufficient stage movement (guests intermingling, circulation of drinks etc.), to which the dance music can relate, particularly at the beginning of sections when its role is first established.

The joins between consecutive dances need careful handling both as regards how the tempo change is effected, and also in the timings of the actions which are invariably called for at these moments. There are three very common types of join: the least dramatic is when there is no gap between the sections, the orchestra itself running one dance into the next. The following example shows such a link between sections (b) and (c). The main orchestra, which has been accompanying the ballata will pick up the tempo after any cadential rallentando by the Duke, so as to lead forwards to overlap with the first chord of the new Minuet, played by the band on the stage. It is at that very moment that the court dancers enter, and in the first ten bars of the new instrumental music the Duke has time to seek out and bring forward the Countess Ceprano.

In the ENO production, no new dancers enter, but it is sufficient (to make sense of the musical change) that the Duke should turn ostentatiously from Borsa, whom he has been addressing in his aria, to look across to the Countess Ceprano on the other side of the stage. This moment is captured in the sketch in the following example. The subsequent conversation shows the flexibility of the word setting over the dance. His prosaic enquiry 'You're leaving?', leads to her cold reply in which the grace note on 'sposo' is less an affirmation of the dance than an emphasis of her loyalty to her husband. Thus far the conversation, as with the Count's in the *Figaro* scene, is detached from the essential spirit of the dance, and the singers' tone will no doubt reflect it. But the Duke's impassioned reply, extolling her beauty, moves to a quite different operatic dispensation. It is no accident that the key of the music now changes to the dominant, a renewal of musical interest at the very moment that the level of the orchestral role changes and he can now feel the accompaniment as fully supporting his amorous advances.

At the end of the minuet there is another kind of join, with a voice, not the orchestra, controlling the pacing into the next dance. The singer is Rigoletto himself, and it is a telling piece of characterisation that this, his first appearance in the opera, should be as an interruption to the entertainment of a society against which he is so deeply at odds, even if in the context he is not able to say so. The following music shows his little cadenza leading into section (d), the first reprise of the opening dance. In addition to Rigoletto's entry, the musical change into the next dance is marked by another action on the stage, the exit of the Duke with the Countess, who has given in to his flirtatious advances. They start to walk off as he sings his last phrase leaving Rigoletto to cover the musical gap between the sections. This moment is shown in the sketch.

The irony of Rigoletto's words is heightened by the notes he sings, repeated C's rising to E flat, a quotation from the 'Curse' theme from the Prelude to the opera. However, we do not yet know the dramatic implication of this because Monterone has not yet uttered the curse, and the phrase is softened by the fact that the E flat is here accompanied by a relaxed E flat major harmony. In other words, this is no more than banter, and does not call for the fatalistic tone he will save for the same music in later contexts. A little rubato is allowable, indeed probably intended, so long as the phrase drives forwards to the accented second syllable of 'Ceprano', on which the new tempo must strictly start, so as to re-establish the scene's momentum. In the ENO production, the taunted Ceprano throws his drink in Rigoletto's face at that precise moment, an action not incompatible with the disruption to the music of the dancing. Rigoletto is behind his bar at that moment, but soon comes forwards for his further taunts, which still linger on the repeated C's and use the dance as an ironic background to his rather malicious exposure of the effect on Ceprano of the Duke's amorous success.

Duke
love intoxicates, overwhelms, destroys my heart
(gives his arm to the Countess and goes out with her)
mo - re i-ne-bria, con-qui - de, di-strug ge il mio co - re!
Rigoletto (to Ceprano)
In te sta che a
265
Rigoletto
(Ceprano makes a gesture of impatience and follows the Duke)
What is on your head, Signor Ceprano?
(to the courtiers) He's fuming!
ve-te, si-gnor di Ce-pra - - - no? Ei sbuf-fa! Ve-
Tempo I (𝅗𝅥 =112)
270
(Off-stage band)
f

The effect of the join can be equally dramatic when the composer brings one dance to a firm conclusion and then leaves a short articulating silence before the next, a device often used by Mozart in his finales. As in them too the momentary disruption of continuity is immensely effective on the stage if the gap coincides with an event of some dramatic importance, most often an entrance. Verdi employs such a break between sections (e) and (f), in order to bring our attention back to the main subject of the opera. Marullo's eagerness as he enters, at the exact moment of the musical divide, must surely attract the attention of all on the stage, and the six bars of music before he sings are enough for him to move to a good position for his announcement about Rigoletto's alleged mistress. This is the start of the last and the longest section, and it is extended at the end by running straight into the climactic più vivo without a break.

To return to the general principles of the operation of dance sequences, the question of the overall musical form must be raised, and in this particular case the music is cast in a rondo structure with the recurring material in sections (a), (d) and (f). It could be argued that this form is not as exactly matched in the dramatic form as that, say, of the Mozart movement in Example 3.9, though the idea of flirtatious love certainly links these sections. A study of other similar dance sequences suggests that not even this degree of musical integration is always felt by composers to be necessary. However, another type of musical structuring is almost invariably to be found, involving an increase in pace and loudness towards the end, with the greater participation of the chorus, so that the whole scene comes to a climax there.

At the very end, as in Mozart, the dances are interrupted by an event of considerable dramatic power, expressed musically by a striking change of texture and tonality. The whirling dance, in A flat, is suddenly cut off to reveal Monteroni's grim voice off-stage, with its fatalistic modulation to C minor. The reiterated note C will have, at least for the moment, a chilling effect on all those on the stage (with the possible exception of the Duke), as well as on the audience, who will remember it from the opening of the orchestral Prelude and this time, as there, the harmonies change to the diminished chord on the E flat each time it comes, sung first by the chorus and then Monteroni. In the ENO production on video the singer enters earlier than marked so as to be seen as soon as he sings. This perhaps demonstrates a difference between the mediums of video and opera proper, for in the theatre, if not on film, the unseen voice required by Verdi is immensely effective. In either interpretation the weight of a whole climax rests for a moment on the intensity of a single singer. Those on the stage will surely 'freeze' when they hear his voice and turn in his direction as he enters.

The essential concept behind the last example, the flexible treatment of an orchestral reference to a background activity, was varied in many ways in nineteenth-century opera. In the last act of *Il Trovatore*, the musical continuum is not a dance but a Miserere from a chapel service taking place off-stage. This is a prayer for the souls of Manrico and Azucena who are about to be executed, and when Leonora arrives for an ill-fated rescue bid, she stops to listen to the chanting before singing of her own feelings.

Example 4.4
Verdi *Il Trovatore*, Act IV

The short excerpt shows one of the magical moments of interchange. Verdi does not actually keep up the chanting but transfers its characteristic A flat minor chord and dotted rhythm to the orchestra for Leonora's accompaniment. In the theatre we understand this to be the sound of the Miserere ringing on in her ears rather than literally continuing, but this is enough to preserve the essential continuity and it frees the orchestra to revert to their traditional role of simply supporting the singer. The orchestral intensification of the short notes of the Miserere's dotted rhythm from semiquavers to the harder pairs of demisemiquavers provides the perfect complement to the anguished solo line.

When Britten employs the same device in Act II, Scene 1 of *Peter Grimes* we are kept more aware of the continuing off-stage service by the frequent references back to it: the pious members of the village are at Matins in the church. However, again we do not hear the whole service, but only snatches of it, including the beginnings and ends of the various canticles and prayers, all neatly dove-tailed into the orchestral accompaniments of the scene on-stage, where Ellen is talking to Peter's new apprentice, and will later quarrel with Peter. The dove-tailing can have ironic force, as when the beginning of the confession in the church leads into the scene where Ellen discovers the first signs that Peter is treating the boy roughly. The church choir are accompanied by an off-stage organ, whilst for Ellen it is the pit orchestra who, although they start from the same notes or chords (as though it were the organ continuing), are in fact entirely identified with her, and with the events unfolding on the stage.

Looking at it another way, we can think of the service as providing a background continuity across the joins of the main divisions of Ellen's aria and the following duet. The whole scene is a veritable source-book for this technique in that Britten subtly varies its use with each new section. For the first section the chords of the opening hymn become the chordal accompaniment for the first section of the aria: for the second, it is the melody of the four-note chant of the Gloria which is taken over by the orchestra as a melodic ostinato. The entry of Peter shortly afterwards evidently called for a more intense treatment, and for this a fast unison setting of the Benedicite is sung throughout the section to provide an agitated background to the two voices on the stage. The breathless pace is maintained by the division of the off-stage singers into two choirs, the one immediately taking over from the other at each cadence. This is so fraught as to be, in effect, a distortion of the church music, as though heard through the ears of Peter and Ellen and caught up in their quarrel. Even here though, it is the pizzicato chords in the pit orchestra which are really, in the traditional sense, accompanying them. Indeed, for all its ingenuity this scene is conceptually simpler for the singers on the stage than the *Rigoletto* dances because the main orchestra is supporting them throughout: the only problem for them (in this sense) is the very minor one of what to do when the music only comes from the church, and this is one of the matters to be thought about in our next example.

Example 4.5
Britten *Peter Grimes*: opening scene of Act II

The extract begins at the end of the hymn in E flat. Ellen is sitting knitting while the boy is playing at her feet. The phrases of her aria pick up from the ends of each line of the hymn in turn, sometimes using notes suggestive of a certain emotional distance from the hymn itself. However, in this last phrase the foreign F sharp is only an appoggiatura onto the G and her line seems to settle happily into the E flat key of the hymn.

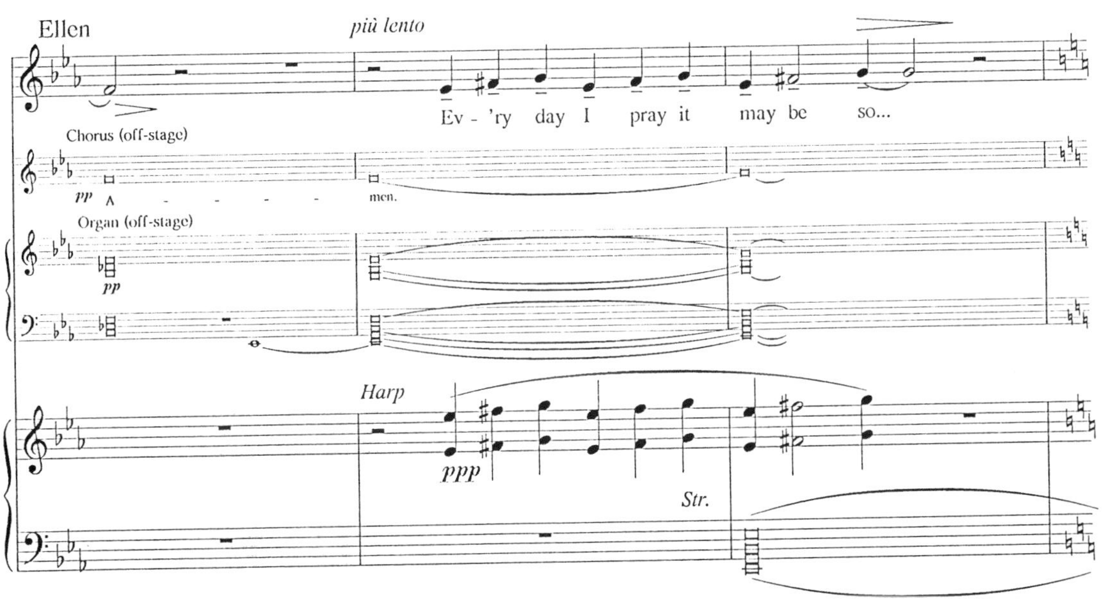

The Rector's intonation for the following prayer, the general confession, begins on a rather strident new note, B. Clearly this off-stage music is not at this moment expressive of the situation on the stage and so it is sensible, in the video film, that Ellen should turn to the direction of the church when the Rector's voice is heard. This makes it all the more dramatic when, at the beginning of the prayer itself she turns back and her eye alights on the boy's coat.

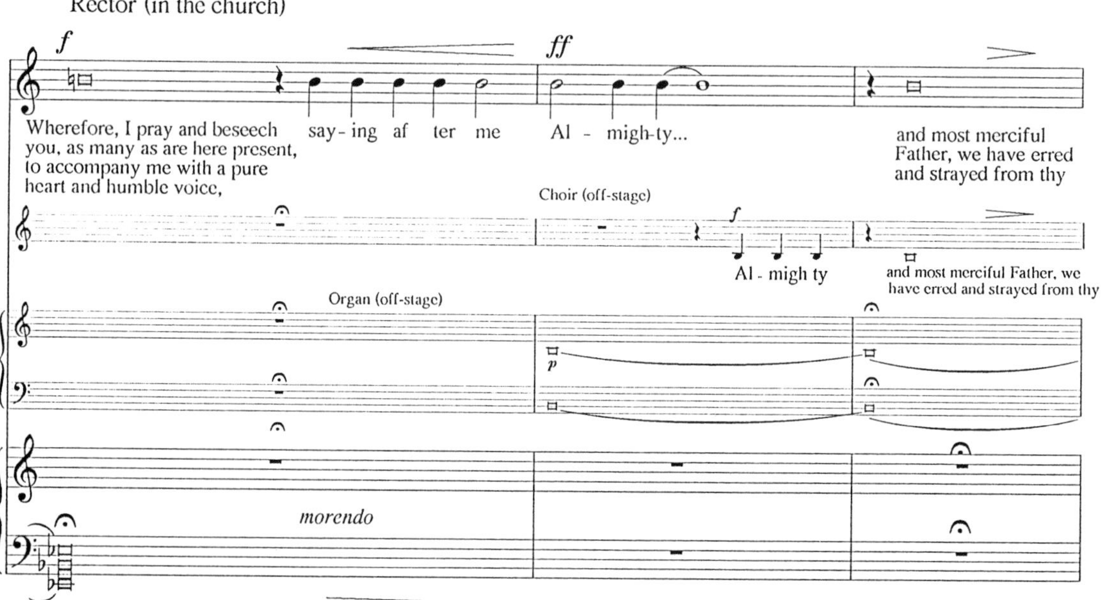

There now follows one of the most moving moments of the opera, when we first sense from Ellen's viewpoint the inevitability of the tragedy to come. The note B of the confession is taken over by the orchestral strings as a hushed but deeply agitated trill: this simple transformation is in itself a telling example of Britten's skill. Equally telling is Ellen's use of the very same notes as those she has just sung at the end of the hymn for the words 'There's a tear in your coat.'[12] In the new tonality of B these have a quite new urgency and poignancy, for the highest note G, the earlier point of rest, is now made restive. The instructions on the score would seem to suggest that she remains seated, lost in her own thoughts perhaps, throughout the three bars after Figure 9 up to the moment of the trill. However, in the Glyndebourne video, on seeing the tear she at once puts her knitting down, rises and walks down to the boy, so that at the exact moment the orchestral trill begins she has her hand on his coat. That is a powerful gesture entirely at one with the music. As she questions the boy he tries to resist her probings and we see Mrs Sedley witnessing the uncomfortable discovery. The simple agitation of the trill gives enough musical interest for all of this stage action.

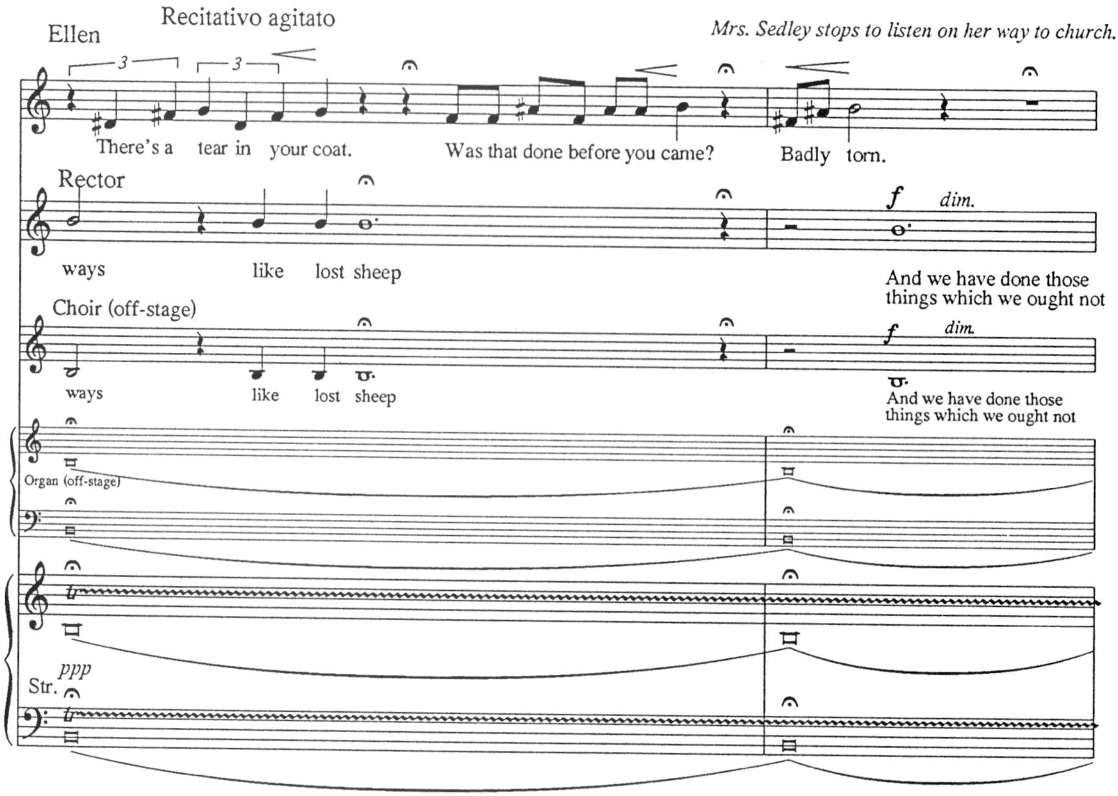

Recitativo agitato

Mrs. Sedley stops to listen on her way to church.

Ellen
There's a tear in your coat. Was that done before you came? Badly torn.

Rector
ways like lost sheep
f *dim.*
And we have done those things which we ought not

Choir (off-stage)
ways like lost sheep
f *dim.*
And we have done those things which we ought not

Organ (off-stage)

Str. *ppp*

Mrs Sedley's snooping presence adds further tension in the build up to the discovery of the bruise. By now the tension is made tonally explicit too, the B major–minor of Ellen and the orchestra pitted against the C minor of the responses in the church. The same tonal dichotomy is transferred into the following section of Ellen's aria, but with a quite new meaning when the four notes of the Rector's Gloria become a melodic

ostinato for Ellen's continuing aria. The common note between the keys, the assertive minor third of the C minor Gloria becomes a more gentle, compassionate major third of B (notated as D sharp). It was no doubt to emphasise this aspect of Ellen's feelings that she and the boy are still seated here in the original stage directions: indeed according to them she does not stand at all until just before Peter's entry. However, the other C minor notes of the ostinato, F and D, transferring into the Phrygian E sharp and the minor C double sharp, seem to point to Ellen's underlying unease and concern for the boy, and they lend some justification to the interpretation on the video with both of them standing. These points are not pedantic, for a concern for the meaning of the music should inform all opera production.

III Storms and Bohemians

We have followed some of the ramifications of the concept behind the Fandango in *Figaro*. There was another and even more important innovation in the role of the orchestra, which also grew out of an eighteenth-century usage, particularly in France,[13] and blossomed in the next century; its use as atmospheric background. In the magical orchestral writing of the arioso 'Che puro ciel' from his *Orfeo*, Gluck was using the new orchestral virtuosity to say something about Elysium quite over and above what a singer can convey. Orfeo in the prelude will not so much 'time every gesture so as to make the audience think that it is his inward emotion which causes the orchestra to play the appropriate phrase',[14] but will rather look around him so as to suggest that it is to those surrounding Elysian fields that the orchestral music refers, as well as to his own emotions in seeing them. This apparently small distinction led, in the next century, to a whole new technique of enlarging the stage by atmospheric orchestral writing. At first composers were content to explore the new dimension, as in Gluck, without the orchestra losing its role of supporting the singer. Thus the orchestral introduction to Act II of *Fidelio* (1806–14) says something universal about darkness and suffering; yet when the orchestral role moves from the general to the particular to accompany the singing of the imprisoned Florestan, the same material functions quite naturally as the accompaniment to his recitative, leading on from his rather broken phrases and bridging the gaps between them, as in the traditional accompanied recitative.

In the full-blooded Romanticism of Weber's *Der Freischütz* (1821), the scoring of the supernatural music is more picturesquely atmospheric, and the use of it is on a larger scale. When there is singing, the orchestra still fully supports it, but there is a tendency for the orchestral role to become more dominant. Indeed in the Wolf's Glen scene the singing stops some four or five minutes before the end; after that there is only speaking or shouting over the orchestral music which now assumes the main burden of the drama. The subsequent developments in German opera, e.g. the storm in Wagner's *The Flying Dutchman* (1841), were to lead to the Music Drama, the subject of the next chapter. For the moment, though, let us explore further how this detachment of voice from orchestra was developed in Italy.

We might ask why composers in a tradition dominated by the singer should have wanted to develop in this way. One factor may have been the desire to extend into the main stage drama something of that evocative power already being explored in the overtures, painting the background against which the drama was to unfold. Perhaps even more important was the search for dramatic realism, moving closer to the spoken theatre. This in opera would involve moving across the vocal levels, from parlando to bel canto, more flexibly than hitherto, yet in such a way as to give an overall musical thrust across a bigger canvas. The inherited musical forms were not proving sufficiently adaptable for this, as Rossini noted in a letter to Wagner in 1860, a play '. . . if one simply considers the rational, rapid and regular development of the dramatic action, makes no use of conventional forms. So how can the independence required by the literary conception be maintained in an alliance with musical form which is wholly dependent upon convention?'[15] It was Verdi's genius to realise most fully the possibilities of using the atmospheric orchestra to solve this dilemma: to give dramatic freedom within big musical structures, yet without compromising the essential Italian vocal tradition.

The thunderstorm in the last act of *Rigoletto* is an example of the pathetic fallacy, in which the growth of the storm is associated with the grim development of the plot up to the murder of Gilda. At the beginning of the scene there is an almost uncanny stillness, with unaccompanied secco recitative of grim bleakness. Then, after some static bare-fifth chords, the first signs of the approaching storm are heard at the vocal cadence points. Introduced in this way, they have the double operatic virtue of giving continuity by bridging the gaps between vocal phrases and also, because the voices are momentarily silent, of making the maximum musical impact. This means in turn that when they reappear later on in an accompanimental role, we are aware of their significance.

Example 4.6
Verdi *Rigoletto*, Act III, storm scene

The passages below are taken from the beginning of the scene where Rigoletto is negotiating with the assassin Sparafucile. The extremely simple use, over many bars, of a held open fifth chord on D, gives just enough continuity of orchestral presence to give a slight shiver of fear for that uncanny stillness which presages a storm. Then gradually the first tangible signs of the storm arrive, including an economical use of the piccolo for distant lightning, trill-like figures on violas and cellos for thunder, and a remarkable evocation of the wind using tenor voices (behind the scene) in chromatic thirds. The vocal lines at this early stage consist mostly of short, unmelodic, declamatory phrases, with words such as would normally have been set as recitative, and to be sung in that way too, though Verdi is careful to direct that the usual appoggiaturas are not to be added. One of the virtues of this technique of Verdi's is that the overall musical design, built up gradually from the various orchestral fragments, is not in the least compromised by the singers' parlando and rhythmic freedom at this stage: in other words, the recitative is contained within the larger musical structure. The flexibility of vocal levels is illustrated by Rigoletto's 'Egli è Delitto . . . (*His (name) is Crime, mine is Punishment*)', a significant affirmation calling for full tone and firm rhythms. The sketch shows a typical gesture at this moment: he turns away from Sparafucile towards the audience, as if making a more universal statement about himself.

Sparafucile
I can throw him in the river myself
Rigoletto
No no, I myself must do it.
Sparafucile
Very well
A get-tar - lo nel fiu-me bas-to io so-lo. No, no, il vo' far io stes-so Si- a! Il suo
26 Ob.
pp
Vcl.

Rigoletto
what is his name? You should also know mine?
His is Crime, Punishment is mine.
(exit)
no me? Vuoi sa-per an-che il mi-o? E - gli è De- lit - to, Pu- ni - zion son i - o.
30
35

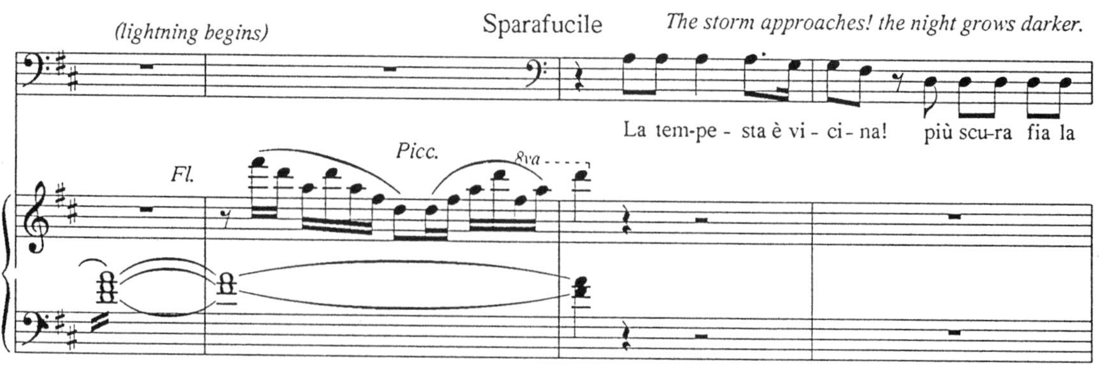
(lightning begins)
Sparafucile
The storm approaches! the night grows darker.
La tem-pe - sta è vi - ci - na! più scu-ra fia la
Fl.
Picc.
8va

The interest has been centring for the moment on the conversations outside the inn. The Duke, meanwhile, has been flirting with Maddalena and will doubtless make a more flamboyant gesture when the appearance of his theme on the solo clarinet diverts our attention to him. At the next appearance of the storm music there is a little more overlap with the voice and there will be more still as the scene progresses, so that from bar 188 onwards the storm is virtually continuous. There are other changes, too, both in the orchestral and vocal writing, to propel the relentless momentum towards the climax: the rhythmic pulse of the orchestral storm gradually quickens and the vocal writing becomes more sustained so that over the whole scene there is something not unlike a progression from the condition of recitative to that of an *arioso agitato*, but held by the orchestra into a tight and dramatic crescendo.

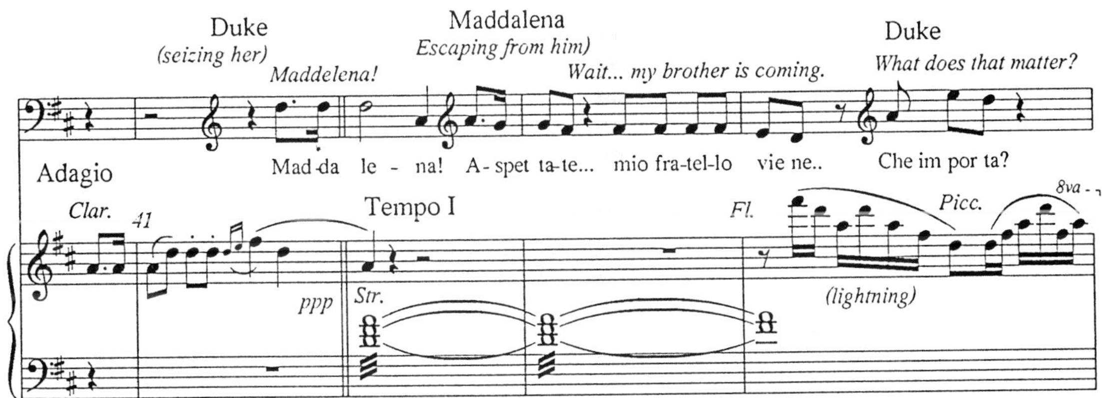

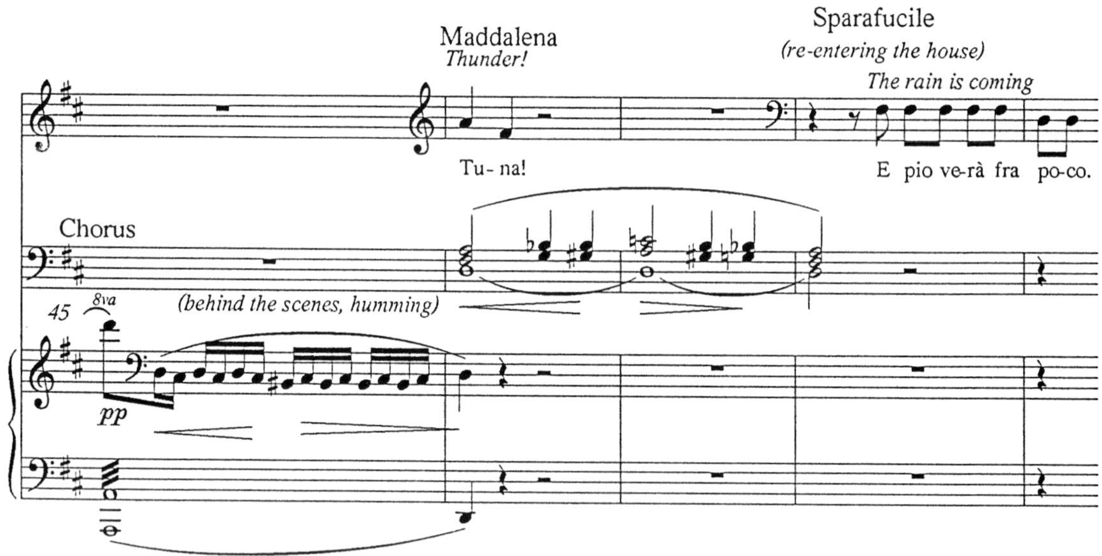

The next short extract comes from later in the scene when Rigoletto has left the stage and Gilda has returned, preparing to sacrifice her life to save the Duke. The natural affinity of the pathetic fallacy to opera is evident in that the orchestra can both represent the storm and also support the increasingly turbulent emotions of the characters on the stage. Yet the singers themselves must maintain a certain aloofness from an orchestral storm whose outward manifestations are not necessarily part of their own experience. Two instances of this are shown here. The *fortissimo* outbursts in the orchestra in bars 276 and 280 are timed to cover the gaps between the singers' phrases, yet they do not in a musical sense arise from them. The first of the phrases even dips down to its cadence and is hardly meant to be sung so as to lead forwards to such an orchestral climax: the second stays on a monotone. The last notes of both are likely to be drowned by the accompaniment. Thus the situation for the singers would seem to be that they should take their general mood from the orchestra, but that in following their own words and projecting them clearly, they may well feel that at times they are actually singing against the orchestra. Gilda's 'Pieta d'un mendico', is not of course sung in her real character but with an assumed voice (this is often done with a slightly forced tone). The gap in the storm allows this new characterisation to be entirely achieved by the voice without any more orchestral competition than the suddenly soft *tremolando* orchestral strings, to be taken up into the imminent climax of storm and drama when she walks in to her death.

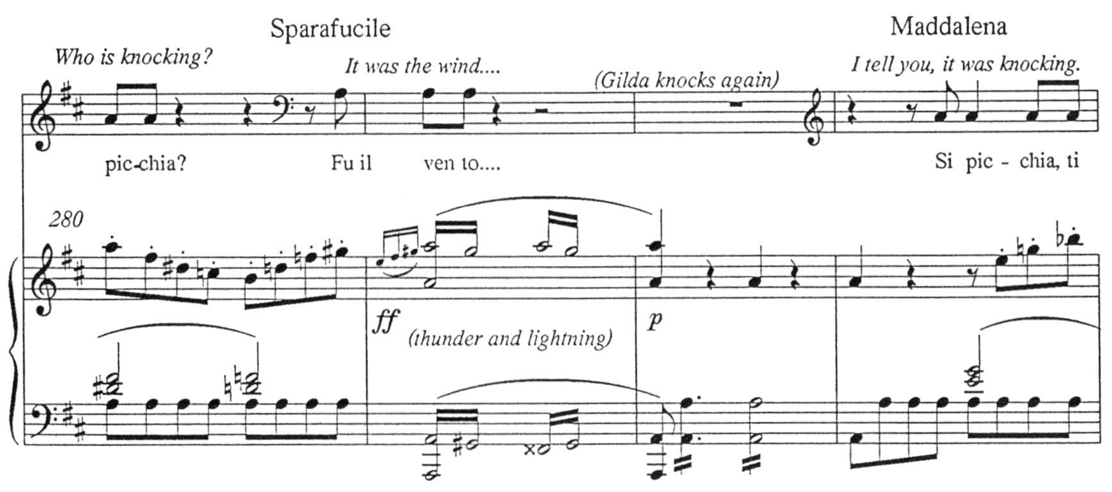
Sparafucile
Who is knocking?
It was the wind....
(Gilda knocks again)
Maddalena
I tell you, it was knocking.
pic-chia?
Fu il ven to....
Si pic - chia, ti
280
ff
(thunder and lightning)
p

Sparafucile
That's strange...Who's there?
Gilda
Have pity on a beggar; grant refuge for the night.
di-co. È stra-no!.. Chi è?
Pie-ta d'un men-di - co; a - sil per la
285
pp

Example 4.7
Puccini *La Bohème*, Act I, Scene 1

There is a development of these ideas in the first act of *La Bohème*. One feature which Puccini may well have noted in Verdi was the overall structuring of the scene in a sort of ritornello form. In the same way as the storm music in *Rigoletto* appears successively in the sequence of keys D, G, B, E, A and D minor, Puccini, too, uses atmospheric orchestral music in a succession of keys C, F, B flat, E flat, A flat, D flat, etc. It is even possible that he may also have looked back to baroque music in that, like Bach's, his ritornello material[16] is a group of themes (a), (b), (c), which first appear as a continuous thread, but are devised so that they can later be used separately.

The frequent reappearances of this material give a sufficient musical unity to the whole scene while the constantly changing key gives a sense of moving forwards with the unfolding drama. It is quite clear from the moment the curtain rises that the music is to be identified with the group of lively Bohemian young men whom we see in their garret; and the occasions of its return at later moments of the opera reaffirm this meaning. Each time it reappears they can go about their characteristic stage business, blowing on their fingers, wrestling with a chair, standing back to look at a painting, etc. and they can feel that the music underpins their thoughts and actions. This is not, of course, to suggest that all of them should engage in actions throughout such passages. Stanislavski, when rehearsing the opening of the opera thought that the audience would not understand the situation if its attention was divided:

> Let us, for the time being ignore Rodolfo, who is externally calm, and turn the music of the beginning of the act in the direction of Marcel. With impatience, even a touch of violence, he is applying his chilled paint to the canvas. That accounts for the persistence, the annoying repetitions of the melody . . . you have to mix your paints, which have thickened with the cold, and blow on your stiff fingers. So go ahead and do that in the rhythm prompted by the music.[17]

Above all it is the energy and liveliness of these young men which captivates our interest, and it is worth studying the scene if only to see how Puccini achieves and maintains such an exhilarating pace. Pace is a quality that every operatic composer and conductor needs to know about, and every producer and singer to respect, for it is a fragile virtue, easily lost if there is a wrong timing on the stage or in the pit. It is by no means synonymous with melodic speed, for often the quickest notes in a score are decorations of slow music; nor necessarily with harmonic speed since surface harmonies also can be elaborations of a slow underlying movement. Puccini's melodic material does in fact move quickly, with (a) and (b) of the last example having a good rhythmic spring. Yet the harmonies here are essentially static, being only mobile decorations of a single chord, a third inversion dominant seventh, and (c) too has a static note throughout, a pedal C.

Puccini puts this to good use when Marcello sings a recitative-like phrase on a monotone (bars 2–5 of the next example) whilst the pace is kept up by (c) in the orchestra. In the gaps between the vocal phrases the continuing pace of the orchestral music can be matched by stage movement and generally Puccini suggests what this should be: in the following passage Marcello the artist moves to different vantage points to view his work. Such actions will be complemented with perhaps more moderate movement, or at least stances suggestive of energy, in the sung passages. To maintain the pace over a long span there has to be a constant renewing of invention and creative energy by both composer and performers. Puccini achieves this in part by the mercurial way he moves from his ritornelli into vocal arioso and back.

Perhaps the most important single element in the achievement of pace in this scene is Puccini's treatment of the cadences which are wonderfully varied, for no two of them in this scene are exactly the same. In bar 11 of the above example there is a perfect cadence to underline Marcello's confident feeling of power over his work, while that in bar 6 of the following example from a little later in the scene is interrupted, giving ironic force to Rodolfo the writer's rather precipitate decision to burn his manuscript to keep their fire going. As is common in Puccini, the singer holds the floor in the immediate lead into the cadence and can even relax the tempo *a piacere*, so long as he keeps the intensity and the musical interest moving forwards into the orchestral entry at the moment of resolution. It will help too if a movement or gesture comes to fulfilment at that exact moment. In the video film at bar 6 Rodolfo impetuously raises his manuscript aloft on the very point of the cadence. Thus the resolution, which might otherwise lead to a slackening of tension and pace, is immediately caught up in the momentum of the new statement of the ritornello.

Rodolfo

Let the manuscript turn to ashes page by page, and my poetic fires fly back to their heavens.

ce ner la car ta si sfal - di e l'es tro ri vo - li a suoi cie - li. Al
string.
f
string.

Puccini stresses the punctuation at this place in the scene by having two cadences in quick succession, each similarly treated so far as the singer is concerned. The second one, in bar 8 shows another very common continuity technique of the composer's. This time, when the orchestra enters at the cadence point, it is not with the ritornello material, but with the melody of Rodolfo's earlier aria[18] played by the flute accompanied by tremolando strings and harp, and this both gives the passage its significance (for Rodolfo is now the prime agent of the dramatic action), and also its continuity, for again the singers only have recitative-like dialogue above it. It is typical of Puccini too that the notes they sing here are just notes taken from the flute melody. Although these little phrases look to be suitable for secco treatment the emotional warmth of this orchestral background with which they have to blend seems to require a more lyrical quality of singing. Puccini may have had this in mind when he wished his dialogue to have 'as much singing, as much melody as possible'.[19] On the Covent Garden video the action is spaced over each of the three little orchestral interludes: both men move forwards in the first of them in bar 9; in the second (bars 14–15) Rodolfo, with a gesture of painful sacrifice, gives Marcello the first handful of torn out pages; and they move over and put the pages into the stove in 17–20.

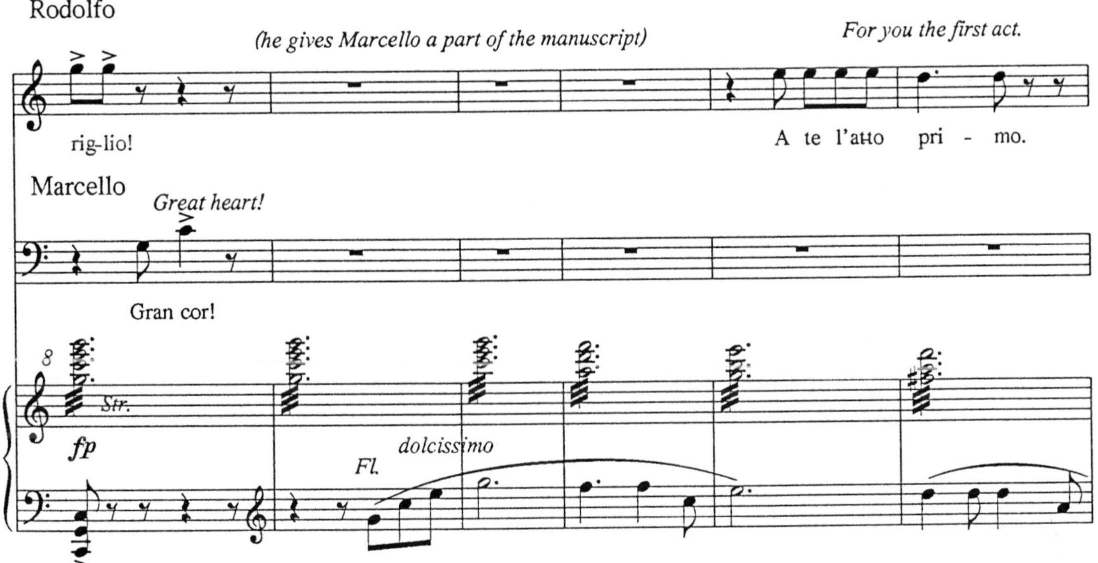

Rodolfo
Tear it up.
he lights a candle and they go over to the stove....
Strac-cia.
Marcello
Good!
Set it alight.
Qua!
15
Ac- cen-di.
p.
Fl. ob. clar.
f

(What a merry blaze!)

(The door at the back opens violently and Colline enters angrily throwing a bundle of books on the table.)

glior!

25

ff *un poco sostenuto*

A Tempo

Colline

The signs of the Apocalypse are appearing!

f Già dell' A-po-ca-lis-se ap-pa-ri-sco-no i se-gni.

30

f

ff

Typically, it is at the next cadence that a new dramatic development takes place. Colline's entry is heralded by his new theme in the orchestral cellos and basses, a modulation to the new key of F, and a new *ff* dynamic, the beginning of a tiny episode in the musical structure. This music suggested to Stanislavski that Colline is 'awkward, makes one think of a bear'.[20] Perhaps from the way he brandishes his umbrella the performer on the video thinks of the music in a rather similar way. Certainly we may infer from the strength of the music that at first he is entirely concerned with himself and with his anger that his books were not acceptable to the pawnbrokers on Christmas Eve.

Then suddenly, at the next cadence in bar 41, the *ff* return of (a) and (b) from the ritornello tells us that he notices what the others are doing and joins them around the stove, singing to recitative above an orchestral music which expresses the pace of the action by its quick modulations to B flat and D flat. The cascading descending figure in 46–7 is suggestive of the rapid dying of the fire caused by the burning paper of Rodolfo's manuscript. Looking at this passage as a whole it will be noticed that as the scene builds up there is a greater musical continuity and that the later cadences are not allowed to have so disruptive an effect on the tempo as the earlier.

Rodolfo
my drama is given...
dà il mio dram-ma...

Colline *...to the fire.*
...al fuo co. Lo

45 8va

Britten's technique for handling the atmospheric orchestra in *Peter Grimes* is not unlike this. In Act I, Scene 1 the sea music, which dominates the whole scene until the gradual intrusion of the storm, is well established in the Interlude before the curtain rises, and it also functions as the accompaniment to the choral setting of Crabbe's words. Between the verses of this are solo passages for some of the Borough characters, whose short-breathed phrases might well break the spell for a moment were they not accompanied by a held chord or repeated figuration from the sea music, which will then be more fully re-established at the cadences. The continuity and unity is kept up in this way for some ten minutes of music until the moment when the composer breaks the spell in order to stress Peter's arrival on the scene. All this is as would be expected from someone who knew his Verdi and Puccini well.

In relation to the earlier discussion, Britten is here closer to Verdi than to Puccini in that the sea music is referring to something tangible outside the stage and independent of the singers. As with Verdi's storm there are moments when the singers are thinking of the sea, and the sea music in the fullest sense accompanies them. At other times, when their thoughts and words are concerned with other things, they must project their recitative words to the audience over the sea music and, in a sense, against it. There is also an intermediate technique which is, I think, unique to Britten, of transforming the background music so that, without losing its identity, it can adapt to supporting the singer. A witty example of this (not illustrated here) occurs at Figure 16 in the score, where the characteristic string chord of the sea music is employed with a new and vigorous rhythmic articulation to support Balstrode's chasing away the small boys who are scrambling over the boats. He can forget about the sea for a moment in his actions, leaving the orchestral harmonies to keep it in our minds and to preserve the unity and continuity of the scene.

There is another interesting use of the same technique in Act I, Scene 2, where the music of the storm interlude similarly dominates the whole scene, but with this difference: that the scene is indoors in The Boar while the storm continues to rage outside, and we only savour its full fury when the door opens. As soon as the door shuts again the continuing presence of the storm is sufficiently suggested by a soft roll in turn on a variety of percussion instruments. This is another of Britten's brilliantly simple ideas, and it works very well in the theatre, providing a musical and dramatic continuity as effective as if the storm were being more fully represented. The libretto of the scene is particularly varied and colourful,[21] and the technique enables the composer to use a wide range of vocal recitative and arioso styles without the whole scene falling apart. The singers don't get much support from the orchestra, but yet they can rely on the sustaining power of the percussion continuum, and interpret their parts with more liberty than would be effective if the continuity were solely in their own hands.

Example 4.8
Britten *Peter Grimes*, Act I, Scene 2

The extract is taken from the very beginning of the scene, where the continuum is provided at first by the bass drum. Although, as in classical recitative, pace and clear articulation of the words are paramount for the singers, there is such character in these words that each phrase can be sung with rather more relish than would be usual in secco recitative. Certainly Mrs Sedley's 'Room from the storm', a studied lie, calls for full and sustained tone, and Auntie's reply with its fourfold repetition is in effect a tiny aria. In the picture from the Covent Garden video film she is seen adopting a characteristic stance, hands on hips. Her very last word 'sight', can be heard on the video, where the balance is contrived, but will almost certainly be lost in the theatre: this doesn't really matter in that it is obvious how the sentence will end. However the singer must bear in mind Britten's direction presto and be aware of the crescendo of the bass drum trill into the a tempo, spitting out the words over the drum so as to drive forwards into the double bar. In other words the ending of the section, like the cadence points in Puccini, involves something of the change of level to be found at the end of a classical recitative.

Recitativo animato (senza misura) *(Inside the Boar, the same night. Auntie is admitting Mrs. Sedley. The gale is now at hurricane force and they push the door shut with difficulty)*

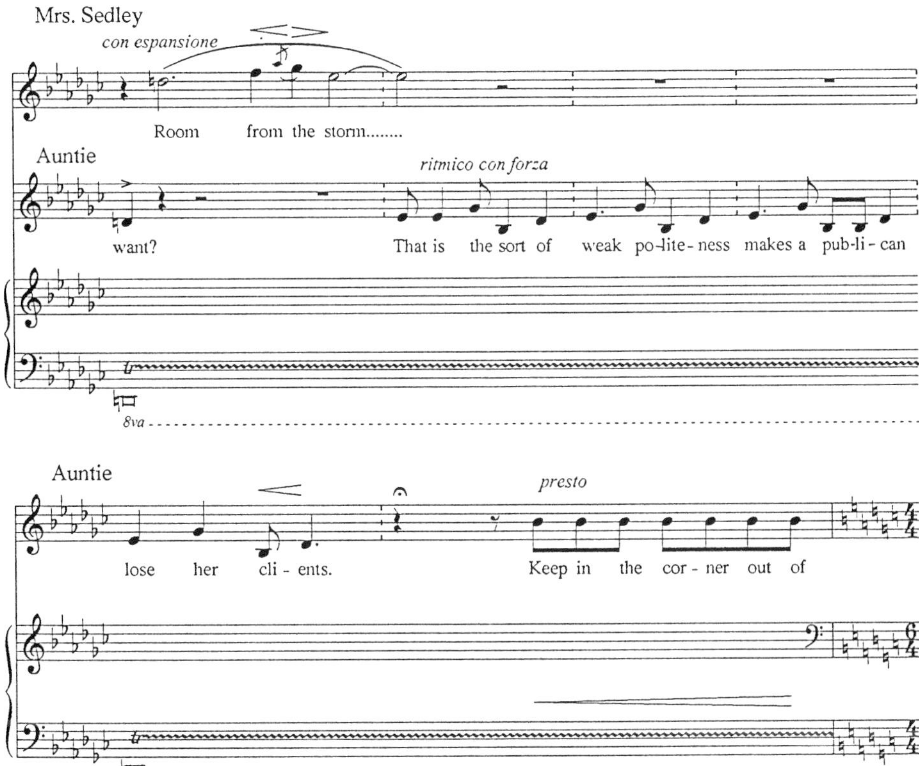
Mrs. Sedley
con espansione
Room from the storm........
Auntie
ritmico con forza
want? That is the sort of weak po-lite-ness makes a pub-li-can
8va
Auntie
presto
lose her cli - ents. Keep in the cor - ner out of
8va

The storm suddenly intrudes into the room when the door opens to let in some fishermen including Balstrode who is seen here taking off his wet coat as he walks in. The freedom allowable in the performance of the vocal passages must not extend to the timings of the openings and closings of the door on the stage which have to synchronise exactly with the orchestral outbursts. The openings are easy, and there will probably be a member of the musical staff behind the scenes with a score to get it right. But the shutting, which normally has to be entrusted to one of the singers who have just entered, does tend to go wrong in performance. The reader may be tempted to surmise that the difficulty is an instance of the proverbial unmusicality of most opera singers (a very unfair prejudice nowadays), but this would not be true in this instance. The problem for the singers stems from the fact that the orchestra, being solely concerned with the storm outside, is not supporting their actions in the usual way when they get inside the pub. To act a part while having to listen to an independent musical argument and achieve an exact synchronisation with it is not easy, and it is, perhaps, an exceptional demand to make of a singer. Of course, in practice, the conductor can give the cue or the problem can be avoided altogether by dispensing with a visible door, as in this Covent Garden production. Here, the blowing of the curtain by the wind through the door assumed to be offstage is effective and more easily controlled, though it could be argued that the forceful proximity of the storm is somewhat diminished.

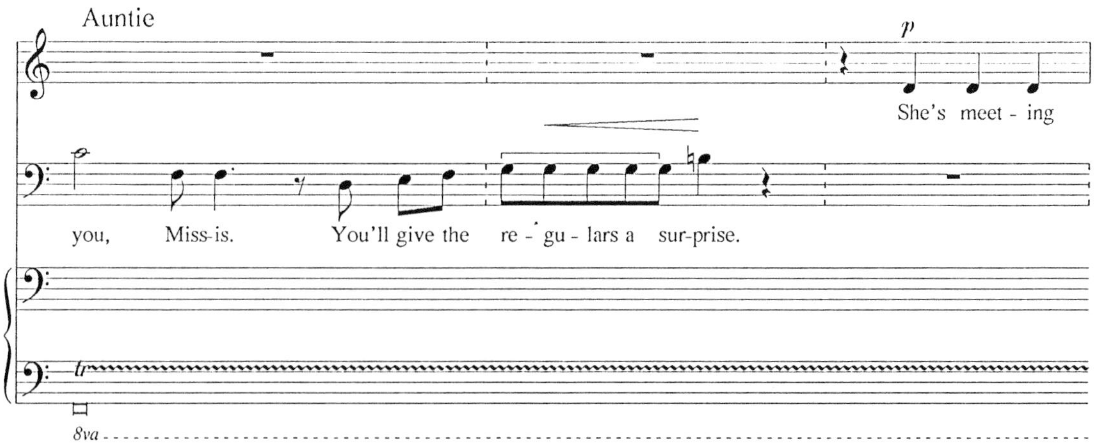

The new section of recitative is underlaid with a side drum roll, a more focussed sound than the bass drum. It makes as wide use of the singers' resources as the previous one, including a whistle, everything still being contained by the roll. At the end the drum has a longer crescendo than before and Balstrode's final tirade and Auntie's final vocalising are even closer to the change of level one would find at the end of a recitative. At the next intrusion of the storm the door stays open longer because, we are told later, the shutters are blown in. The force though not the momentum of the wind will abate just for a moment (i.e. the orchestral music maintains its presto tempo but reduces to *pp* for two bars) to give Bowles, one of the new arrivals, a chance to deliver his news that the sea has broken over the Northern Road. This he will do, as in Puccini, on a monotone parlando sung in tempo. The picture shows the scene at the moment just before he sings.

Auntie
pp
f
Ned.
The quack!
He's look- ing af- ter her heart
at-tack.
It's
Balstrode
f
Which Ned?
Bring us a pint.
8va

Auntie
clos - ing time.
The
Balstrode
ff
3
You
fear- ful
old
fe - male,
why should you
mind?

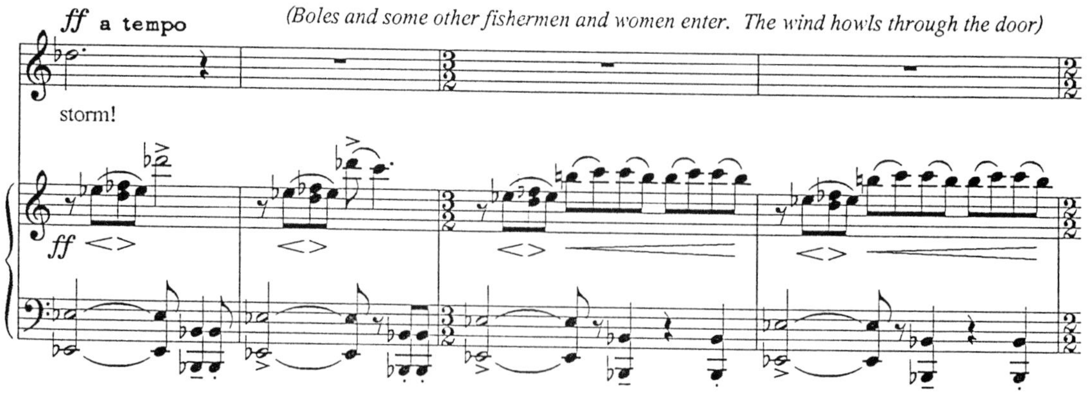
ff a tempo
(Boles and some other fishermen and women enter. The wind howls through the door)
storm!
ff

One further aspect of the scene, only to be appreciated from studying the whole of it, is its overall structuring. As in so much good opera the drama and the music grow together in intensity towards the end. At first, when the door is shut, only a single instrument is used, a different one each time: bass drum, side drum, cymbal, harp tremolando, tambourine and timpani. But at the end, for the climactic entry of Ellen with the new apprentice, the background ostinato is enlarged to a con fuoco figure from the main orchestral storm interlude, played pianissimo at first by the unison strings. From here onwards the singers have less liberty. They must keep up the intensity, following on from each other strictly in accordance with the rhythms of the score, so that the scene grows inexorably into the final curtain music.

Notes

1 See Erber (ed.) (1978).
2 The production was given in Florence, as part of the 1984 Maggio Musicale, under Roger Norrington, and it later toured England.
3 See Erber, op.cit.
4 Quoted from John Whenham, 'Five acts: one action' in Whenham (ed.) (1986), p. 65.
5 A different view of the role of these reappearances of the La Musica prologue is given in Drummond (1980), p. 135. Drummond sees them as having the formal function of framing Acts III and IV, the scenes in Hades in which Orfeo is put to the test, and also as following acts in which Euridice has been lost and preceding those in which she is to be regained: so he too (although differently) sees them as looking forward in time.
6 See Curtis Price, 'Dido and Aeneas in Context' in Price (ed.) (1986) p. 36, for further discussion of this.
7 Quoted from Auden (1963) p. 471.
8 See Mann (1977), p. 421, footnote.
9 The relation of action to musical interest is pursued further in Chapter 7.
10 See Noske (1977), p. 36. The key of the dance, A minor, is associated in Mozart on several occasions with exoticism.
11 See Chapter 26, 'The Originality of Rigoletto' in Kimbell (1981).

12 The motivic structure of this section is explored by David Matthews in 'Act II, scene 1: an examination of the music', Chapter 6 of Brett (ed.) (1983), pp. 126–34.

13 Notably in the operas of Rameau, whose achievement is summarised, with a bibliography, in Grout (1988).

14 Quoted from Dent (1940, rev. 1949), p. 141.

15 Michotte 'Souvenirs Personels: La visite de Wagner a Rossini', cited in Kimbell op.cit. p. 64.

16 But not the key structure, which goes perpetually flatwards and makes no effort to return to its starting point. The thematic material is from a work he wrote as a student, *Capriccio sinfonico*.

17 Quoted from Stanislavski and Rumyantser, (1975), p. 214

18 This also is from an earlier work, *La Lupa*.

19 Quoted in Carner (1974), p. 337.

20 Quoted from Stanislavski and Rumyantser, op.cit. p. 221.

21 Asked what were the qualities he most desired in a libretto, Britten said, 'What I require is memorable and thrilling phrases. I think the pub scene in *Grimes* was successful partly for this reason.' Quoted from Shafer (1963), p. 116.

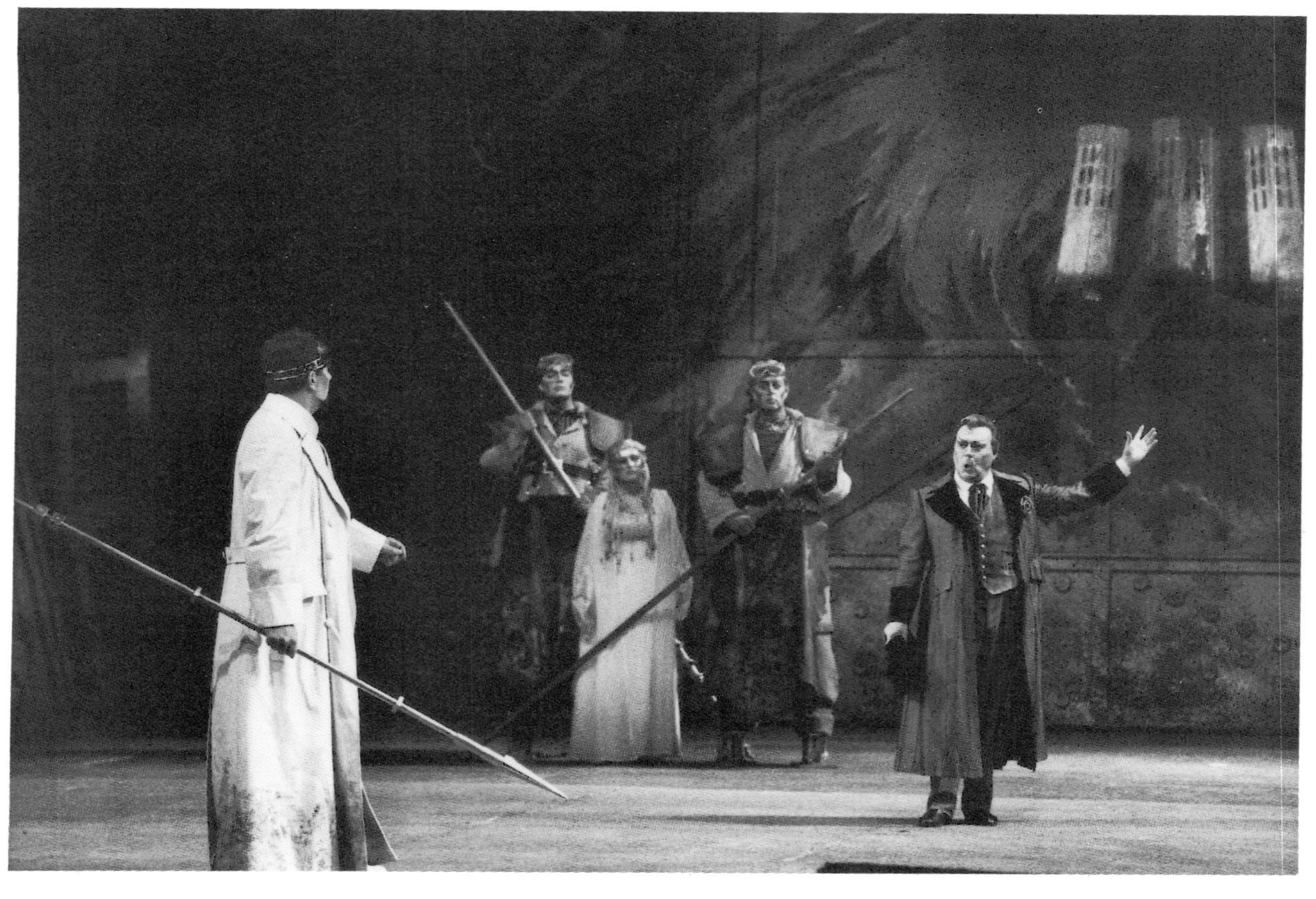

A dramatic moment from Loge's Scene 2 narration in the 1991 Royal Opera House production of *Das Rheingold*. At the back of the stage Freia (Deborah Riedel) is held captive by the two giants (Gwynne Howell and Franz-Josef Selig) as the agreed payment for the building of Valhalla. At first Loge (Kenneth Riegel) seems to be playing for time, but when he begins to tell of the theft of the gold Wotan (James Morris) wheels round towards him in astonishment. This is at bar 74 of the music example on p. 194 and is accompanied by a striking reappearance on a horn of the 'Gold' motif, not in its original major mode but now in the key of B minor. The passage is discussed in the context of a different interpretation on a video film from Bayreuth. *Photograph Zoe Dominic*

5 The Symphonic Dimension in Wagner

I Harmony and Leitmotif

The main concern of this chapter is to study a famous passage, Loge's monologue from Scene 2 of *Das Rheingold* and, before that, to look at some of the innovations which make the understanding of Wagner's music dramas difficult for performers brought up on traditional opera. There are the difficulties for singers, for example, who are puzzled by vocal writing which seems to be pitched somewhere between the standard recitative and aria, but yet calls for a different approach from either, not only in vocal technique but also, conceptually, in the relationship with the orchestra. Wagner certainly did his best to explain these things himself, as witness his several hundred essays and pamphlets which, although they are generally taken to be addressed to his audiences, do contain much that is relevant to the understanding of his performers too. That is true of much that he wrote in the long period of gestation for *The Ring*, from the time of the first prose sketch in 1848 until the completion of the first opera of the cycle, *Das Rheingold*, in 1854, and in particular of the extended essay 'Opera and Drama' of 1851.[1]

The growth in Wagner's mind of the whole concept of *The Ring* makes a fascinating study in itself and has inspired an immense literature.[2] Of particular interest to our study is Dahlhaus' view as to why, when Wagner started with the intention of writing a single opera *Siegfrieds Tod* (which was eventually incorporated into the fourth opera of the cycle, *Götterdämmerung*), he gradually felt impelled to write three preparatory operas.[3] This, he argues, was for musical reasons. The story of a hero whose death brings about the downfall of an old order of law and force and inaugurates the dawn of a new utopian age, needed a great deal of narrative explanation. Wagner came to realise that the music for this could only have dramatic meaning if it had already been given clear dramatic reference points, and it was the primary function of the earlier operas to set these up. Of course, the earlier operas did more than just that, and indeed in our example, from as early as the second scene of the first opera, the music is already concerned with reinterpreting motifs whose dramatic identity has been established in the first scene.

Among the many aspects of the music drama there are two in particular which it is crucially important the performers should understand, the harmony and the motivic structure. We shall look at these separately in a general way, before exploring their interaction in the main example.

Harmony

The important role of the orchestral harmony was stressed by Wagner himself in the third part of 'Opera and Drama', 'Poetry and Music in the Drama of the Future'. To begin where Wagner finishes, he sums up the role of the orchestral harmony with a striking analogy: the singer's words and melody function like a boat on the deep waters of the orchestral harmony, the harmony expressing what is inexpressible in verbal language. Earlier, he had rejected the idea of rhyme in the words because that depends on 'musical' vowel sounds whose effect, he argues, would be lost when the orchestral harmonies take over the deeper musical dimension. Instead he posits the use of the older German alliteration as the appropriate discipline for his verse, since it depends only on the 'unmusical' consonant sounds. This, incidentally, has the further advantage of being associated with an irregular metrical and sentence structure, enabling him more easily to avoid the regular phrase structures of traditional arias,[4] and throwing extra weight, as we shall see, on the phrasing of the orchestral accompaniment.

Wagner demonstrates how alliterative verse would be set to music with a short illustration, from which it will be seen at once that the pattern of the harmonies (modulations) is independent of the pattern of the alliteration, aiming rather to bring out the deeper feeling and structure of the words.

Die Liebe bringt Lust und Leid
(*Love brings joy and grief*)
(Harmony) *A* *B*
doch in ihr Weh auch webt sie Wonnen.
(*yet in her woe she also weaves delight*)
B *A*

The scale of Wagner's example is misleading in that it seems to be referring to no more than word painting. He explains that the same principle operates over bigger structures and that the term 'harmony' must be taken to mean not just chord colouring but also key and modulation. How this works over a bigger span can be seen in the chart opposite of the key structure of the first scene of *Das Rheingold*, extending over some twenty three minutes: the scale of the chart is given by rough timings based on the Boulez recording. The brackets on the left indicate the periods of dominance of the main keys.

The E flat at the beginning stands for the primal innocence of the Rhine and, at this stage, the integrity of the Rhinemaidens. When Alberich appears the key is disturbed, occasionally referring back to E flat when the Rhinemaidens sing, and triumphantly reasserting that key for the reprise of their song at 11′ 14″. The whole act so far, then, is enclosed by the one key which, like the dramatic situation it represents, has been disturbed but not overcome. Then, beginning at about the twelfth minute of the scene Alberich makes an enormous final effort to catch one of the maidens and it is during the ensuing chase that the key of E flat is finally lost. The tonality settles into a new centre, C major, when Alberich's attention (and ours too) is diverted from the chase by the appearance of the gold.[5] After this the key centre of C dominates the whole of the remainder of the scene. However, there is a change from major to minor, at first tentatively at the discussion of the possibility of obtaining the gold by renouncing love, and then emphatically over a time span of some three minutes when Alberich actually does steal the gold, taking it down with him into the Niebelung depths.

Within this very simple overall structure, E flat – C major – C minor, the details of the harmony and the variations in the harmonic rhythm can be seen to relate equally closely to the drama on the smaller scale. The calm of the opening is obtained by having no harmonic movement at all; pure E flat triads. With the appearance of the Rhinemaidens the harmony begins to move to diatonically related chords but there is still no change of key centre. However Alberich's music immediately threatens the key by introducing minor and diminished chords and many chromatic notes; it also speeds up the harmonic rhythm, an indicator of the increased emotional tension. The new key, C major, is introduced in nearly as static a way as the E flat of the opening (there are 24 bars of the same chord), for Alberich is wonderstruck at the sight of the gold. Again the Rhinemaidens' song disturbs the harmonic rhythm but not the key, and again it is Alberich whose music threatens the stability of the key. At the end of the scene the harmonic stasis returns but under the tragic mood brought about by the reiteration and prolongation of the C minor chords.

Dahlhaus[6] has done a survey of the role of C major in the whole opera, concluding that it is never used again with the strength of the passage in the first scene (13′ 20″ – 16′ 45″). For example it reappears in Scene 4 when Wotan contemplates the ring forged from the gold: but he can't keep the ring, as Wagner makes quite clear harmonically by setting the passage in the context of the stronger B minor of Alberich's curse, to which key it returns so that Wotan's dreams sound as no more than an extended Neapolitan episode. There is a similar use of the key in Loge's narration when he is telling Wotan of the Rhinemaiden's prayer that the gold should be returned to them.

Even so brief a survey as this reveals that Wagner is a master of the controlled use of harmony to articulate the drama, and the performers of any mature work of his will always find this aspect of it worth studying and trying to understand. Until recently it has been comparatively neglected by the Wagnerian musicologists despite the clear leads given by the composer in his essays. On our next subject however,

DAS RHEINGOLD SCENE I

Time	Key	Subject	Motives
0'00		Primal Innocence of the Rhine	1
1'			
2'			
3'	E Flat		
4'		Rhinemaidens' song	2
5'00	(G minor) (E flat)	Alberich appears taunted by Rhinemaidens	3
6'	(E minor)		
7'			
8'	(A minor)		
9'	(E flat minor)		
		Flosshilde flirts with him, mocks him	
10'00			
11'	E flat	They escape from him Reprise of Rhinemaidens' song	2
12'	(various)	Alberich renews chase	
13'			4
14'		He sees the gold	
		Rhinegold song	5
15'00	C major		
16'		He asks what it is They explain power of ring	6
17'	(E)	He questions them further They explain renunciation	
18'	C minor		7
	E→C	Rhinemaidens song reprise	2 4
19'			
		He contemplates renunciation	6 4 7
20'00			
		He renounces love, and steals the gold	
21'			
22'	C minor	Orchestral interlude	6 7
23'			

the use of motifs, there is an immense literature yet, paradoxically, Wagner himself tended to be rather guarded about it.

Leitmotifs

The term was first coined by the historian Ambros in 1865 and systematically used by Baron H. von Wolzogen in his thematic guide to *The Ring* of 1876,[7] the year of the first performance of the whole cycle at Bayreuth. Wagner evidently felt that Wolzogen's list went too far in tying each motif to a particular dramatic entity while saying too little about its role in the overall musical form. Nevertheless Wolzogen and his many successors[8] do give a starting point for the performer's necessary investigation, even if the truth about the meaning of the leitmotifs is less simple than they sometimes suggest.

An important association for each leitmotif, if not the full meaning, will be obtained by looking at the dramatic context of its first appearance. Sometimes it may actually be sung, in which case the words will give a further clue: examples of this include No. 2, the song of the Rhinemaidens, No. 5, the Rhinegold song and No. 7, the 'Renunciation' motif which is first heard when Woglinde explains to Alberich that the ring can only be forged by one who renounces love. More often, though, it will first be heard in the orchestra and will be associated with something or someone seen on the stage, the river Rhine, the gold, Loge, Freia, etc. Indeed it was partly in order to establish these visual musical associations that Wagner first felt impelled to embark on the earlier operas of *The Ring* cycle, and it behoves the producer and performers to make the associations clear, especially on the first occasion. Some recent productions have gone too far, I believe, in neglecting this obligation: for example the very opening of *Das Rheingold* really must be seen to be taking place in water, whether this is simulated by rippling lights or fan-blown streamers or by having the Rhinemaidens water-borne by suspension from cables.[9] Not to do this makes the music sound wrong because there is nothing on the stage to which its clear figurations can refer: it has no raison d'être.

However this is not to say that the meaning of this music is narrowly confined to the representation of the flowing waters of the Rhine, for it helps us to make associations, birth experience, utopian innocence, etc. and later on the same, or very similar music, may refer to other natural phenomena. Dahlhaus makes the point that Wagner's conception of the elements and landscape was anthropomorphic and 'the flowing waters of the Rheingold prelude, the tongues of flame in Loge's motif are psychograms'.[10] This richness of meaning is not confined to the nature motifs. The Valhalla theme at the beginning of Scene 2 could well refer also to the noble qualities of Wotan himself, whose sword motif could also signify the concept of true manhood, and so on. Robert Donington and others have worked backwards from these more generalised meanings to show that the motifs of *The Ring* tend to fall into groups, each group containing themes which are not only motivically related but whose referential meanings share some common symbolism. Often the first such group to be listed will be that defined musically by a triad with an added sixth (melodically or harmonically) and relating to nature (and innocence) in some form. The ramifications of this motif embrace not only the song of the Rhinemaidens, as children of nature, but also the glitter of sun in the water accompanying the gold motif, the forest and birdsong in *Siegfried*, and even, perhaps more contentiously, the magic sleep of Brünnhilde at the end of *Die Walküre*, 'innocent sleep from which she will be woken into womanhood'.[11] The same motif with yet another reference appears in Loge's narration as a prelude to his account of his journeyings across water, earth and air.

If one way in which Wagner draws his vast canvas into a unity is by relating different motifs in this way, an even more potent technique is by the conscious transformation of the individual motifs so that they clearly keep their original references but reinterpret them to give new depth to each new context in which they appear. In Loge's monologue, for instance, Freia's motif, which was hectic at its first appearance because she was trying to run away from the giants, comes in a new form as a serene contemplation of the ideal of womanhood. The use, after the theft, of the gold motif in the minor key is another instance of change closely linked to a new dramatic situation.

Frequent attempts have been made to codify the motifs according to the way they are used in the symphonic structuring of the music. At one end of the scale are those that recur only at isolated moments

Rheingold Motifs

to make a particular interpretative point. These are similar to the 'reminiscence' motifs which had been a feature of opera since the eighteenth century. Wagner would have been aware of their use in the French tradition, in the works of Méhul, and, of course in Weber's *Der Freischütz* in the German. Wagner is most creative in his use of this technique:[12] sometimes it may involve a comment in the orchestra which not all those on the stage could be expected fully to understand. There is an instance of this in Scene 4 of *Das Rheingold* with the stark reappearance of the curse motif when Fafner kills Fasolt, this being the first working out of the curse. When Alberich laid the curse, earlier in the scene, soon after the ring had been wrenched from his finger, only Wotan and Loge were on stage with him and heard the curse. At its reappearance, then, the other gods stand horrified at the murder but do not understand its full significance. It is almost as if Wagner is speaking over their heads directly to the audience.

At the other end of the scale are what have been named by Kurth as 'developmental motifs'.[13] These are used over larger tracts of the score, and are extensively repeated or developed so as to contribute to the unified continuity of the music. Often they do not have such specific dramatic connotations as other more striking motifs, but their use may be thought of as contributing to the more symphonic aspect of that continuous interaction between the symphony and the drama to be found in Wagner's works. In the chart of Scene 1 on p. 183, the extensions of the semiquaver figuration of the Rhine music are shown, and notated by a line to show constant repetition and a dotted line to show more sporadic continuation. In one way or another the figure permeates the texture of the music over the whole span from the beginning of the scene to the appearance of the gold. It may be taken at first to refer to the watery background of the scene, but in changing its harmony (and figurations to some extent), to underly Alberich's flirtations, his chases, etc., its meaning is in some sense extensible. One commentator, Carolyn Abbate, even goes so far as to argue that the motifs have no intrinsic referential meaning at all, but that they absorb a meaning through being used at particular moments and then tend to lose it and to revert to fulfilling a more purely musical function unless the meaning is purposefully reasserted.[14]

The second part of the scene is similarly underpinned by a more brilliant variant of the semiquaver motif (labelled 5) with a triplet on the first beat, heard some hundreds of times, and extending into the following orchestral interlude. This may be taken initially to refer to the bright glittering of the gold in the water (or perhaps to the associated element of ecstasy in the Rhinegold song) but again it becomes identified with the changing dramatic actions over the period of its influence, up to and beyond the theft of the gold. The little chromatic figure, part of theme 3, has a similar though shorter period of projection. It evidently refers to the way that Alberich disturbs the diatonic nature of the Rhine and the gold, and it follows him through various moods and adventures, again in such a way as to lose too specific a dramatic reference. It is through these themes in particular that the atmosphere is maintained or changed and the larger scale symphonic web is woven.[15] Here, Wagner's incomparable art of transition is exercised, a musical journeying from one place or mood to another. There is just one final point to make: the dramatic meaning of any of these motifs can be changed or enriched by conjunction with one or more of the others, either in contrapuntal combination or by their being placed one immediately after the other as a continuous melody. These techniques too are exemplified in Loge's narration.

II A Note on Performance Practice

The early music movement has extended its attentions forwards into the nineteenth century, but has not yet, to my knowledge, addressed the very considerable difficulties of re-creating an authentic Wagner performance. The intractability of the problem stems from the fact that Wagner was highly dissatisfied with the conventions and practices of his time: there would be little point in expending much musicological effort to reconstruct a style of performance against which he was rebelling. It is better to appreciate that the larger issues he was aiming to address in his operas were such as to transcend any narrow definition of correct style. Nevertheless a brief summary of some of the salient features of Wagner's own approach to performance may be helpful, if not to be followed slavishly. The main source, apart from Wagner's own writings is Porges' account of Wagner's direction of the first complete production of *The Ring* in 1876.[16] This book is required reading for anyone involved in performing the work.

Perhaps the biggest difference between Wagner's performances and those of our day (so far as we can tell) is the greater emphasis he put on overt expressiveness, involving more inflection of tempo and dynamics than is now fashionable – after all it could only have been achieved with some loss to the longer-term flow of the music. Time and again we read of Wagner taking one passage slower, another quicker, highlighting certain moments with rallentandi, etc. It is as if each theme was given its own tempo and expression. Wagner's own essay on conducting[17] makes the same points. There is little evidence as to just how this was done, though David Breckbill analyses in some detail a 1928 recording of Richard Strauss conducting the Prelude to *Tristan and Isolde*, which was interpreted in this way. He argues that Strauss would have learnt the style from von Bülow, who conducted the first performance of the work.[18] We have noted the crucial importance of the first appearance of a motif. Wagner, it seems went to the length of having it played 'in a grand style, slowly and broadly, but when serving as a reminiscence . . . it should be slightly faster and with accents less pointed – as it were in the throw-away style of an experienced actor delivering an interpolated sentence'.[19]

Questions of balance between singer and orchestra clearly preoccupied Wagner a great deal. In his view it was essential that the orchestra should be entirely covered (out of sight of the audience) as was possible at the Festspielhaus at Bayreuth, and later at the Prinzregententheater at Munich.[20] Even so he insisted on orchestral dynamics being reduced in accompanimental passages so that the singers' words should come across clearly. He enlarged on his, by then, famous analogy of the singer as a boat on the surface of the deep orchestral harmony, insisting that the orchestra should support the singer as the sea does a boat, rocking perhaps, but never upsetting or drowning.

Wagner's biggest problems in the performances of *The Ring* (financial difficulties apart) lay with the singers on whom he devoted much time. Porges is helpful in explaining how a singer is to pace and to plan a role: for example in Scene 1 of *Das Rheingold* Alberich is to begin with a certain rough dryness of tone, the voice growing warmer and more impassioned as he is 'swept by lust compounded by hatred and fury at the climax of Fing' eine diese Faust!', (*Could I but lay hands on one!*) just before the sight of the gold calms him down. The tempi should be set, it would seem, so that the dialogue is essentially at the same speed as speech. However, once the tempo of a passage is set the notes must be sung in strict tempo, not as classical recitative. The dynamic markings must also be scrupulously observed so as to enunciate the words with clarity yet, in the result, with an impassioned and poetic mode of delivery. 'Distinctness!' Wagner said at one point, 'The big notes will take care of themselves; the little notes and the text are the main thing.'[21] Accents too are to be scrupulously observed, and it is unfortunate for us he made rather less use of them in his later works.

It is evident that in Wagner's day vibrato was less used by singers, as by string players, than is normal practice today. It was saved as a special expressive effect. For the singers there was more use of portamento, and it is unfortunate for us who have lost the tradition that no-one indicated on the score or the parts where it was to be used. It may perhaps have been indicated by a slur, when the slur would not have another meaning, e.g. between two adjacent notes having different words or syllables. Another point made concerns vowel sounds. The singer should get to know the accompanying harmonies intimately and colour the vowels so as to blend with them. This, I believe is good practice for any vocal music, though one rarely hears of it being discussed. Looking at all of this one is left with a feeling that Wagner saw the art as rather more sensitive and gentle than it tends to become in our large opera houses.

It is clear that for Wagner the general style of the actions and indeed the actions themselves were to grow directly out of the music. A typical injunction, when the gold appears in the first scene of *Das Rheingold*, requires the movements of the Rhinemaidens to match the smooth motion of the orchestral violins who are accompanying the main motive on the horns (theme 4 on page 183). Sometimes this correlation is more literal than would now be customary. In the last scene of the opera the justifiably truculent giants are directed to 'thrust their staves into the ground one after the other, each thrust coinciding exactly with the strong beat of their rhythmic motive',[22] and such precise co-ordination is not exceptional. As would be expected, importance is attached to strong stage positions, reflecting the dramatic situations, and those not involved in the actual dialogue must nevertheless show involvement in the drama by their gestures: they are 'living sculpture'. We shall explore how some of these ideas can be worked out in the following example.

III Loge's Narration

Firstly a synopsis of the scene and its context. Wotan is in deep trouble, having rashly agreed to hand over Freia, the goddess of youth and love, to the giants in payment for the building of Valhalla which is now complete. The other gods and goddesses, including Freia herself, are scandalised when they realise the price to be paid. Wotan pins his hopes on Loge, the trickster fire god, who had promised to help him. Loge arrives rather late in the scene to find an ugly situation with the giants about to take Freia away while Wotan, unable to break his contractual agreement with them, is trying to prevent the other gods assaulting them. Loge at first tries to win the giants' confidence by praising their handiwork (which does nothing to placate the anger of the other gods), and he has to remind Wotan that he only promised to do his best to help; he can do no more.

As the narration proper begins he appears to be explaining that there isn't much he can do anyway because wherever he has been on his extensive travels he has always found womanhood to be more highly valued than any other prize. This is taken to imply that the giants are unlikely to accept any substitute for Freia, but it is really Loge's cunning way of introducing the subject of Alberich's theft of the Rhinegold, an action which indeed prized wealth above love. We must accept the operatic convention that the orchestra, in supporting Loge, enables him to project an almost magical evocation of the splendour of the gold, so that the giants can be lured into accepting it as a substitute for Freia. Indeed in one sense Loge is almost too successful, because Wotan is also tempted by the thought of the gold, and when he goes off with Loge at the end of the scene to trick Alberich into giving it up his motivation is more than simply liberating Freia. It is only the intervention of the goddess Erda in the last scene of the opera that will eventually persuade him to allow the giants to keep it all.

Porges devotes several pages to his account of Wagner's own rehearsing of this scene.[23] Loge is to enter not from the side of the stage but from the rocks in the middle, presumably to stress his more devious itineraries, and should remain upstage at first, only gradually moving forwards later. His accompanying music is to be pointedly yet lightly played, (including even the Valhalla theme used when praising the giants), and the ironic tone in his voice should be without affectation or mannerism. The singer 'should make a point of accompanying his speeches with gestures and movements suggestive of the restlessness of his nature as a fire god', and for his first phrase in the extract Wagner suggested that he should 'reinforce the words with swaying movements of his upper body'.[24]

The first bars of the music are accompanied only by non-motivic chords (apart from the brief reference to Loge's chromatic music in bar 7), a reversion to a texture not far removed from traditional accompanied recitative, but presumably to be sung rhythmically as Wagner insisted elsewhere. The two slowings of the pace and the rising vocal line (C, D, E flat, E and F in bars 15–20) suggest that at the end the recitative moves with a quite traditional change of level into the 'aria' beginning in bar 21: however, as we shall see,

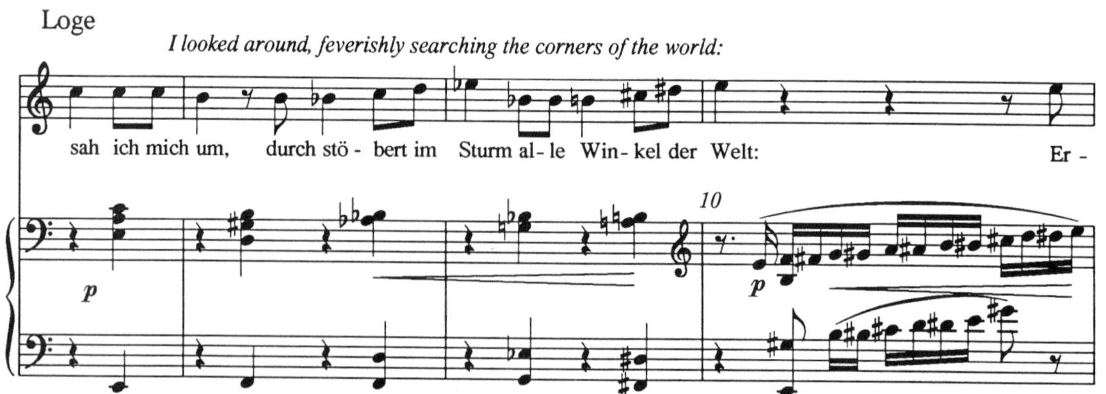
Loge
I looked around, feverishly searching the corners of the world:
sah ich mich um, durch stö - bert im Sturm al- le Win- kel der Welt: Er -
10

to find a substitute for Freia, so as to be a just settlement for the giants. In vain I searched,
satz für Frei-a zu su- chen, wie er den Rie - sen wohl recht. Um-sonst sucht' ich, und

and now see full well, that in the whole world, nothing is so rich that men will accept it as a substitute
se - he nun wohl: in der Wel - ten Ring nichts ist so reich, als Er satz zu mu- then dem Mann für

this proves to be no traditional aria. Given Wagner's demands for expressive positioning, one can picture the staging as showing the tensions as illustrated in the first sketch: Loge now in front, with Wotan separating the infuriated gods on one side from the giants holding the reluctant Freia on the other.

'Weibes Wonne und Werth' (*woman's beauty and delight*) is a splendid example of the use of alliteration to stress a striking idea and on this occasion it coincides with an equally striking musical idea, bringing about a change of musical level as Loge, the consummate story-teller begins to bewitch his audience. Wagner highlights the phrase by bringing in four of his horns at this point, a wonderfully rich sound after some 20 bars with only strings in the accompaniment. In passing it must be said that it is always worth looking at his scorings for clues as to his intentions. We know he took particular care with the orchestration of *Das Rheingold*, working out the instrumentation on a separate pencil draft before writing up the fair copy.[25] The motif used for 'Weibes Wonne und Werth' is something of a puzzle because of a certain similarity to the Renunciation motif (number 7 on p. 183), which might on one level be taken to have the opposite meaning. Perhaps the common link is simply the generalised concept of womanhood.[26]

What is more important, though, is to realise that in contemplating this idea with Loge, we enter a new and magical musical world. The horn chord in bar 23 is sustained over the next few bars as, with beautifully intricate scoring, each section of the elaborately divided lower strings enters in turn with the nature motif discussed earlier, and with its associated static harmonies. Never, at the end of a recitative in the eighteenth century did obbligato instruments enter to define the new level of the beginning of an aria with greater effect than this. It is often difficult to assign a precise dramatic meaning to such developmental figures as the nature motif here: the difficulty is usually only a verbal one, for the purely musical meaning is invariably simple and clear. In this instance there are a few intriguing clues in the music itself. The eight successive string entries (four cellos, two violas, two second violins), weave a pattern not unlike that of the eight horns in the prelude to Scene 1, and the crest of each string phrase has diatonic appoggiaturas similar to those of the joyful beginning of the Rhinemaidens' song (theme 2). Thus the music associates womanhood with the basic creativity of nature, and with what, referring to the song, Donington defines as 'the state of nature from which joy comes'.[27]

However, all this turns out only to be the backcloth for a serene transformation of Freia's theme, which was heard earlier in a more frenetic form (No. 10 on p. 183), but now floats high on the first violins: Freia as idealised womanhood indeed! Porges, never one to play down the emotional depths of his mentor's music, speaks of a flood of tender feeling, to be played very lyrically but also very calmly and evenly. It is indeed an idyllic passage. The music, to revert to a concept of Chapter I, is supporting Loge in the sense that he is conjuring up these visions, and it calls for gestures (or perhaps only stances are needed at this particular moment) to match the stasis and serenity of the music.

Loge's vocal phrases in bar 31–5 look almost like fanfares. They are not that, but are nevertheless moulded to cut through the atmospheric orchestra – not to disturb it, but so as to get the 'surface' words across clearly. The singer needs just the tone to do that, not a very full tone. The notated rhythms are to be exactly observed. Perhaps a touch of vibrato on 'Luft' (*air*) is appropriate, this being one of those big notes which would 'take care of itself'. The key changes to B minor in bar 35 as Loge refers to the frustration of his enquiries, and this is significant because it is a key to which he will return in bars 59–76 and again at bar 113 to give pathos to the ending. Wagner marks this first move into the key with exquisitely overlapping woodwind and horn chords, a different colour on each beat of the bar, still over the backcloth of the nature music in the strings. He merely indicates (via Porges) that they are to be played very smoothly, without any trace of accent, leaving the accentuation to Loge's voice part, as earlier. The longer note on 'Manne' (*a man*) is a hint for him to warm the phrase to lead forwards to the second 'Weibes Wonne und Werth', in the major mode. This time, to give greater continuity, Wagner closes the phrasing in so that Freia's serene theme (now on the clarinet), actually overlaps with the singer's last note. The new orchestral interlude lasts only for a bar before the narration continues.

The second section of the narration, beginning in bar 43, is a shortened and modified restatement of the first, notable for its greater impregnation with Freia's motive, which cuts through the texture on the very characteristic tone of the cor anglais in bar 49, and even more assertively on the horn solo in the next bar. These lovely entries prepare the way for the singer's long notes at the end of the section, a climax to be

for woman's beauty and delight
Langsam
sehr breit.
(All show astonishment and perplexity)
etwas bewegter, doch sehr ruhig.
Wei - bes Won - ne und Werth!
Cor A.
21
p
+Horns
Cellos div.
3
piu p
25
V. I
Ob.
dolce
Wherever there is life and being
Loge
So weit Le-ben und We - ben,
29
Vln.
30
Flt.
p

In water, earth and air
I asked much, seeking from all, where
In Was - ser, Erd' und Luft,
viel frug ich,
forsch-te bei al - len, wo
piu p
35
p Clar.
Hn.
Bsn..
Clar.
Hn.
Bsn..

force stirs
and seeds sprout,
What would a man think greater than
Kraft nur sich rührt,
und Kei-me sich re-gen:
was wohl dem Man - ne
mächt'-ger dünk', als
vln 2
cresc.
40
vln 1

woman's beauty and delight.
rall.
a tempo
Yet so
Wei - bes Won - ne und werth?
Doch so
tr
Clar.
Ob.
f
dim.
p

sung with full voice. There is an interesting production idea in the Bayreuth/Boulez video recording. In these interludes Loge moves freely around the stage, as though addressing each group in turn, and on these excursions he makes big arm and body movements, with Freia's long shawl streaming after him to weave graceful rippling patterns in the air. The mobility and grace of this express well his ethereal qualities as fire god. He had taken the shawl from her at the beginning of the narration, to suggest perhaps that he refers to her obliquely throughout his story (see overleaf).

Loge comes to the crux of his message in bar 58. As he begins to retell the story of the stealing of the gold the music reverts for the moment to 'recitative' whose orchestral rests enable him to point the words very clearly indeed and so to emphasise the new interest. The music reverts in bar 60 to B minor as the gold motif is heard on the solo horn in that key, reminding us of the minor playings of the motif in Scene 1,

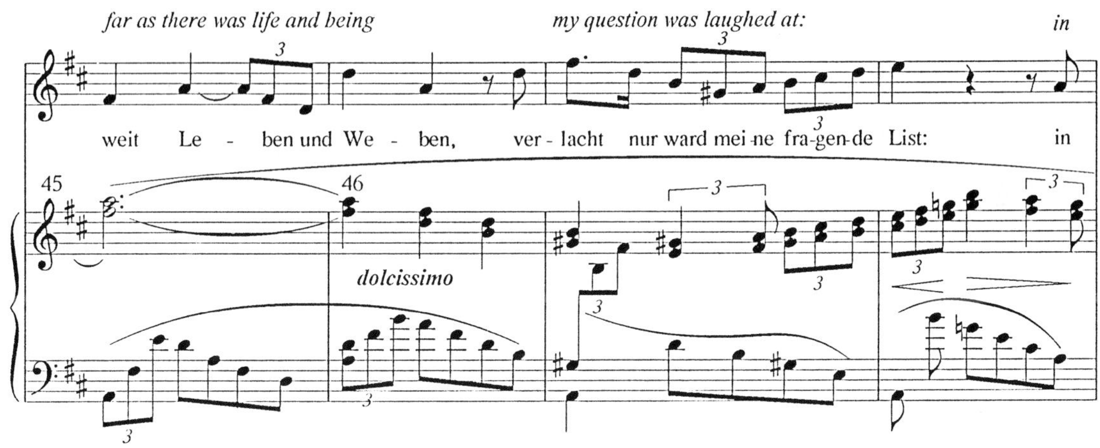

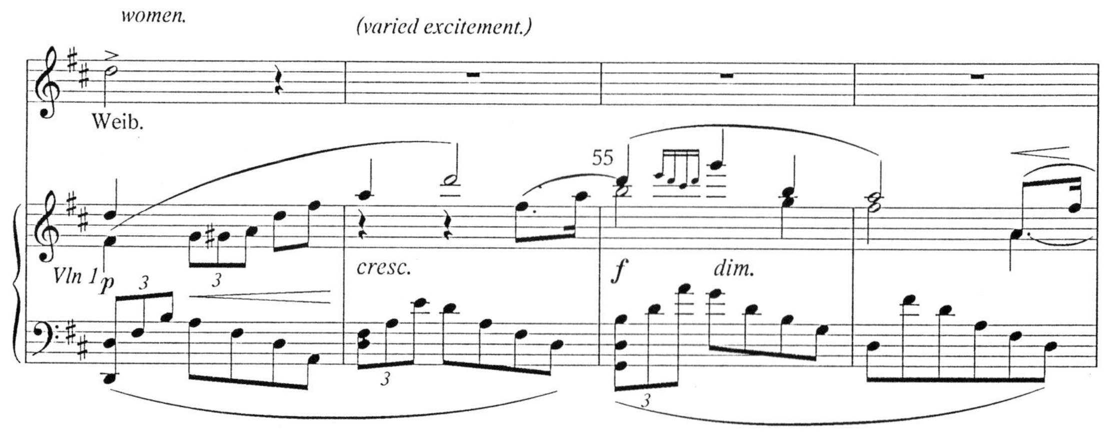

after the gold was stolen. This brings us to a passage of great subtlety and complexity in the harmonic and motivic working: there was surely nothing like this in opera before. As Loge tells of the Rhinemaidens' loss of their gold the orchestra recalls the Rhinegold song, but now with the plaintive sounds of the cor anglais and with poignant harmonies in E minor, the sombre violas simulating the original glittering figure. In bar 67 the music does actually go back into the original key of C major for the second strain of the melody, only to get pushed fatefully back to the prevalent B minor at the word 'Noth' (*woe*) in bar 69. When Loge recalls the original happiness of the Rhinemaidens, their first song is recaptured with the fresh sound of the flutes in A major. However at the mention of the theft in bar 73 the harmony changes colour at once to a diminished chord back in B minor, and the horn again sounds the gold motif in that key. This time, though, the motif is continued into the ring motif (on cor anglais) as if the two of them were simply parts of the one melody, and we in the audience, if not yet those on the stage, can understand this as a reference to the forging of the ring from the gold. It will be later in the scene before Loge explains the ring and its power to them. Again in this passage we could regard the singer's role as projecting the words clearly without musically competing too much with the rich orchestral commentary. However at the end of the section, bars 79–82, Wagner as usual gives the singer a more lyrical phrase to sing, harmonising with the 'Weibes Wonne und Werth' motif on the orchestral strings in a sad C sharp minor context.

Let us now for a moment turn our attention away from Loge's and the orchestra's ecstatic visions to consider how the others on the stage are reacting. At first they are not taken in by Loge's tale at all, but are impatient at what seems to be a waste of time. The music is certainly not supporting them and their feelings, and their acting must suggest that this is so, though any movements should not distract attention too much from Loge when he is actually singing. If he wanders near them in the course of his excursions they could even show disdain by looking away. In the video film, during the orchestral interlude in bars 53–8, there are some interesting actions which are against the meaning of the music but which can be justified on the grounds that the music is only supporting Loge anyway. The other gods (apart from Wotan and Loge) protectively surround Freia, and the giants walk threateningly across the stage to take her back into their custody. It is true, of course, that the orchestral music here refers to Freia, though in too calm a way to imply any such stage movement. However, the action does create a very good stance for what is now to come. Loge's recounting of the theft of the gold immediately grips their attention, filling them with astonishment and embarrassment. Wagner, according to Porges, wanted each god to express this in a characteristic way, and he suggested that Freia, Wotan's wife, should be the quickest of them to react with her facial expression. He also took trouble to ensure that the grouping of the characters at this point should create a significant and vivid stage picture.[28] This is certainly obtained in the video film when they swing round from their momentary conflict to hang on every word coming from Loge's mouth. Wotan's special responsibility as leader is shown by his walking a few paces over towards Loge at this moment.

The Rhine's innocent children
told me of their plight:
Des Rhei-nes kla - - - re Kin - - - der klag-ten mir ih-re
65
Cor A.
Hns.
sempre p

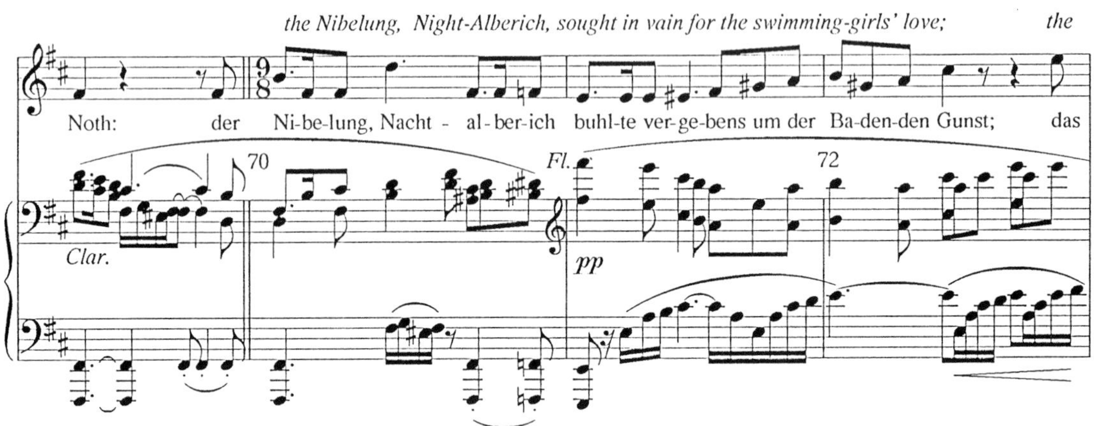
the Nibelung, Night-Alberich, sought in vain for the swimming-girls' love;
the
Noth: der Ni-be-lung, Nacht - al-ber-ich buhl-te ver-ge-bens um der Ba-den-den Gunst; das
70
Fl.
72
Clar.
pp

Rheingold
he stole from them in revenge:
he now regards it as of
Rhein - gold
da raub-te sich räch-end der Dieb:
das dünkt ihm nun das
Hn.
75
76
Cor A.
fp
mf
p
f

The main part of the narration now moves to its end in a splendid climax. From the Rheingold motif's lament in the remote C sharp minor, Loge twists the key right back to the original C for the Rhinemaiden's prayer that their original joy should be reinstated by Wotan's returning the ring to them. The gold motif in the resplendent C major is heard first on the bass trumpet in bar 90 and then, a wonderful moment, on the high trumpet in bar 95. The effect of this is to reinforce the fine rhetoric, now vocal as well as orchestral, of the cadence in bars 96–7. Then there are five resplendent bars of C major, recapitulating the Rhinegold music from the first scene in its full former glory.

Of course all this fine rhetoric is really insincere because Loge knows full well that Wotan is in no position to return the gold even if he wanted to. The insincerity is at once made clear in the music when Loge adds his own modest cadence to the Rheingold passage (bars 102–3) taking the music back to the much darker key of B minor: so the flurry of C major has turned out to be a Neapolitan episode after all.

grace.
For the gleaming toy,
torn from the deep
Huld.
Um den gleis- en- den Tand,
der Tie-fe ent-wandt,
83
p
piu p
p

the daughter moaned to me:
to you, Wotan
they entreat
to bring
er - klang mir der Töch-ter Kla - ge:
an dich, Wo - tan,
wen-den sie sich,
dass zu
85
88
p
p
Horns

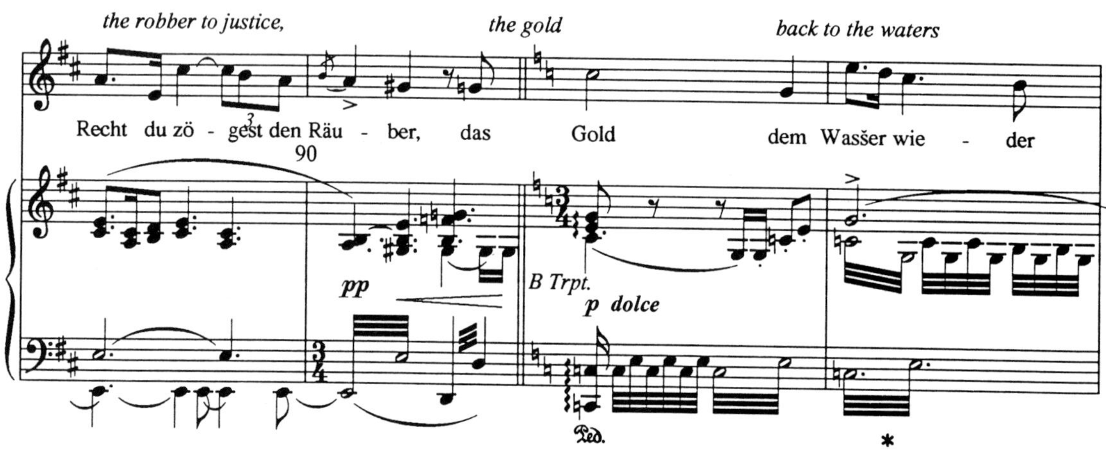
the robber to justice,
the gold
back to the waters
Recht du zö - gest den Räu - ber,
das
Gold
dem Wasser wie - der
90
pp
B Trpt.
p dolce

to return
to remain theirs for ever.
ge - best und e - wig es blie - be ihr ei - - - -
93
Trpt.
95
tr
poco cresc.
p
Ped.
*
Ped.
*

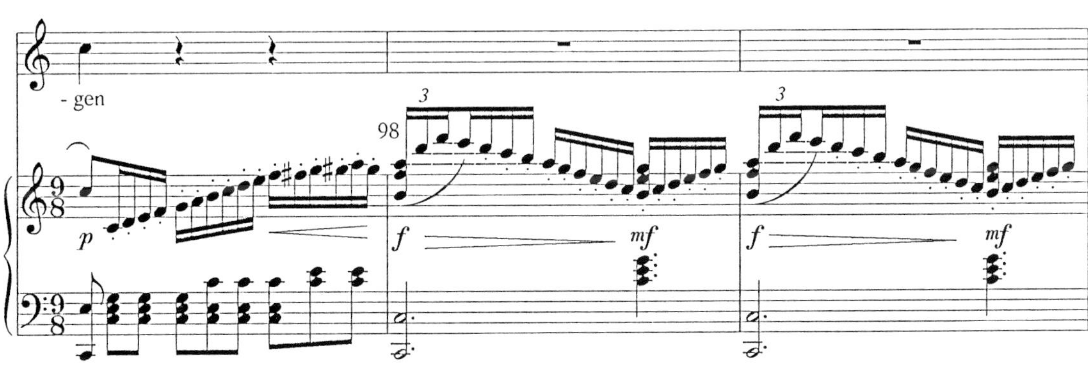
- gen
98
3
p
f
mf
f
mf

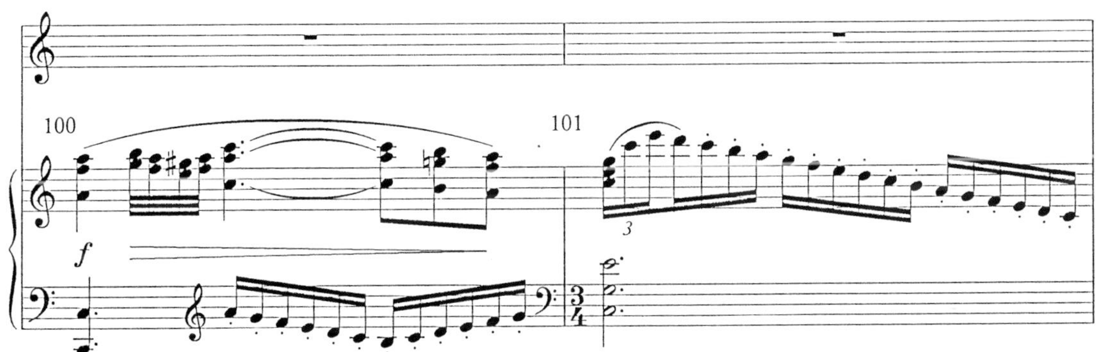
100
101
3
f

From now onwards the interest turns away from Loge to the results of his cunning, and we will hear the various reactions of the other characters supported in the orchestra in the usual way. Wotan at first doesn't see the point, but chides Loge for apparently expecting him to do the impossible when he has other more pressing problems on his hands: however, the reaction of the giants is indeed as Loge planned, and that is what really matters. They are immediately jealous of Alberich and show interest in the possibility of wresting the gold from him. Thus Wotan is forced into an action which is to generate the plots of three operas still to come.

Notes

1 See Ellis (tr.) (1892–9, repr. 1972), vol. 2. A good summary of *Opera and Drama* is given in Abraham (1974). The term 'opera' is used here and later for convenience, but Wagner himself called *The Ring* a Buhnenfestspiel. He took a good deal of trouble in his prose writings to distinguish his Music Drama from opera.

2 A survey of the subject and its literature is to be found in Sadie (ed.) (1984). Wagner's own account in his autobiography, Wagner (1983), is compelling reading but not wholly accurate. See also Donington (1990), footnote 1 to Chapter 12, p. 223, for a good recent selected bibliography.

3 See Dahlhaus (1979), pp. 83–7. A summary of this is given in the same author's article on Wagner in Sadie (ed.) (1984), vol. 20, pp. 103–45.

4 Further comment on Wagner's use of alliteration and the patterns of his 'lifts' (stresses) is in Stewart Spencer's chapter 'Wagner as Librettist' in Millington (ed.) (1992).

5 Interpretations of the underlying meaning of this are legion. Bernard Shaw in Shaw (1898) saw the gold as representing the power of money; Robert Donington in Donington (1963) sees the whole scene as a birth experience, and this moment as the dawn of consciousness.

6 See Dahlhaus (1979), pp. 112–16.

7 An English translation was published in London in 1882.

8 There is a good synopsis of the plots of *The Ring* with the associated leitmotifs in Newman (1949).

9 Perhaps not, though, the elaborate trollies used in the original production and which the original Rhinemaidens in 1876 were not courageous enough to use. There are illustrations of these in Donington (1990), p. 107.

10 Dahlhaus, op.cit. p. 118.

11 See Donington (1963), appendix examples 26–32, pp. 272–4.

12 See Thomas S. Grey's chapter 'Reminiscence motif and leitmotif' in Millington (ed.) (1992).

13 See Kurth (1920).

14 See Abbate (1989), pp. 92–124.

15 I realise that the word 'symphonic' here is something of a misnomer, for the symphonies of Wagner's day were not constructed like this, and he was inclined to exaggerate his own indebtedness to the symphonic procedures of Beethoven. The word is simply used to mean motivic and tonal development of musical material in the orchestra. Wagner's own words on the art of transition are contained in a letter to Mathilde Wesendonk: 'My subtlest and deepest art I might now call the art of transmutation. . . . My greatest masterpiece in this art of subtlest and most gradual transition . . . is *Tristan* Act II sc. 2 . . .'. Quoted from Goldman (1964) p. 213, a very useful anthology of his writings.
16 Porges (1876) tr. Jacobs (1983).
17 Wagner R. 'Uber das Dirigieren', (1869), tr. Ellis (1892–9, repr. 1972), vol. 4.
18 Breckbill D. 'Performance Practice' in Millington (ed.) (1992), p. 354.
19 Porges, op. cit., p.12.
20 Wagner himself had a hand in the design of the pit at Bayreuth. It should be added that the covering of the pit also had the effect of changing the quality of the sound by damping the high notes and so helping the balance even more. This and other features of the Bayreuth Festspielhaus are discussed in Forsythe (1985), pp. 186–92.
21 Quoted in Breckbill 'Performance Practice' in Millington (ed.) (1992), p. 357.
22 H. Porges, op. cit., p. 36.
23 Ibid, pp. 20–7
24 Ibid, p. 21.
25 See W. Darcy, 'Autograph Manuscripts', in Millington, op. cit., pp. 217–9.
26 For another view see Donington (1990), pp. 194–5, where it is related to other motives in *The Ring* cycle.
27 Donington, op. cit., p. 197.
28 Porges, op. cit., p. 22.

Part III
Further Studies

Rocco the gaoler (Robert Lloyd) and Leonora, disguised as a man Fidelio (Gabriela Benackova) look down on the sleeping Florestan (Josef Protschka) as they descend into the deep dungeon for the melodrama scene in Act II of *Fidelio*. As yet she cannot see whether or not it is her husband. When Rocco tells her that the prisoner is not dead but only asleep his spoken words are supported in the orchestra by a reassuring pastoral phrase on the oboe: see p. 218. *Photograph Catherine Ashmore*

6 Speech and *Sprechgesang*

I Spoken Dialogue between Musical Movements

The exciting dramatic possibilities of the juxtaposition of music and the spoken word were being explored in the spoken theatre in Europe long before the days of opera. It is worth starting by looking briefly at how a great playwright handles the speech/music tension, even though the essential nature of opera, that the drama is primarily articulated by the music, means that this tension is felt in a different way. One thing that the two genres have in common is that the moments of change from speech to music and vice versa need especially careful handling, for they have to carry a dramatic weight as signifying changes of level or intensity.

Shakespeare, who was working in a theatrical tradition which made much use of music, handles these changes with great resource. It would seem that moving into the musical dimension was easy if there was a reasonable pretext for it. The problem for the dramatist (and often for the actors too) was to make the return to speech equally justifiable. In *The Tempest*,[1] where music has the clear role of signifying the magical dimension,[2] we experience a sense of pleasurable anticipation at the moment we hear the first notes of Ariel's song in Act I or the music for the entry of the masque in Act IV. It is the endings of these little musical scenes which are especially noteworthy. In the first, Miranda sees the bemused Ferdinand and immediately falls in love with him, and this happens at the very moment when the music stops, presumably at the end of line 407 in the following short extract. It is a new dramatic twist of such compelling interest that we in the audience have no time to lament the loss of the musical dimension.

Shakespeare *The Tempest*, Act I, Scene 2

Ferdinand

The ditty does remember my drown'd father:
This is no mortal business, nor the sound
That the earth owes: I hear it now above me.

Prospero

The fringed curtains of thine eye advance,
And say what thou see'st yond'.

Miranda

What is't? a spirit?
Lord how it looks about! Believe me, sir,
It carries a brave form:

The Act IV masque ends even more dramatically when Prospero suddenly interrupts it and dismisses the dancers, in order to cope with the impending assault from Caliban and his fellows.

Shakespeare *The Tempest*, Act IV, Scene 1

Enter certain reapers properly habited: they join with the nymphs in a graceful dance: towards the end whereof Prospero *starts suddenly, and speaks: after which, to a strange, hollow, and confused noise, they heavily vanish.*

Prospero (aside)

I had forgot that foul conspiracy
Of the beast Caliban and his confederates
Against my life: the minute of their plot
Is almost come. – (*To the Spirits*) Well done; avoid; no more.

The primacy of the words as the main vehicle of communication is re-established very soon after this when Prospero, in the famous lines 'The cloud-capped towers, the gorgeous palaces / The solemn temples, the great globe itself, / Yea all which it inherit, shall dissolve / And like this insubstantial pageant faded, / Leave not a rack behind' takes up the recent musical experience of the masque into the even higher level, in this play, of his poetry. These two little scenes are almost opera[3] in that their music is sung and played over a period of several minutes; and it is because the musical dimension establishes itself so firmly that Shakespeare had to use such strong dramatic gestures to justify the return to speech. Where the music is of less consequence, as in Stephano's songs, there was no such necessity.

If we now compare this with Singspiel opera we see the other side of the coin. The tensions of the medium are still felt at the moments of change but now the other way round. In a context where the main thrust is musical we welcome the change to prosaic speech, the more so because (and this is a respect in which the dualism of play/opera breaks down) the musical movements in classical opera invariably announce their closure with a firm cadence: they seem positively to be demanding a new beginning. It is in the return to music that the greater musical and dramatic skill is needed. There is the further difficulty, for both composer and performers, of relating the musical movements across the spoken gaps so that the music can be experienced as an entity. Let us then look at some of the moments in *The Magic Flute* when music is reintroduced after speech.[4]

The arrival of a new character will invariably make a new musical beginning seem quite natural, and if that arrival heralds a new twist to the plot then a new key will be all the more appropriate. Both points are illustrated at the joins of Scenes 1 and 2 of Act I. The Trio No. 1 finishes firmly in C major as the three ladies leave the stage, having rescued Tamino from the serpent. Tamino, left on his own, regains consciousness and tries to remember what has happened: this is the first use of the spoken voice in the opera and so it sets up the pattern for what is to come. But very soon a new kind of music strikes up in a new key: he immediately understands this to refer to the arrival of someone else, so he looks round and the sight of the approaching Papageno so astonishes him that he hides behind a tree, leaving the stage clear for the new character and his first aria.

There are several simple things to be noted about the way this action is handled by the composer. Because the interval between the two movements is only of about 30 seconds duration,[5] and because Tamino's speaking, unlike recitative, has no tonal dimension (musically speaking), there is nothing to dislodge the memory of the C major across the gap, and so we hear Papageno's aria quite clearly as in the dominant key. In other words, the tonal drama can be even clearer in Singspiel than in opera with recitative. Papageno's long ritornello is, of course, fully supportive of his character and has the effect of buoying him up so that his entry can be a sustained, perhaps slightly stylised, exhibition of his character. The libretto seems to suggest that we should first be made aware of his approach by the slightly inane sound of his pan pipes in the distance. Even when his ritornello begins, (making musical sense of the phrase played by the pipes), he still customarily doesn't actually appear for several bars. The effect is comic because of the deliberate withholding of something to which the music is making such strong reference.

Humour of this kind is in the best traditions of the interpretation of the part because it involves the music: for despite his occasional speaking Papageno, unlike Ariel, is a completely operatic character whose every emotion and motivation is in the music. Indeed, in the very first production in 1791 Mozart himself played an even simpler musical trick on the audience in Papageno's second aria in Act II. Schikaneder himself was playing the part and Mozart had been watching the performance from a box close to the orchestra:

> But during Papageno's aria with the glockenspiel I went behind the scenes, as I felt a sort of impulse today to play it myself. Well, just for fun, at the point where Schikaneder has a pause, I

played an arpeggio. He was startled, looked behind the wings and saw me. When he had his next pause, I played no arpeggio. This time he stopped and refused to go on. I guessed what he was thinking and played a chord. He then struck the glockenspiel and said 'Shut up'. Whereupon everyone laughed. I am inclined to think that this joke taught many of the audience for the first time that Papageno does not play the instrument himself.[6]

Again, to spoil the joke by analysing it, the essence is in the unexpected dislocation of the music and the staging.

Example 6.1
Mozart *The Magic Flute*, Act I, No. 2

The example begins with just the few bars of the Trio, No. 1, the exit music for the three ladies who have just rescued Tamino from the serpent. The dialogue as he wakes up is spoken and this is inevitably quite a dramatic surprise because it is the first speech in the opera and it comes after some twenty minutes of music (counting the overture) the effect of which is to establish music very firmly as the primary medium of communication. For these reasons he can take his time for the moment and articulate the words quite slowly and clearly. The first video still shows him wheeling round in concern at the new musical intrusion on his spoken soliloquy, the sound of Papageno's pipes.

End of Trio No. 1
(The three ladies go to the door of the temple, which opens and closes behind them.)
f
3

Tamino (*spoken*)
(*awaking and looking nervously around*)

Wo bin ich? Ist's Phantasie, dass ich noch lebe? Oder hat eine Hohere Macht mich gerettet? Wie? – Die bosartige Schlange liegt tot zu meinen Füssen?	*Where am I? Is it a dream that I'm still alive? Or has a higher power saved me? How? The evil serpent lies dead at my feet?*

(*He stands up and looks around. In the distance pipes sound, softly accompanied by the orchestra. Tamino follows the sound.*)

Was hör' ich? Wo bin ich? Welche unbekannter Ort? Ha, eine männliche Gestalt nähert sich dem Tal.

What do I hear? Where am I? What unknown place? Ha, someone in the form of a man is approaching.

(*He hides behind a tree*)

The music will normally have progressed this far before Papageno is actually seen, and various birds and nets are seen too to signify his engagement in his professional calling. On the video film he makes a very leisurely entrance from the back of the stage and when the time comes for him to begin his first verse he is still exploring the locality. The photograph shows him gingerly prodding the serpent to make sure it is not still alive, a typical piece of stage business at this point.

8va
8va

cresc.

A more dramatic instance, not illustrated here, of the same musical device of a move to the dominant across a short spoken divide, occurs between movements 11 and 12 in Act II. In the forecourt of the temple the two priests lecture Papageno and Tamino on being vigilant against the guiles of women: the music for this is in the temple key of C. When the priests leave, the other two have time for only a few lines of dialogue before a temptation does indeed arrive in the form of the three ladies. They must enter quickly, for Mozart forces a lively pace by dispensing with a ritornello: the only introduction before they sing their Allegro in the dominant key of G is a single unison chord which must surely come hard on the heels of the short spoken dialogue. This is a very dramatic event, an attempt to subvert the two friends from their quest, and it is clearly underpinned by the pacing and the strong tonal tension of the music.

To return to Example 6.1 for a moment, the real justification for the new music in the dominant key is the entry of a new character. However at the end of the same movement there is a very different treatment of the interface of speech and music. The aria itself finishes with an orchestral flourish to cap a third verse in which Papageno has been revealing some of his most intimate thoughts. His dreams of his future wife are often supported by some such action as his cradling his arms in a manner suggested by the very last lines:

Sie schlief an meiner Seite ein,	(*She'd sleep at my side,*
Ich wiegte wie ein Kind sie ein.	*I'd rock her like a child.*)

As the music ends there is a much longer passage of spoken dialogue, so long that the structural force of the eventual change of key back to the E flat of the overture is somewhat weakened, though this time there are other factors at work.

Example 6.2
Mozart *The Magic Flute*, Act I, No. 3

The dialogue begins with the mutual introductions of Tamino and Papageno and continues with the arrival of the three ladies, who are still the agents of virtue at this stage of the opera. They padlock Papageno's mouth as a punishment for his having lied that he had rescued Tamino from the serpent. They also give Tamino a portrait of Pamina, the daughter of their mistress the Queen of the Night. Then the dialogue finishes as shown with some jesting remarks to Papageno, but these are nothing whatever to do with the sonorous E flat chords that we immediately hear on clarinets, bassoons, horns and strings. This music is for Tamino who has been looking at Pamina's portrait with increasing rapture. He will surely move a few steps to the front or centre stage during this short introduction with such a sense of purpose that whatever other action is taking place at the time (the third lady going off, Papageno still gesticulating), it is clear to the audience even before he sings that he now holds the stage. The music lifts us up at once into a quite new dimension of passionate devotion in the obverse way from the moment in *The Tempest* when the music stopped to reveal a similarly exciting new love interest.

First Lady

Du willst vermuthlich wissen, warum die Fürstin dich heute so wunderbar bestraft?

Would you like to know why the Queen has punished you today in this strange way?

(*Papageno nods*)

Second Lady

Damit du künftig nie mehr Fremde belügst.

So that you will tell no further lies to strangers.

Third Lady

Und dich nie der Heldenthaten rühmst die And're vollzogen.

Nor boast of heroic deeds done by others.

First Lady

Sag' an, hast du diese Schlange bekämpft?

Tell us, did you kill this serpent?

(Papageno signifies 'No')

Second Lady

Wer denn also?

Who did, then?

(*Papageno indicates he doesn't know*)

Third Lady

Wir waren's Jungling, die dich befreiten. Zittre nicht, dich erwartet Freude und Entzücken. Hier, dies Gemälde schickt dir grosse Fürstin; es ist das Bildniss ihrer Tochter.
Findest du, sagte sie, dass diese Züge dir nicht gleich-gultig sind, dann ist Glück, Ehr' und Ruhm dein Loos! Auf Wiedersehen!

It was us who rescued you, young man. Don't be surprised, joy and delight await you. Take this portrait sent by our great queen. It is the likeness of her daughter. If you find that you are not unmoved by it then fortune, honour and glory will be yours. We meet again!

(*Exit the three Ladies and Papageno*)

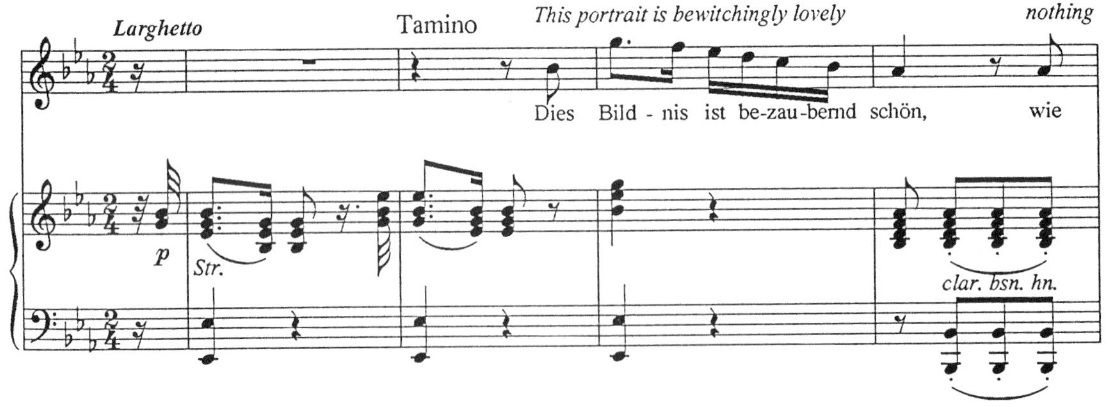

Example 6.3
Mozart *The Magic Flute*, Act I, No. 4

Tamino's aria finishes, of course, in E flat and is followed again by quite a long passage of spoken dialogue parts of which are often cut in performance, with the good effect of enhancing the dramatic key change to the dominant for the next music, the Queen of the Night's first aria. The dialogue begins with some banter between the Ladies and the mute Papageno but continues with more important business when they tell Tamino that it is his duty to rescue Pamina from an abductor, as yet unnamed. Only the last few lines of this dialogue are given in the example here. As in the earlier scene the new music in the new key announces the arrival of a new character, but this time the dramatic tension is enhanced by a change of scene too. Mozart's tense, urgent ritornello is preceded by thunder as the stage darkens to reveal the awesome queen on her throne. In fact the Haitink video ignores Schikaneder's instruction that she should be 'seated on a throne which is sparkling with stars', but it nevertheless achieves the dark regality which the music surely requires. In dispensing with the throne the queen is free to move, starting at the back of the stage as a silhouette against the night sky and moving forwards into the light to sing, as shown in the photograph. This is particularly effective because of the way it matches the music which crescendos from *piano* to *forte* in the first five bars of the ritornello.

(About 30 lines of dialogue omitted here)

Tamino

O sagt, Mädchen, sagt wo ist des Tyrannen Aufenthalt?

O tell me, ladies, tell me where the tyrant lives?

Second Lady

Sehr nahe an unseren Bergen lebt er in einem ange nehmen und reizenden Tale. Seine Burg ist prachtvoll und sorgsam bewacht.

He lives near to our mountains in a pleasant and charming valley. His castle is impregnable and closely guarded.

Tamino

Komm't Mädchen, führ't mich! Sie sei gerettet. Das schwöre ich bei meiner Liebe, bei meinem Herzen!

Lead me there, Ladies! She shall be rescued. I swear it by my love, by my heart!

(Thunder)

Ihr Götter, was ist das?

Heavens, what is that?

The Three Ladies

Fasse Dich!

Be strong!

First Lady

Es verkündet die Ankuft unserer Königin.

It heralds the arrival of our queen.

(Thunder)

The Three Ladies

Sie kommt! Sie kommt! Sie kommt!

She comes! She comes! She comes!

Going right through the opera in this way it will be found that every musical entry has a similarly clear dramatic justification; but it must suffice here to look at one or two later moments where the process works in slightly different ways. There are some places where the music resumes in the same key across the speaking gap, and the effect, of course, is that it re-establishes a dramatic identity too. This can be a very powerful correspondence, and in fact its first use in *The Magic Flute* is across only a very short stretch of dialogue, and with a correspondingly stronger effect. The Queen of the Night's aria, No. 4, finishes in B flat, and the scene changes back at once to the rocky terrain of the opening. Tamino has time for only a few (spoken) reactions to the aria before the orchestra starts up again for the reappearance of Papageno, who is still gesticulating because his mouth is padlocked. The fact that the key at this point remains in B flat is a potent reminder that Papageno (and Tamino too, for that matter), are still under the strong influence of the queen.

There are several features making the next example of the same device quite different from this. There is a much longer dialogue gap between the F major Priests' March, No. 9, and Sarastro's next aria in the same key. Moreover, this dialogue is three times interrupted by the threefold temple chord of B flat. These chords don't quite have the effect of destroying the key because they are heard, in retrospect at least, as subdominant chords in a longer term F major tonality, and indeed it is the overall unity of key which makes for such a moving experience when Sarastro, in his aria at the end of the scene, lifts the music from the level of the March to the exultation of prayer.

This last move has a difficulty for Sarastro, in that he has to move straight from speech into an uplifting aria without there being a perceptible 'bump'; in other words to do what in opera seria would be achieved by purely musical means through the sensitive handling of the end of a sung recitative. The reappearing temple chords throughout this dialogue also contribute to the generally elevated level of the whole scene; indeed the interaction of spoken and musical levels as a result of the chords brings this scene close to the condition of melodrama, to be discussed shortly.[7]

Example 6.4
Mozart *The Magic Flute*, Act II, Nos. 9–10

The extract begins with the end of the March of the Priests, enough to show its firm F major tonality. The priests process onto the stage during this music and the first photograph shows them assembled at the end waiting for Sarastro to address them and to answer their questions. This is all conducted in spoken dialogue (the words not given here[8]) until the intrusion of the first set of threefold chords, the effect of which is to elevate their speech into a higher, ritualistic level, or rather, since the speech has already assumed such a tone, to support and confirm it.

(*Dialogue, Sarastro and Priests*)

The pattern now repeats twice more, with further spoken dialogue punctuated by the threefold chords. After the third set of chords Sarastro alone speaks and he has the difficult task of taking the speech right through into his aria. There is more than one way of doing this – he could raise or otherwise intensify the voice, or slow the pace of the words – but whatever is decided must be done with discretion, for the words themselves do not have the force of Shakespeare's verse. In the performance on the video Sarastro both slows and raises his voice: it is certainly as if he is declaiming poetry rather than prose, especially towards the end. As with earlier examples of recitative leading into aria, he suggests the desired continuity by not moving at the transition into the aria. The photograph shows his dignified stance at this moment.

(*Dialogue, Sarastro, Speaker*)

Second Threefold Chord (B flat)

(*Dialogue, Sarastro, Speaker*)

(*Dialogue, Sarastro*)

Sarastro

Man führe Tamino mit seinem Reisegefährten in den Vorhof des Tempels ein.	*Tamino is to be taken with his companion into the forecourt of the temple.*

(*to the Speaker who kneels before him*)

Und du, Freund, den die Götter durch uns zum Vertheidiger der Wahrheit bestimmten – vollziehe dein heiliges Amt und lehre durch deine Weisheit beide, was Pflicht der Menschheit sei, lehre sie die Macht der Götter erkennen.	*And you, friend, whom the gods have appointed as the defender of the truth – fulfil your holy office and through your wisdom teach them both the duty of men and to know the power of the gods.*

(*Exit the Speaker with one of the priests*)
(*The priests assemble with their palm fronds*)

Adagio
Sarastro
O Isis and Osiris,
O I - sis und O -
p

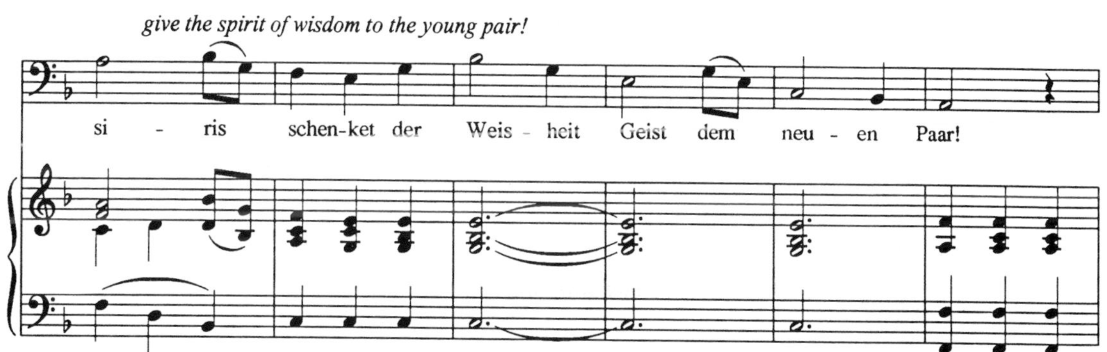
give the spirit of wisdom to the young pair!
si - ris schen-ket der Weis - heit Geist dem neu - en Paar!

The join into Sarastro's second aria, No. 15 in Act II, is even harder to bring off in performance because the preceding dialogue doesn't have the same uplifting aura of temple chords, nor the long-term tonal dimension, and its ritornello is even shorter: yet the aria itself is as exalted as the earlier one. In this case, moreover, Schikaneder is less considerate in giving some very prosaic words for the lead-in from the spoken dialogue, words whose effect is rather negative.

Pamina (*spoken*)

Herr, strafe meine Mutter nicht! Der Schmerz über meine Abwesenheit –	*Sir, do not punish my mother! Her grief at my absence –*

Sarastro (*spoken*)

Ich weiss Alles. Weiss dass sie in unterirdischen Gemächern des Tempels herumirrt und Rache über mich und die Menschheit kocht . . . deine Mutter soll beschämt nach ihrer Burg zurückkehren.	*I know everything. Know that she is lurking in the cellars under the temple and plans revenge against me and mankind . . . your mother will retreat in shame to her castle.*

Anthony Besch re-wrote the last speech for the 1980 production at the London Coliseum and gave the performer a much better springboard into the music at this point:[9]

Sarastro (*spoken*)

I know everything. She is planning vengeance on me and all humanity. By her own laws she deserves to be punished. But we follow different rules.

II Melodrama

The term is not to be confused with the Italian 'melodramma', a general word for opera, nor with its common meaning in the spoken theatre,[10] but refers here to the use in a stage work of action with speech (not singing) accompanied by or alternating with the orchestra. The presence of the background music has the effect of heightening the speech, and to that extent melodrama, when used occasionally in *Singspiel*, can be regarded as the equivalent of accompanied recitative. This is as distinct from the unaccompanied dialogue we have been looking at, whose function corresponds more to secco recitative. The relationship between melodrama and accompanied recitative also has a structural dimension in that they are both often built up as a series of sections following the changing moods and imagery of the words: a glance at the next example from *Fidelio* will make this clear.

We know that Mozart at one time of his life was very excited by the dramatic possibilities of the technique, which he had seen in the work of Benda:[11] but eventually none of his completed operas used it.[12] However, Beethoven incorporated it to wonderful effect in *Fidelio*, having seen and admired its use in the work of Cherubini, whose opera *Les deux Journées* (1800) may well have served as a model in this regard.[13] In the *Fidelio* dungeon scene it contributes powerfully to the overall expression of dereliction and suffering over which (to even more powerful music), Leonora's heroism is eventually to triumph.

Example 6.5
Beethoven *Fidelio*, Act II, Melodrama

The second act of the opera begins in a dark subterranean cell. Florestan sits on a stone, his body chained by a fetter to a wall. The music opens with a long and powerful orchestral prelude in F minor, whose symphonic motifs are later used as an accompaniment to Florestan's recitative, reflecting on his grim situation. This leads into his famous A flat aria 'In des Lebens Frühlingstagen' looking back on his earlier life and leading into an F major cabaletta when he thinks of his beloved wife Leonora. Florestan sinks back exhausted, the music calming to a quiet orchestral coda. The melodrama begins as Rocco the jailer enters with Leonora, who is disguised as a man, Fidelio, employed as Rocco's assistant. They descend the steps into the dungeon by the light of a lantern, carrying a jug of wine (for their own refreshment) and tools for digging Florestan's grave.

The opening dotted rhythm of the example is suggestive of the traditional opening of an accompanied recitative, except that here it is in bare octaves, ending with a figure which can only be understood as a sort of musical shiver, evidently referring to Leonora. At first the unaccompanied dialogue is prosaic and to be spoken sotto voce as Rocco and Leonora grope their way down the dark steps.

A second, somewhat similar, orchestral phrase takes the key into an uncertain tonal area and ends on a *pianissimo* sustained string chord over which Leonora speaks, still quietly, I think, and perhaps a little slower. Although this diminished chord can be heard as a sequential answer to the last chord of bar 2, it still has a quality of suppressed tension which supports the anguish she can put into her words, lifting them emotionally above the level of the earlier unaccompanied dialogue. The three quick chords in bar 7 momentarily clear the tonality and the atmosphere as Rocco sees the prisoner, raising his voice to tell her of this. They will go over to him during the next dialogue and the sudden urgency of her 'Ihr meint es?' is allayed by the pastoral calm of the *Poco Andante* oboe solo as he reassures her, perhaps at a more measured pace, that the prisoner is only asleep. The music is now back in F major, the last key of Florestan's aria, and it may also express Leonora's relief that he isn't dead, though of course she is still concerned as to his identity. However, the sudden short *Allegro* in bar 13 evidently refers only to Rocco, who is concerned to get the grave dug as soon as possible, and it is the cue for him to walk over to the cistern.

Since the quick notes refer to Rocco, his next business-like lines can be delivered more quickly too, but the sustained and expressive orchestral passages which now follow refer only to Leonora: to her almost uncontrollable feelings as she reflects that this as yet unrecognised man may well be her husband. Each of her speeches is backed by a sustained string chord (Rocco in bars 22 and 24 only gets a held note), and the three passages in bars 16–17, 18–19 and 20–21 sustain an increasingly profound emotion. The last of them is a quotation (in the same key, E flat) from an equally emotional moment in an earlier duet[14] when she first heard she was to be allowed to accompany Rocco on this expedition. The held string chords are quiet enough background for her to be able to speak without raising her voice too much, but their expressive intensity (especially with the C flats in bar 20) will demand that her speech betrays a corresponding depth of feeling.

Although it is Rocco who has the next few passages of dialogue, being concerned mostly with the practical details of the digging of the grave, Beethoven's little musical interludes continue to stay with Leonora who, even when she picks up her spade to walk over to Rocco, will still be tempted to look back at the prisoner if the music is to make sense. Then at the end of the passage, when she does actually get down to helping Rocco with the digging, the music moves into a fully sung duet.

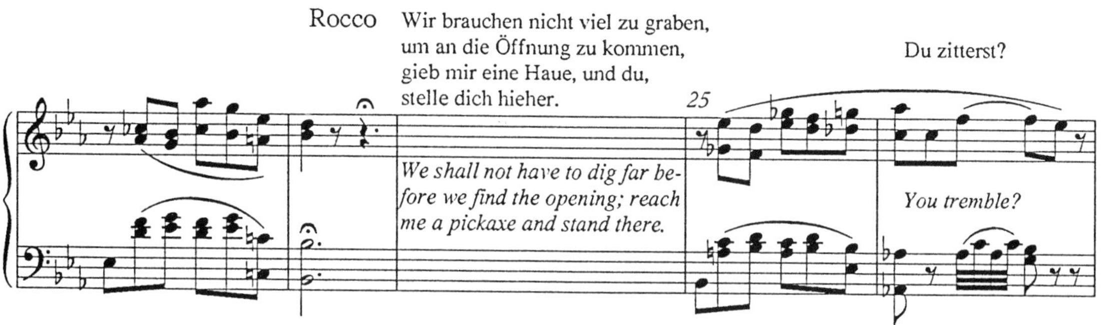

What did Beethoven achieve by the use of melodrama in this scene? The usual answer to the question is that the slightly macabre combination of unpitched speech with music contributes to 'the gruesome significance of the scene'[15] and this is undoubtedly true. The same thing could be said, despite a very different manner and context, of Weber's Wolf's Glen scene in *Der Freischütz* (1821). Over and above that, however, Beethoven was able to give some sharp characterisation (Rocco's practical concerns, Leonora's feelings as she shows bravery and love in an impossible situation) in such a way as to leave the music open for all the extra depth in the fully sung passages which were to follow. The characterisation inevitably means that where the accompaniment is specifically supporting Leonora it is not at the same time also supporting Rocco. We now turn to a passage of melodrama from another opera where the accompaniment supports neither of the speaking characters.

Carmen is a difficult work to study because there are so many different versions in circulation. The problems have all been sorted out at a scholarly level,[16] but all of this has yet to come to fruition in a reliable edition. There is not even general agreement as to its real genre. Bizet wrote the work as an opéra comique (unusual as it is in that genre in some ways) and that involved the use of spoken dialogue, which he handled with very great skill. He realised that the adoption of the work by the world's great opera houses at that time involved its being sung throughout and there is evidence that he intended to rewrite it with recitatives replacing the dialogue, but he died before he had time to do it. The task was undertaken by the composer's friend Ernest Guiraud with results that are felt by many to be less than fully satisfactory.

The very excellence of the original adaptation from Merimée's novel made Guiraud's task all the harder. For one thing the details of Jose's past life, explaining his character and motivation, had already been so skilfully condensed by Bizet's librettists that it was a thankless task to make the further cuts necessitated by the slower pace of the recitatives in the French tradition at that time. Another and even bigger problem lay in the fact that Bizet had planned what was to be spoken and what sung with such dramatic flair that the conversion to singing throughout meant the sacrificing of some potent dramatic effects, two of which are to be found in our next example.

Example 6.6
Bizet *Carmen*, Act I, No. 9

The extract is taken from the beginning of the Song and Melodrama from Act I (Song and Recitative in Guiraud's version). Carmen has been arrested after a fracas in the factory (off-stage), and brought out into the square by the corporal José for questioning by Zuniga, the officer in charge. In Bizet's original version of this scene Carmen sings, and the two men only speak. The force of this is twofold. Firstly, as Susan McClary has well shown,[17] Bizet had carefully arranged that in Act I José only sings when roused to high emotion (on seeing his mother's letter earlier in the act, and when seduced by Carmen, later), a subtlety quite lost by Guiraud's added recitatives. The other matter is even more crucial to our extract. Carmen is weaving a spell of sexual infatuation around the two men and that is the sole concern of the music, both of what she sings and of the orchestral support for it. The two men, in resisting this temptation (for the time being at least), express this on the musical level by speaking against the music, in as staccato or otherwise unmusical a way as is appropriate. That is an effect which is certainly lost in the sung revision (not shown here). Although Guiraud sets the recitatives of this scene in 4/4 or 2/4 time they lapse frequently into triplet rhythms which are bound to sound very similar to the lilting 6/8 of Carmen's Tra la la's, and make it very hard indeed for Zuniga to project commands like '. . . dit le répondre, réponds!' in a sufficiently brusque way and without sounding as though he has been beguiled by Carmen's singing.

The first video still shows a suitable position for the opening of the scene: Zuniga at a table, suggestive of his authority, Carmen guarded by the corporal José and other soldiers holding back the crowd. Carmen's first phrase is directed to be sung quietly, and in this interpretation she is looking down as if she were just singing to herself. Her sheer insolence in singing at all, rather than answering the charge against her in the spoken language in which it is put, is enhanced by her apparently wayward approach.

Zuniga (*spoken*)

(*to Carmen*)

Eh bien! . . . vous avez entendu? . . . Avez-vous quelque chose a répondre? . . . parlez, j'attends. . . .

Well! . . . You have heard?. . . . Have you anything to say in reply? . . . speak, I'm waiting.

I will tell you nothing!
moi, je ne te di - rai rien! Tra la la la la la la
4

I'll brave all the fire, the steel and even heaven.
la! Je bra - ve tout le feu, le fer et le ciel mê - - me.
7

Carmen is supported most wonderfully by the orchestra when a solo flute in its sensuous low register takes over her melody at the end of the second phrase. The phrygian cadence in E doesn't quite bring her music to rest in bar 11: we are left with a feeling of more seduction to come and it is against that background that the unseduced Zuniga must ensure that his spoken lines cut through clearly. There is a beguiling new twist of harmony in each new section of Carmen's song: the second section, near the end of the extract, moves off in C (which is not felt as the home key) as she tempts them, particularly José, deeper into her alluring world. As suggested in the libretto she now looks up and, in the video film, shows greater boldness in smiling at them.

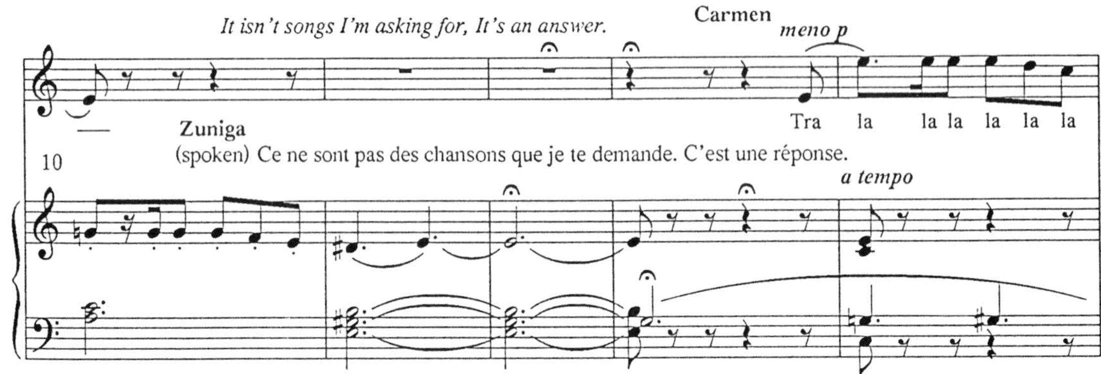

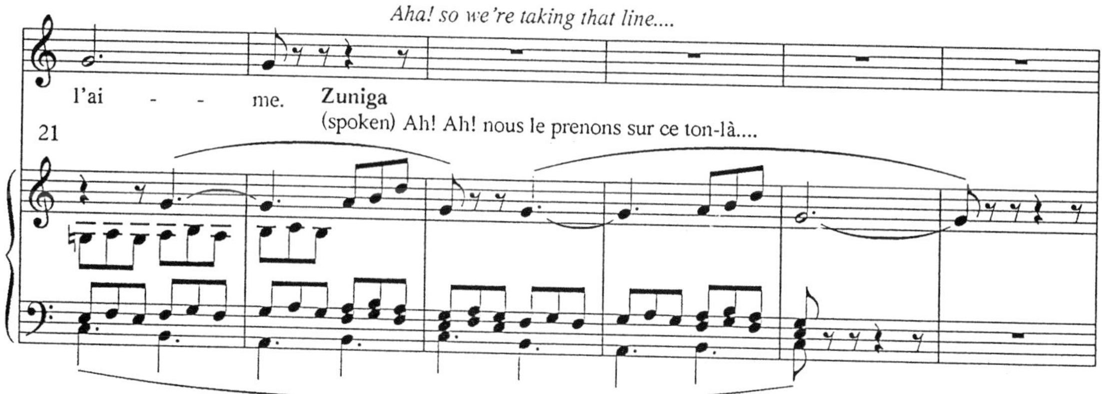

There is not now, I think, the same prejudice against opera with spoken dialogue: opera houses worldwide which can accept *The Magic Flute* and *Der Freischütz* in this form can surely accept *Carmen* too. The fact is that Bizet was more at home at the Opéra Comique. In a letter to Guiraud he wrote 'Your place is at the Opéra; I'm afraid of making a poor showing there. . . . I shall shine at the Opéra Comique; I shall enlarge and transform the genre'.[18] This he certainly did.

A somewhat similar operatic concept was much favoured by Berg: the orchestra identifying strongly with someone on the stage while others show their alienation from this by talking over it. At the beginning of Act I, Scene 3 of *Wozzeck*, Marie sings in harmony with the orchestral March as she enthusiastically watches the soldiers on parade. Then, turning from them for an acrimonious banter with her neighbour, she speaks (shouts) over the continuing march. Near the end of the opera in Act III, Scene 4 the device has great ironic force. Wozzeck is drowning, and the sliding chromatic orchestral chords represent his drifting into unconsciousness. The unfeeling reaction of the Captain and the Doctor, who hear that someone is in difficulties in the water but choose not to investigate, is expressed by their speaking against the orchestral background.

There is a very different use of the technique in *La Bohème*. Puccini gives it enormous weight by saving it until almost the last moment of the opera, to highlight Mimi's death. The musical climax of this final act, well before the extract, is her last duet with Rodolfo: in fact the main music is now over, to all intents and purposes. Once Mimi has died Puccini is concerned to bring the opera quickly to an end, yet he evidently wanted to dramatise as much as possible Rodolfo's reaction. This he does by having her die quietly, unnoticed by Rodolfo who is at the other side of the room at the time and thinks her to be asleep. Those on the stage who have noticed the death seem to him to be behaving strangely, and this is the context for a hushed melodrama over a binding pedal note in the orchestra, just enough to give musical continuity.

Example 6.7
Puccini *La Bohème*, ending of Act IV

The first video picture shows a typical staging for the scene at the moment of Colline's entry, Mimi on a bed to the right and the others dotted around the room. When the speaking starts it is very unexpected because the device hasn't been used before in the opera. Puccini highlights it by having five complete bars of rest for the cast on the stage beforehand, the space being filled by a pianissimo reference to a theme earlier associated with Mimi.

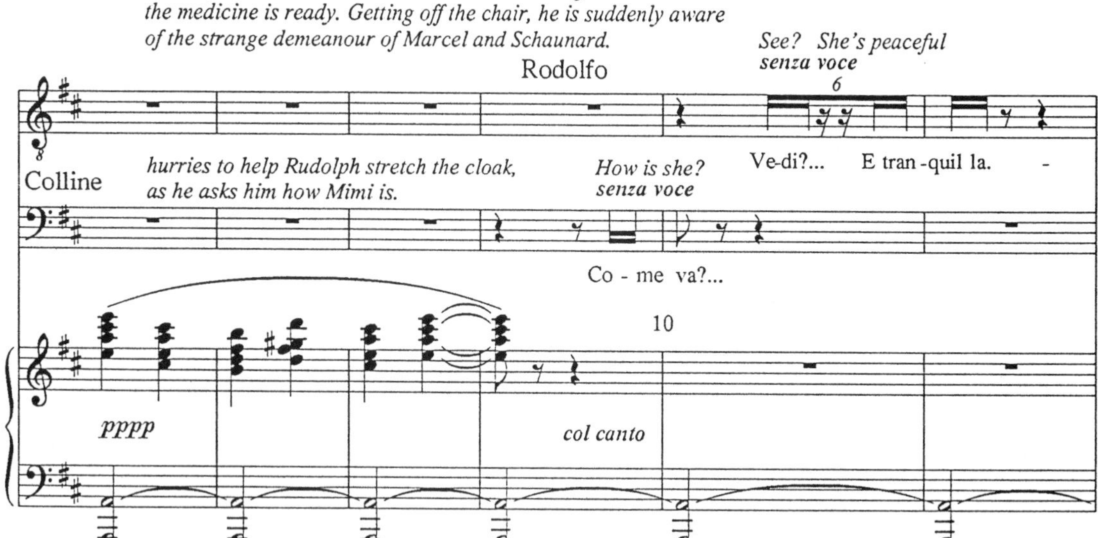

The use of the technique here has some distinct advantages: by being non-musical it expresses well the momentary confusion of those on the stage, a confusion of such dramatic interest that no music is needed to sustain the attention of the audience. It also serves to provide the maximum contrast to the singing of Rodolfo's heart-rending cry when he realises what has happened. The timings here, as always in Puccini, are carefully gauged, the rhythms of the speech being exactly notated, though I would suppose that Puccini intended them to be taken with a little freedom, particularly after the pause in bar 12 as Rodolfo's fears suddenly increase. There is a temptation for him to raise his voice in bar 14, but a subdued desperation makes stronger drama of what is to come. At the change of key a silence of precisely one and a half (slow) beats heightens the emotionally devastating effect of the sudden *fortissimo* chord for Marcello's impulsive action. This in turn triggers off the single sustained phrase of the opera's final gesture (an impassioned recapitulation of a melody to which in the preceding duet, Mimi had expressed her love for him[19]) as Rodolfo rushes to her bed, where he is seen in the second photograph.

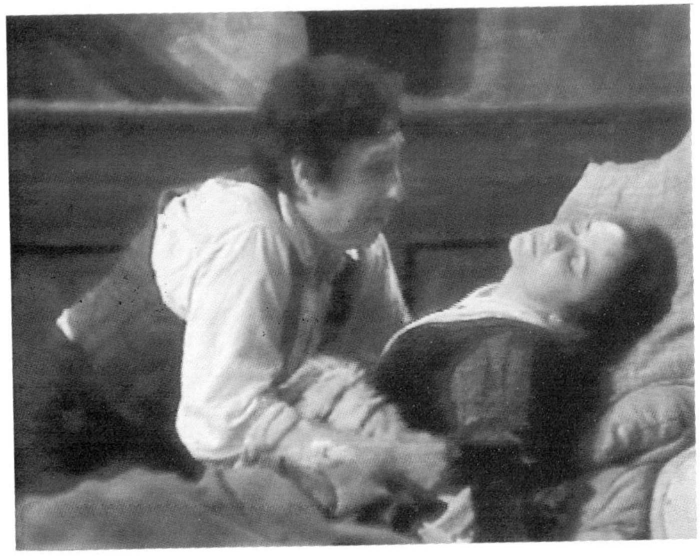

III *Sprechgesang*

The twentieth century has seen the emergence of several distinct types of vocal writing in the rather grey area between speech and song. The rhythmic dimension, whether free or strict, is usually easy to notate and interpret. It is in the interpretation of the freedom of pitch that most difficulties arise. Three types are used in *Wozzeck*, each with its own notation. When the notehead is replaced by a cross the words are to be spoken fairly strictly in the given rhythm but with the pitching of the voice left entirely to the performer, as with any spoken passages. This is, in effect, the same thing as the words notated without noteheads in the previous Puccini extract. There is an effective use of a variant of it in Britten's otherwise vocally conservative *The Rape of Lucretia*, when the Male Chorus describes Tarquinius creeping through Lucretia's house at night.[20] Here the vocal notation shows relative pitch so that the points of climax, where the voice is most raised, are more tightly controlled.

At the other end of the speech/song divide, Berg uses a normal notation with a single line through the stem to denote what is almost normal singing. This might mean singing with more than the usual amount of portamento between the notes, or perhaps with a slightly husky tone, nearer to speech in that sense. It is important in such passages that the melodic line of the vocal part is clearly recognisable.

When, in Act III, Scene 1, Marie reads from the Bible the third time,[21] the music is fugal and her line must clearly enunciate the fugue subject at the outset since if the form is to make sense this must be recognised when it is subsequently taken up by the orchestral instruments. Later she must contribute to the harmony when she is doubled by a solo violin in the middle of the contrapuntal texture. The singer's difficult task is to achieve all that without losing the point of the differentiation at the change to normal singing at the end of the section.

Example 6.8
Berg *Wozzeck*, Act III, Scene 1

An even more difficult problem comes with the type of *Sprechgesang* between these two extremes, notated by Berg with ordinary noteheads but with a cross through the stem, as in the following example. In the preface to *Wozzeck*, Berg defines this as meaning that the singer 'strikes the note but leaves it immediately by rising or falling in pitch, but always bringing out the relative pitches of the notes', and further warns the singer 'not to fall into a singing manner of speaking'. This is merely a summary of Schönberg's directions in the foreword to *Pierrot Lunaire* and in a margin note in *Die Glückliche Hand*, where the same notation is used.

How exactly this is to be interpreted is still a matter of controversy. It may be helpful to observe that the background to *Pierrot Lunaire* was Schönberg's experience with cabaret 'melodramas' early in his career. There is a recording of Schönberg's own interpretation of the work with Erica Stiedry-Wagner, on which Boulez comments '. . . in the case of the spoken intervals the pitch is more than approximate, while the few notes actually sung are for the most part precise in pitch; on the other hand the perpetual glissando from one note to the next soon becomes irritating'.[22] One big difficulty for the singer is that the speaking voice is normally more restricted in its frequency range than is the singing voice and, particularly in the case of women, is often in a lower register too. This means that the extreme notes of the *Sprechgesang* range, especially the high notes in the female roles, are beyond the normal speaking register and simply must be sung if they are not to sound very ugly. Boulez[23] advocates changing the pitches by lowering them (but keeping the relative intervals as far as possible) rather than destroying the desired distinction by reverting to singing.

Example 6.9
Berg *Wozzeck*, Act III, Scene 1

The second short extract is taken from the very beginning of the scene. Marie is in her room reading the Bible by the light of a candle.[24] The words she reads are set as *Sprechgesang* and then she reverts to singing for her own reactions to them. Berg often uses *Sprechgesang* to make this sort of dramatic distinction: e.g. in Act I, Scene 2 for the hallucinations of the demented Wozzeck as contrasted with the comparative sanity of his friend Andres who sings. The singer will surely be tempted to sing at figure 5 of the example because the given notes fit so easily into the sensuously gentle harmonies of the accompaniment, a rare moment in this work. For most singers, however, this lies in their speaking range and the notes must be regarded as speech and left as soon as they are sounded. However, the high D of 'erfunden' is another matter because it may well be above the speech range and moreover it makes a most poignant dissonance with the orchestral harmony, a moment whose beauty is too intense simply to be thrown away. In other words the note will probably have to be sung, and sustained long enough to register its harmonic potency. Then the singer must slide down to the A, thus keeping up the aura of *Sprechgesang* so as not to pre-empt the singing to come. This is certainly difficult, but it is just possible at the slow tempo of the passage. The distinction between the *Sprechgesang* and the singing can be brought out in a very simple way by actions such as those suggested here: her head is down in the book as she reads but she looks up when she sings, clasping the Bible to her. We must be in no doubt that these are now her own innermost feelings.

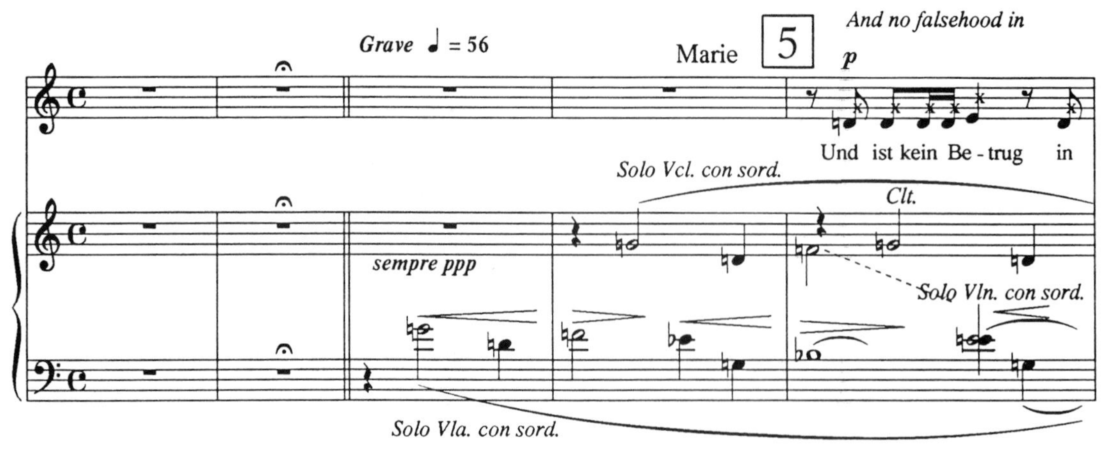
Grave ♩ = 56
Marie
5
And no falsehood in
p
Und ist kein Be - trug in
Solo Vcl. con sord.
Clt.
sempre ppp
Solo Vln. con sord.
Solo Vla. con sord.

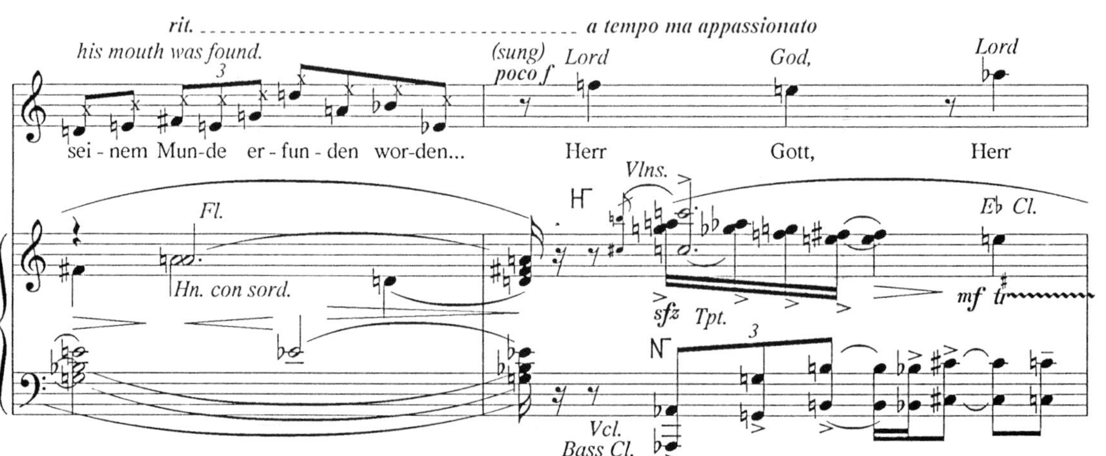
rit.
a tempo ma appassionato
his mouth was found.
(sung)
poco f
Lord
God,
Lord
sei - nem Mun-de er - fun - den wor-den...
Herr
Gott,
Herr
Vlns.
Fl.
Eb Cl.
Hn. con sord.
sfz
Tpt.
mf
Vcl.
Bass Cl.

Notes

1 In some respects this play is very close to the court masques of its day, (and to that extent to opera). Certainly, the earliest recorded performance of the play occurred in 1611 for the Court at Whitehall and J.H.Long, in *Shakespeare's Use of Music, The Final Comedies*, Da Capo Press, 1961, pp. 93–127, suggests how it may well have been staged like a masque.

2 It has been argued that the symbolism of music in the play goes further than that to embrace love and harmony in the highest sense: see Wilson Knight (1953).

3 W.H. Auden (1963), p. 524, argues that Ariel is an operatic intrusion into the play because the magical dimension of his character is expressed in music. Even if this were so, he is not completely operatic because other aspects of his character, his motivation and the bargaining with Prospero for his freedom, are only to be found in spoken passages.

4 Since the discussion in this chapter is exclusively devoted to this one aspect of the opera the reader may wish to refer to W. Mann (1977), for a good general account of the work, and to J. Chailley (1972), for a study of its masonic symbolism.

5 The reader should be aware of the fact that Schikaneder's text is generally regarded by producers as being even less sacrosanct than are those of Shakespeare: one rarely, if ever, hears it in full. However, this particular passage is not generally changed to the extent of invalidating the points made.

6 From a letter to his wife dated 8–9 October 1791, translated in E. Anderson (1966).

7 The reader should be warned that in the Sawallisch performance the Trio, No. 19 (in B flat) is interpolated into this dialogue, presumably to enlarge our understanding of the feelings of Pamino and Tamino at this juncture. Whatever its merits, this does somewhat weaken Mozart's tonal scheme.

8 A convenient complete libretto with a singing translation is in *The Magic Flute, Mozart*, ENO Opera Guide, ed. Nicholas John, Calder (1980).

9 see N. John ed. op. cit. p. 105.

10 'a sensational dramatic piece with violent appeals to emotions and a happy ending'. *The Concise Oxford Dictionary of Current English*.

11 See his letters of 12 and 14 November, 3 and 10 December 1778, translated and edited in E. Anderson op. cit.

12 It is used in an unfinished Singspiel, *Zaide*, and in incidental music to a play, *Thamos König in Aegypten*, both completed in 1779, some three years before *Die Entführung aus dem Serail*, his first major Singspiel.
13 See Deane, Basil (1965). Beethoven also used the technique in his incidental music to *The Ruins of Athens*, *King Stephen* and *Egmont*.
14 It is part of the Finale to Act I.
15 Kobbé's Opera Book, Putnam, 1952 edition, p. 130.
16 Notably by Winton Dean: in detail in his article 'The True Carmen', *Musical Times* (1965), pp. 846–55; and more generally in his book, *Georges Bizet, His Life and Work*, London, (1965).
17 See Susan McClary (1992), p. 46.
18 Quoted in W. Dean (1975), p. 107.
19 A convenient thematic review of the opera is in Ernest Newman (1954), pp. 38–85.
20 See Benjamin Britten, *The Rape of Lucretia*, Boosey & Hawkes, 1946, vocal score pp. 122–4.
21 *Wozzeck*, Act III, Scene 1, 3 bars after Figure 50.
22 Pierre Boulez (1986), p. 332.
23 See Boulez op. cit. p. 379.
24 This evocative suggestion was made by Berg himself in 'The Preparation and Staging of *Wozzeck*', reprinted as Appendix I in George Perle (1980), p. 206.

'There's a devil in your eyes.' The Drum Major (James King) draws himself to his full height over Marie (Anja Silja) as he prepares for a final and successful attempt to seduce her. The action is supported by loud brass music: see the chart on p. 258. Somewhat unusually in this opera the 'Pride' motif is heard here in his vocal line rather than in the orchestra as he looks down into her eyes. *Photograph Catherine Ashmore*

7 More Music and Action

I Two Operatic Deaths

The relationship between music and action has been a central concern of the previous chapters. In taking each type of opera in turn, we have explored the meaning and dramatic implications of the music and the text. The purpose of the present chapter is to look at the subject from the opposite direction, starting from certain categories of action and seeing how they have been treated musically. The reader is asked to bear with some repetition of earlier ideas in order to now probe into operatic principles and practices which run across the chronological and national boundaries.

It is a paradox, that opera, dramma per musica, is not primarily concerned with action at all. For example, in opera seria the main action was relegated to the musically unimportant recitative sections, leaving it to the arias and other set pieces to explore the operatically more crucial matters of motivation and reaction. This emphasis is true of almost all opera both before and after the days of opera seria, and indeed there are times when a crucially important action will not in itself be clearly articulated in the music at all: the death of Dido in *Dido and Aeneas* is one such case. The stabbing of Carmen illustrates the point in a particularly striking way because Bizet revised the ending of the opera quite specifically to take out of the music the 'programmatic' references to the action itself. The scene has been the subject of a very thorough investigation by Winton Dean.[1]

Example 7.1
Bizet *Carmen*, end of Act IV

Bizet composed at least four different versions of the ending of the opera, and in the earlier ones the moment of the stabbing and Carmen's slump to the ground are clearly depicted in the music by a sudden *fff* chord and a falling chromatic scale. The extract overleaf shows the third of these earlier versions and the one that is still quite often used in productions,[2] despite Bizet's own clear rejection of it. In Bizet's final version, whose authenticity is beyond doubt,[3] he cuts out the descriptive music and goes straight from José's 'Eh bien, damnée!' into the off-stage chorus, the crowd in the arena praising the victorious Toreador. He saves José's 'Ah ma Carmen adorée' for later, in the brief coda which follows. The effect of these changes is to take the emphasis away from the action itself and to throw the whole dramatic weight onto the irony of Escamillo's victory in the arena at the very moment his lover is murdered. Susan McClary even suggests that we are to understand the conflicts inside and outside the bullring as parallel, '. . . although the particular mapping (who is bull, who torero in the Carmen/José altercation) is left open'.[4] Of course, in removing the musical description of the stabbing, Bizet leaves open the question as to when exactly it should take place, and it is only to be expected that this will vary from performance to performance. There is a strong case for making the main movements of the two characters (her attempt to escape and his catching her), during the brief introductory fanfare in the second bar of the final version and to time the actual stabbing to coincide with the moment the off-stage choir begins to sing. This is not because it is the implied meaning of the music at that point, but in order to make better sense of

Earlier Version

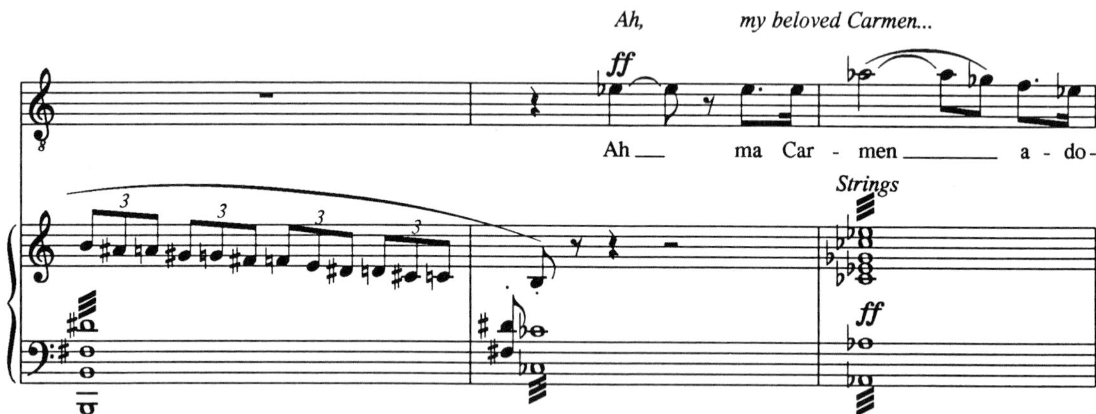

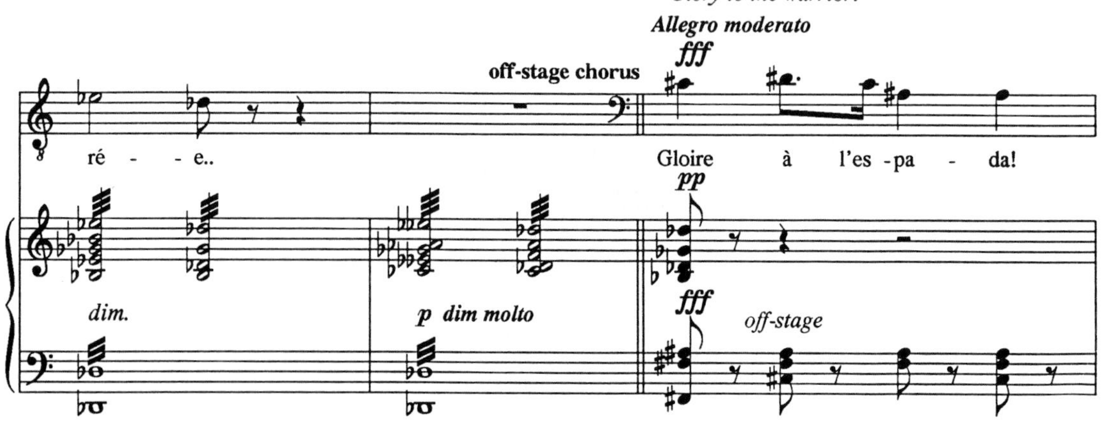

something in the music later, the pathetic counterpoint to the chorus, beginning in bar 4 and coming not from the arena but from the violins in the orchestra pit. This searing melody can best be understood as an orchestral comment on the tragedy of the already dying heroine, and on José's immediate remorse at having killed her.

On the Glyndebourne video film the action is paced out more gradually than suggested above. The fanfare in bar 2 is the occasion for José to draw his knife. Then, from the other side of the stage, where he has gone to retrieve the ring she had just thrown away, he turns and points the knife menacingly at her. As the Toreador music begins he moves over to her and at the expressive counterpoint in bar 4 he opens his arms as if in a last gesture of desperate supplication. This certainly makes sense of that music which, as we have seen, could be taken to refer to him. The actual stabbing takes place in bars 6 and 7 and has no particular relationship to anything in the music, indeed the shock of its violence rather detracts from our listening to the music at all for the moment. However, this music is by now so well known from previous repetitions that it will establish the irony of the situation without needing attentive listening.

Final Version

Chorus
To - ré - a-dor, en gar - - - de! To - ré - a-dor!
3
ff
Violins
4 espress.

And dream well, dream when fighting.....
To - ré - a-dor! Et son-ge bien, oui songe en com-bat-tant,
6

At the death of Peter Grimes in Britten's opera, the function of the music, as in the case of *Carmen*, is not to depict the death, but rather to bring out its irony. After a nightmarish fog scene with a demented Peter, there is a silence, and it is in this musical emptiness that Balstrode, speaking not singing for the first time in the opera, orders him to go out to sea and sink the boat. Then the first sounds of dawn are heard and the opera finishes with the Borough gradually getting back to a normal day's work: the irony is that it is the death which makes this normality possible and indeed cathartic.

Example 7.2
Britten *Peter Grimes*, Act III, Scene 2

The vocal score, reproduced below, is perhaps misleading in that it gives no visual representation of the time scale, which is drawn out much longer than in the corresponding passage of *Carmen*. The problem for the performers is to pace the whole scene so as to give the right weight to the coda which, once started, gives the producer some three and a half minutes to get the whole chorus on stage before the music reaches its *forte*. This must all be done so as to look random enough to suggest the irregular arrivals of the village community coming to life in the morning, and slow enough (the music is slow too) to suggest what in real life would take much longer. The effect of the musical silence following the last Foghorn note (about 1 and a half minutes on the video film), is to throw weight onto the last scene, whose music is a reprise from Act I, Scene 1, and is substantial enough to stand on its own as a coda to the whole opera. The very first note of the dawn music, a pianissimo high E on a solo violin emerging from the silence, is wonderfully evocative and worth being kept waiting for, certainly until any noise of departing footsteps is still: on the video there is a whole minute's silence between Balstrode's last words and the violin entry. That may seem long on the film but it is well judged for this pregnant situation in the theatre.

It should be explained that earlier in this production Peter's demented monologue had finished with him crouching on the ground. When Ellen entered she immediately went over to him, knelt down beside him and put an arm round him. That is shown in the first video photograph. The second one shows Balstrode helping Peter up after speaking to him, and in the third he is seen gently leading him off.

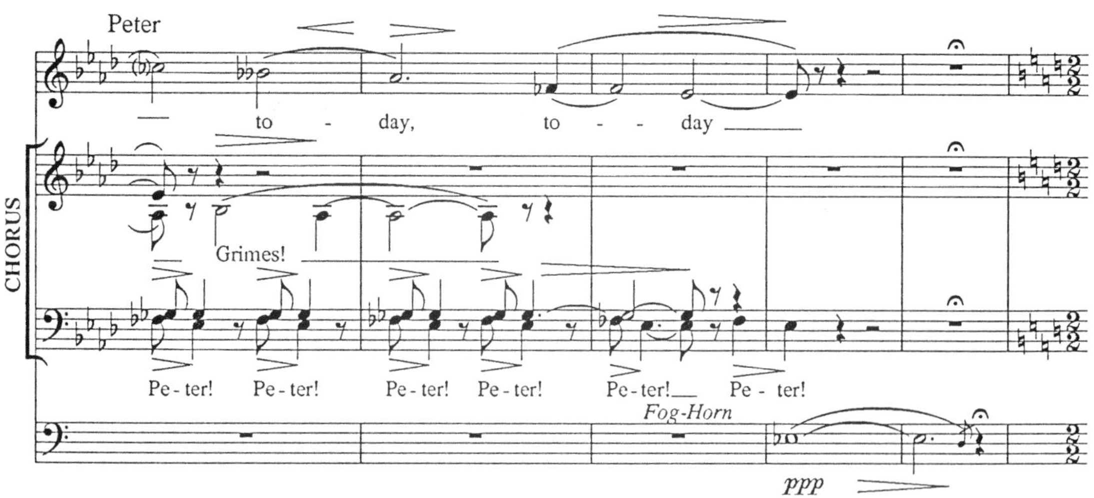
Peter
to - day, to - - day
CHORUS
Grimes!
Pe - ter! Pe - ter! Pe - ter! Pe - ter! Pe - ter! Pe - ter!
Fog-Horn
ppp

Balstrode
(*Crossing to lift Peter up*)
Come on, I'll help you with the boat.

Ellen
No!

Balstrode

Sail out till you lose sight of the Moot Hall. Then sink the boat. D'you hear? Sink her. Good-bye Peter.

(*there is a crunch of shingle as Balstrode leads Peter down to his boat, and helps him push it out. After a short pause, he returns, takes Ellen by the arm, and leads her away.*)

When the orchestral music starts up the lights are very gradually raised. Although the music is very simple, a static three-note chord with grace notes plus an occasional undulating arpeggio, it holds the atmosphere so well that the tiniest gradations of light are enough visual interest, especially if, as here, they gradually illuminate a nicely balanced harbour set, at first seen only in profile. The orchestral sound changes density when the flute enters with several violins in the 13th bar of Figure 53. That is the sonority we remember from Act I and so it might perhaps be the cue for the first fisherman to come on, certainly not before. In the Covent Garden video there are some four or five on the stage by the end of the extract.

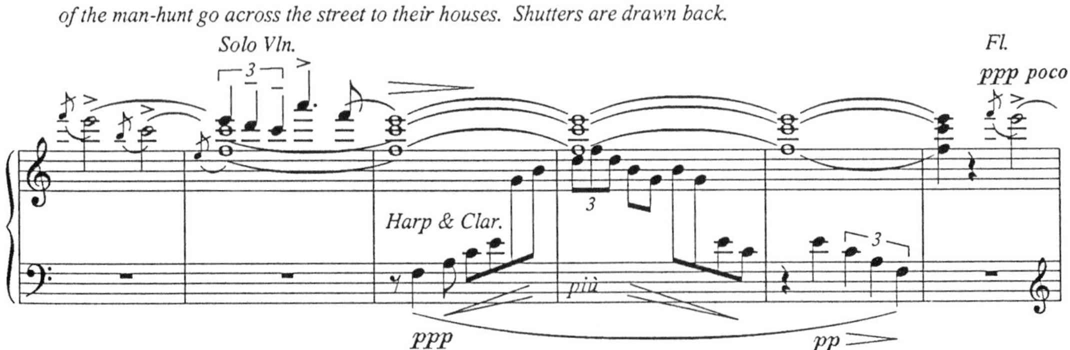

II Structural and Decorative Action

These operatic deaths are examples of what can be called structural actions; actions on which the whole plot of the opera turns. The death of Carmen, for instance, precipitates the end of an opera which can be viewed in retrospect as inexorably leading up to it. Once it has happened Bizet evidently felt he had nothing further to say about the story, and this was perhaps another reason why he was so concerned to tighten up and make the ending more concentrated. Structural action might be any of those actions, an entry, departure, vow, theft, murder or suicide as the result of which the situation on the stage is essentially changed.

However, such action makes up only a small proportion of the expressive stage movements which do so much to bring an opera performance to life. In our very first example in Chapter 1, Cleopatra's aria 'Non disperar' from Handel's *Giulio Cesare*, there was no structural action at all in the above sense. It will be recalled that the entry of Ptolemy, the only such action in the scene as a whole, took place in the preceding recitative, in accordance with the opera seria conventions of the time. Yet Handel's vivid character portrayal in the aria provided rich opportunities for expressive action, not only through the words and melody of the vocal line but also through the expansion of the characterisation into the orchestral accompaniments and ritornelli. We saw that this expressive action did indeed have a structural dimension in that its overall shaping was suggested by the form of the music, so that in each ritornello the singer moved to a new position and the whole stage movement was paced so as to bring the action, like the music, to a climax for the final exit.

In a similar way the Countess's 'Dove sono' from Act III of *The Marriage of Figaro*, Example 1.3, although it called for much more restrained expressive action, could still best be interpreted on the stage with an element of structural thinking, as when the singer sat for the Andantino and stood up for the final Allegro. At the other extreme is Susanna's little aria 'Venite inginocchiatevi' from Act II of *Figaro*, where she is dressing up Cherubino as a girl. Here the vocal phrases and orchestral ritornelli are much shorter than those of the Handel example, giving scope for many little actions, making him kneel, turn, walk, adjusting his collar etc. The structural dimensions of this, too, can be brought out in various ways, one of them suggested by Mozart's tonality. The main action of the dressing can take place in the first part of the aria, accompanying the tonal excursions to the various related keys. However, when the music returns to the tonic towards the end, the words are concerned less with action than with comments about the young man's good looks (Mirate il briconcello, mirate quanto è bello! *Look at the rascal, see how handsome he is!*), and that surely suggests that the dressing is now substantially complete and that Susanna can stand back to admire her handiwork. This means, in effect, that there can be less action as the music reaches its final resolution: but of course that resolution and the greater musical intensity it brings will more than compensate for the reduction in visual interest. Decorative action, then, needs to be sensitive to the structures of the music.

Returning to the main topic of operatic events which are structural in the wider dramatic sense, a few more things can now be said about the arrival of the Messenger in Act II of Monteverdi's *Orfeo*, (discussed in Example 2.1). We are not here concerned with the substantive event itself, the death of Eurydice, which takes place unnoticed by the music and unknown to the audience, perhaps between Acts I and II. The operatic event is the Messenger's disclosure of this news to Orfeo, and we have seen how Monteverdi and his librettist make the Messenger spin it out with a series of partial disclosures before she finally blurts out the whole truth. We saw also how the producer in the Harnoncourt performance on video matched this gradual revelation by having her enter at the top of the stage and slowly move down to Orfeo at the front.

In addition, on the small scale, Monteverdi underlines the tension between the Messenger and Orfeo's gradual comprehension, by the striking contrasts of key: for each of her phrases she wrenches the key sharpwards from his more relaxed flat key comments. It will be found that this differentiation of key does not operate on the large scale over the whole of Act II; that was a device only possible with further developments in tonality later in the century. Instead, Monteverdi articulates the wider action through his use of musical form, the dance-like ritornelli, arias, duets and chorus coming to a climax with Orfeo's ecstatic 'Vi recorda, *Do you remember*,' just before the Messenger's arrival. From then onwards the whole text is set to sombre recitative, broken only by the even more sombre chorus 'Ahi caso acerbo, *Alas, cruel fate*,' this being a contrapuntal treatment of the Messenger's very first phrase. Monteverdi also introduces a new continuo sound for the Messenger, the organo di legno, which further contributes to the change of mood.

In translating this structural change into the staging the Harnoncourt video performance employs two very striking visual ideas. Firstly, the Messenger is dressed in black, and this works well not only because of its death symbolism, but also because it changes the whole visual aspect of the scene from the moment she appears. The other production device is more controversial. The stage lights are suddenly dimmed at that same moment, and remain so for the remainder of the act. Again the symbolism is strong (a cloud has covered the sun perhaps) and the dramatic impact of the entry is enhanced. The fact that the device would probably not have been available in Monteverdi's day would rule it out only in the most narrowly authentic realisation. What is perhaps more controversial is that it doesn't quite fit the music, in which the Messenger's news is only gradually revealed.

There is a moment of action in a later seventeenth-century opera when a sudden change of lighting would be dramatically more appropriate, if still unauthentic. It comes in Purcell's *Dido and Aeneas* some eighty years after *Orfeo*, by which time the longer-term possibilities of tonal planning were being increasingly explored.

Example 7.3
Purcell *Dido and Aeneas*, Act II, Scene 2

Purcell puts the new awareness of tonality to splendid use in his treatment of the main event of Act II, Scene 2, the appearance of Mercury to command Aeneas to forsake Dido and go off to found Troy. The moment of Mercury's entry is articulated in the music by a gesture which Monteverdi could have employed: a juxtaposition of D major and A minor. What is new, however, is that these are now conflicting tonal centres which control much longer stretches of the score. Before this moment the music has been consistently in D since the beginning of the act, some seven to eight minutes earlier; at first in D minor for the hunting party at the grove, then D major when the storm sends them all scurrying home. This gives enormous force to the change to A minor which, never once returning to the D we can still remember, persists doggedly for the rest of the scene, for Mercury's commands and Aeneas' reluctant acceptance of them. Thus, while in its detail the tonal structure is less interesting than that of *Orfeo*, in its longer-term ramifications over some fifteen minutes of music it is stronger, and the tonal dividing point is, quite precisely, the moment when Mercury appears.

End of chorus (voices doubled by orchestra)

(The spirit of the Sorceress descends to Aeneas in the likeness of Mercury)

This prompts a comment on the controversy surrounding the ending to this act. Every scene in the opera except this one ends with a chorus (or chorus plus dance) and the original libretto[5] did indeed provide words for a final chorus (for the Sorceress and Witches) for this one too. We do not know whether Purcell ever set these words: if he did, the music has been lost. It may have been his decision not to set them at all but to end the act with Aeneas' emotional recitative.[6] Attempts have been made to supply a final chorus to the act by, among others, Benjamin Britten and Thurston Dart (using material from other works of Purcell) and there is a pastiche Purcellian setting of the words of the original Witches' chorus by Michael Tilmouth.[7] Each of these is good in its own way, but they all make the mistake of finishing the act in D minor, apparently for the reason that all Purcell's other scenes in the opera finished in the same key as they began (or its relative minor). But none of those other scenes embrace such a strong structural action as this one, or contain such a strongly ramified key change. To finish in the starting key is to finish in the key of the celebratory hunting party, and that is surely wrong.

The earlier suggestion of playing the second part of the scene with dimmed lighting is, of course, anachronistic, but it would clarify the fact that Mercury's intrusion inaugurates a quite new dramatic dispensation for the remainder of the scene. Purcell's careful key schedule says exactly that, and any added material must surely be consistent with it and remain in A minor. The scene gives an early example of the articulation of a structural action by key. In its simple and direct way it is perfect and there is nothing in later opera more effective. It is revealing to compare it with an action from an opera written a century later by a composer making full use of the further dramatic possibilities of tonality then available.

Example 7.4
Mozart *The Marriage of Figaro*, Act II, Finale

The action in question, a surprise appearance by Susanna, comes at the join between the first two sections of the Act II finale. The dramatic context is that the Count, hoping to catch the Countess in a compromising situation, has found her dressing room locked and has reason to believe that she is hiding Cherubino in it. While he goes to fetch tools to force open the door, requiring the Countess to accompany him, we in the audience see Susanna go into the dressing room to take the place of Cherubino, who escapes by jumping out of the window. The extract shows the moment on the Count's return when, to the astonishment of both him and the Countess, the door opens to reveal Susanna, who of course, as the Countess's maid, has every right to be there.

In the following extract the precise instant is shown when Susanna is to appear, to coincide with the orchestral rests in bar 121, and the photographs show some of the moments surrounding that action. In bar 119 the Count is depicted at the moment he turns away from his aggressive confrontation with the Countess, sword in hand, to force the door, but just in time to be confronted by the emerging Susanna in the doorway in bar 121.

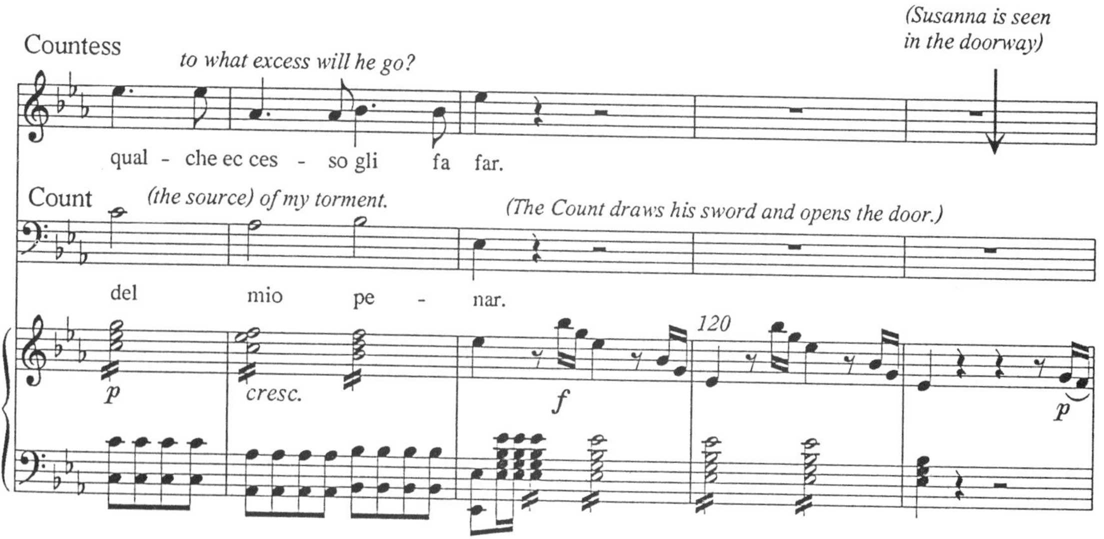

It will be noticed in the second of the photographs that the Countess has turned away as if unable to face the expected Cherubino. The third picture, to coincide with bars 124–5, shows her astonishment at hearing the Count's 'Susanna!': and even after hearing it she still doesn't look round immediately, perhaps because she hasn't yet quite taken in the new situation.

Countess
Su - san-na!
Count
(astonished)
Su - san-na!
122
125
Molto andante
p

In bar 129 another close-up picture shows the Count with Susanna, who has used the first two bars of the Molto Andante to walk forwards a few paces, in this case almost provocatively into his sword, a touch of insolence which, as we will see, is consistent with the music despite its apparent decorum.

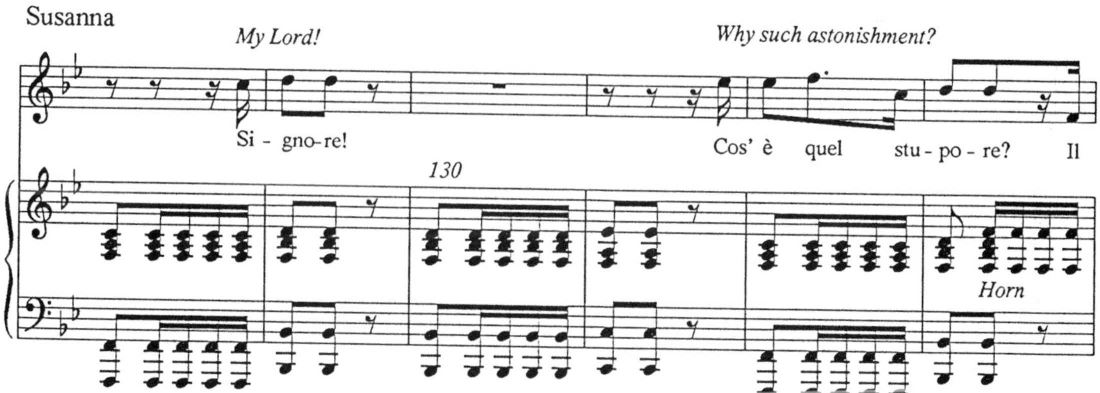

Concerning the new musical idea, the Molto Andante, Frits Noske[8] makes the point that in the eighteenth century this would have been regarded as an aristocratic minuet, i.e. not appropriate to Susanna's station as servant, and so it is a delightful vehicle for her veiled impertinence. As often in such moments it is the orchestra which announces the new musical idea and there is a particular intimacy in the singer/orchestra relationship here because while relying on the orchestra to express and sustain her real feelings, she can sing against it some little phrases, disjointed in themselves, representing what discretion at that moment actually allows her to say (she will take over the second strain of the melody later as she gets a little bolder). Her actions at this point must surely match the decorum of the music and not stress its implied rudeness, i.e. a dead-pan expression and a minimum of dignified (but not pompous) actions will allow the music to make its point.

To understand Mozart's tonal drama we must realise that the bar 121 indicates the end of a long movement whose home key of E flat has by now acquired considerable weight. This tonality is associated in our minds with the Count's aggressive suspicions and so it is musically quite correct that he should go over to force the door in the final E flat orchestral coda, bars 117–9. When Susanna appears in the magical two and a half beats of rest, the whole E flat tonal edifice gradually begins to topple with the little bridge passage, consisting of orchestral moves down first to C and then to the disruptive A natural (bar 125), an appropriate means of expressing the astonishment of the other two; this leads into the new idea in the B flat tonality for Susanna. However, the weight of the previous E flat tonality can still be felt and it imparts to the B flat a tension which only wears off as the Count and Countess come to terms with the new situation. In other words, our growing comprehension of the change to the new tonality is synchronous with the Count and Countess's growing comprehension of the new dramatic situation, and it is for this reason that, on the video film, it is appropriate that the Countess should continue, for the moment, to look away.

This delightful moment occurs at the join of the first two sections of the finale of Act II. The same principle of structural action, underpinned by a change of key, is found in most of the joins between sections in this and other Mozart finales. Usually, the sections follow straight on from each other with only a tiny comma in which the entry or other action takes place. In that respect the little bridge passage in bars 121–6 of the above example, and also the recitative between sections of the Act III finale illustrated in Example

4.2 are somewhat exceptional. Just as the finales are the climaxes of their respective acts, so they themselves move towards a climax at the end, generally a fast movement with all the available characters singing. They are conceived as tonal entities too, coming to a musical resolution in re-establishing the home key at the end. This is appropriate in the long-term for the ending of the Act II finale because by then, after several changes in his fortunes, the Count's aggression is once more ascendant as he contrives that Figaro should marry Marcellina. The return to E flat is therefore dramatically justified as well as being musically right.

Example 7.5
Mozart *The Marriage of Figaro*, Act IV, Finale

The following passage is similar to the previous one in that Susanna again outwits the Count but a comparison is of interest because this time Mozart is less concerned to articulate the action itself than its consequences. The whole situation is more complex. The 'Susanna' with whom the Count has been flirting turns out to be the Countess in disguise, while the real Susanna, disguised as the Countess, is able to make the Count's jealousy look ridiculous when he attempts to expose his wife flirting with Figaro. The first video still shows the veiled Susanna (dressed as the Countess), in a mock contrite stance while the others beg for pardon on her behalf.

When the Count refuses, the real Countess enters and turns the tables on him. Mozart leaves no articulating gap here, but simply registers the astonishment of the Count and his two allies by switching at once to the tonic minor, their mental agitation represented not only by the detached notes in their vocal parts, but also in the restless quaver ostinato in the violins.

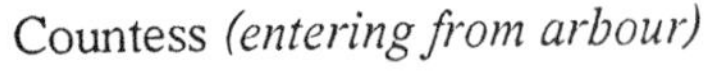

It is only at the end of the section (some dozen intervening bars are omitted from the example) that Mozart arrests the continuity of the music in order to highlight the moment when the Count comes to his senses and asks for forgiveness: that is much more important than the actions which led to it. The pregnant paused crotchet rest in bar 420 becomes the still centre of one of the most wonderful moments in all opera. The stage must now be absolutely still except for the Count who, in the video film, turns slowly and begins to go down on his knees during the silence.

Then, keeping to the principle of there being only significant action during a silence, it is the Countess who turns a little in the following pause in bar 424, just enough to transfer our attention to her for her answering phrase. Later in the phrase, in this performance, she bends down to him as she sings and takes his hands in hers. This action, too, is entirely consonant with the beneficent, hymn-like music, perfectly expressing the forgiveness which alone can resolve the frenetic tensions of the earlier part of the finale, and indeed of the whole opera.[9] As was noted earlier the reconciliation is confirmed in the music by her taking over and completing the Count's melody.

III Ritualistic Action

There is an almost ritualistic quality in the last example, an enactment of a process which had been dramatically pre-ordained, and is now underpinned with music of an almost religious stasis. Some operas have more such moments than others, and if the opera is the enactment of a myth then it is arguably all ritual. That certainly was the view taken by David Freeman for his controversial ENO production of Monteverdi's *Orfeo* in 1981. He stressed the unrealistic nature of his presentation by having the whole story acted out in miniature during the ritornelli of the prologue 'like the argument of a seventeenth-century poem'.[10] He took as his general conceptual model the Oberammergau passion play, and had the cast reverting to their roles as villagers for the final Moresca dance.

Naturally, *Orfeo* has moments with greater and lesser degrees of ritual, among the former being no doubt the underworld scenes of Acts III and IV. Here, Freeman attempted to reduce even further the illusion of reality by keeping the pastoral chorus on stage throughout, thereby arguably weakening the differentiation which Monteverdi's scoring does so much to create. In a quite different approach to the staging of the same scene, the Harnoncourt video changes the lighting of the set to blue and the actions are much more measured than were the cavortings of the nymphs and shepherds in the earlier acts.[11]

Example 7.6
Mozart *The Magic Flute*, Act II, Finale, March

Of the several ritualistic passages in *The Magic Flute*, the fire and water trial is one with particularly interesting production problems. This is the last of Tamino's ordeals, and the only one he shares with Pamina, who shows him how the flute will protect them both, and that is what gives the composer the imagery for the March, a flute solo with accompanying chords on the brass and timpani. There is very little else to be said about this almost simplistic music, which is less dense, musically speaking, than anything to be found in Mozart's purely instrumental music, even in the serenades. The reason, of course, is precisely that it was written not to be listened to but to accompany the ritualistic action, and its utter simplicity is an invitation to the producer to provide something suitable (if simple) for the audience to see. To have the two characters walking away to undergo their trial off-stage unseen is surely as contrary to the intentions of Mozart's music as to Schikaneder's original stage instructions:

> *The doors close behind them: Tamino and Pamina are seen moving; the crackling of fire and the howling of wind can be heard, also at times muffled thunder and the rushing of water. Tamino plays his flute, accompanied by soft drums. As soon as they emerge from the fire they embrace and take up a position at the centre of the stage.*

On the Sawallisch video film (not illustrated here) the producer cleverly achieves a ritualistic quality by situating the action at the back of the stage behind a grill in such a way that the two characters are seen only as silhouettes moving slowly across the background representation of fire and water. The illustration below is taken from the Haitink production and shows the two as they emerge into the light from the second ordeal of water, the moment when ritualistic action gives way to normal action.

Ritualistic opera has been returning to favour in the twentieth century, especially in British opera in works by, amongst others Holst, Vaughan Williams, Tippett, Britten, Birtwistle and Harvey. There are copious production suggestions by Colin Graham in the published scores of the Britten church parables, which call for particularly stylised actions.[12]

IV Music as Commentary on Action

Having begun this chapter with the proposition that opera is not primarily concerned with action, it would not be right to exclude from it a discussion of a scene where the action is indeed a primary concern of the music, though not the only one.

Example 7.7
Berg *Wozzeck*, Act I, Scene 5

The music depicts the Drum Major's seduction of Marie, and some of the actions which lead up to it. The accompanying chart is mainly concerned to show how the intensity of the music relates to the action. At the top the bar numbers are shown, and this also gives the time scale, each bar lasting about three and a half seconds. Underneath this are the actions as given in the score, with an arrow to indicate those places where the synchronisation with the music has to be exact. Underneath that are the words of each phrase sung by the two characters, showing where each phrase begins and ends. At the next level of the chart is a graph showing the approximate dynamic intensity of the music: Berg's intricate differentiations in the orchestral dynamic makes this aspect of the reduction somewhat problematical, but despite the approximations of the chart it is clear how the musical intensity relates to the stage action in this scene. Finally, at the end are listed the main musical motifs to be heard in the music from time to time.

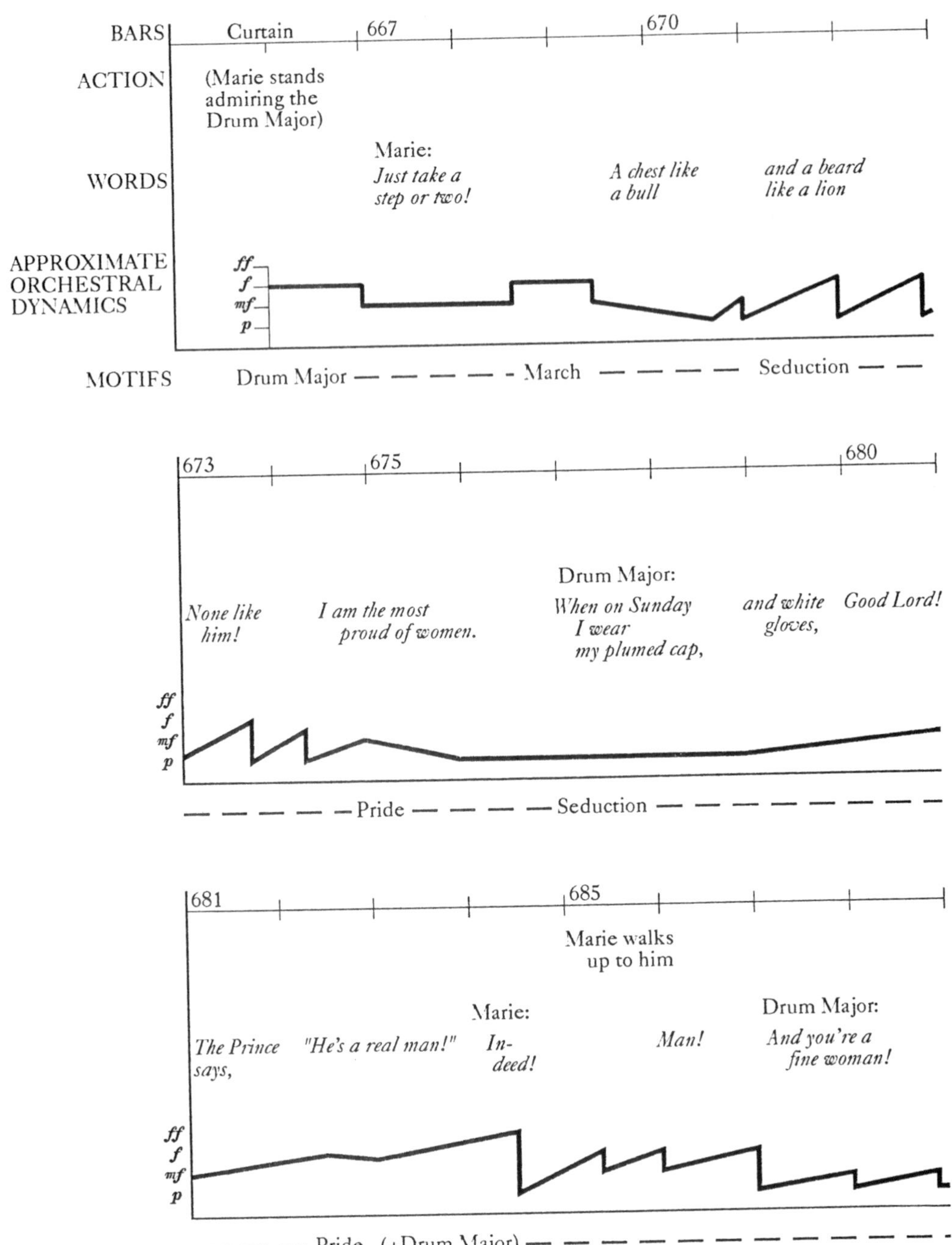

Berg Wozzeck (continued)

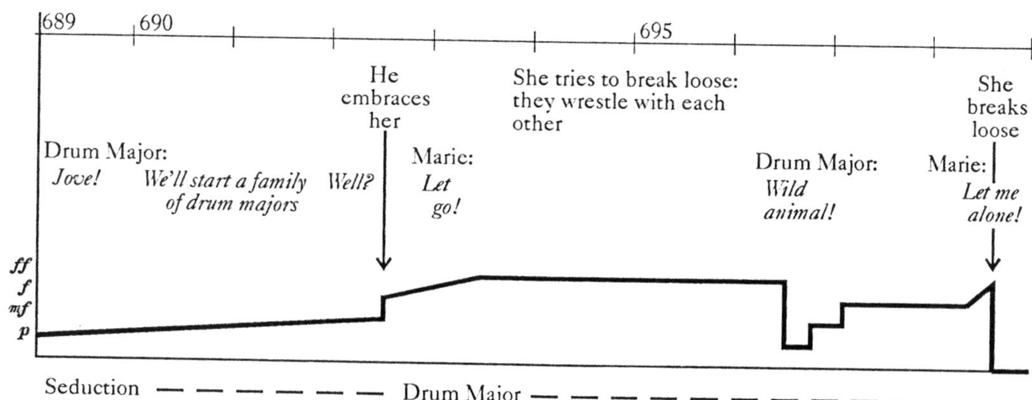
689
690
695
He embraces her
She tries to break loose: they wrestle with each other
She breaks loose
Drum Major:
Jove!
We'll start a family of drum majors
Well?
Marie:
Let go!
Drum Major:
Wild animal!
Marie:
Let me alone!
ff
f
mf
p
Seduction
Drum Major

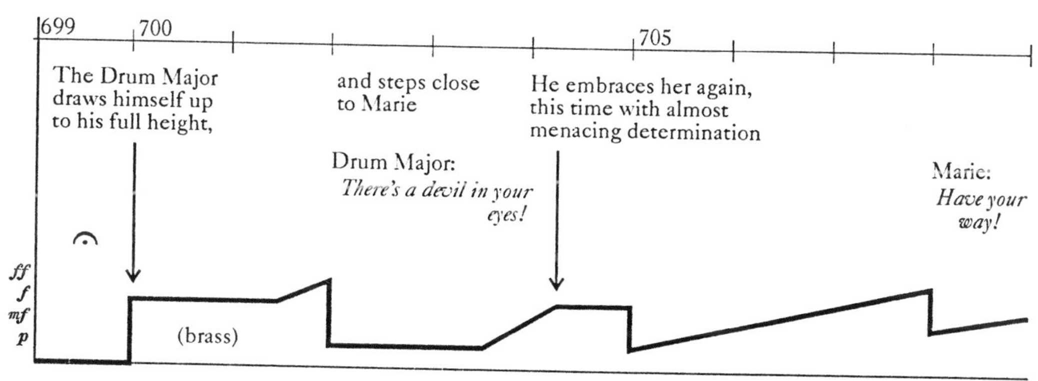
699
700
705
The Drum Major draws himself up to his full height,
and steps close to Marie
He embraces her again, this time with almost menacing determination
Drum Major:
There's a devil in your eyes!
Marie:
Have your way!
ff
f
mf
p
(brass)
Seduction

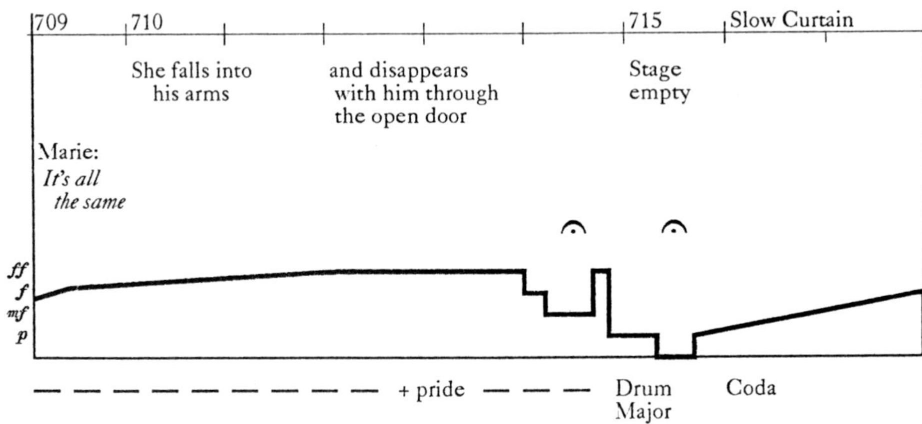
709
710
715
Slow Curtain
She falls into his arms
and disappears with him through the open door
Stage empty
Marie:
It's all the same
ff
f
mf
p
+ pride
Drum Major
Coda

It will be seen at once that the most important actions are all accompanied by short and loud orchestral passages: her breaking loose after their first embrace (bars 693–6), his drawing himself up to his full height (bars 700–2), the second embrace (bars 705–8), and finally her yielding and going off with him into her room (bars 710–14), as suggested in the third sketch. Once they have gone off and the stage is left empty, the orchestra changes its role, and we understand that it is now commenting on the sad turn of events, rather than merely describing them. The harmonies Berg uses here will reappear right at the end of the opera,[13] his final comment on the whole tragic story.

Before looking at the action we must first briefly describe the motivic structure of the scene. George Perle, who has undertaken a thorough analysis of this and other aspects of the opera,[14] has argued for the existence in all of nineteen leitmotifs, three of which are prominent in this scene and have here been given the names suggested by Perle. The reader following the music of this scene may find the music example helpful but should bear in mind that Berg's treatment of leitmotifs is much more elusive than, say, Wagner's, and that reappearing motifs may be developed in such a way as to veil their identity. Thus although the performers of the opera should certainly try to understand the complex motivic references, they should not always expect a clear interpretative lead from them.

Berg himself described the form of the scene as 'quasi rondo',[15] and it is possible to see the Seduction motif as a possible main theme of such a structure, though the Drum Major's theme is more striking and nearly as much used. Certainly, nearly all the music refers to him, and the various aspects of his character, his seductive aspect (from Marie's viewpoint), his military brilliance, his pride in himself, etc., arguably don't need to be distinguished too sharply. There isn't much characterisation apart from this, for the tension in the music is not the result of any clashes between his music and anything associated with Marie: the music is really all his and she, in admiring him, sings his kind of music. The music is essentially symphonic in nature and comes to its climaxes at moments of action, particularly in those places where the singing stops and the orchestra takes over. Thus, unlike some of the operas we have been looking at earlier in the chapter, there is an increase rather than a decrease of musical density at the moments of action.

It is clear from the chart that the final action from bar 710 onwards is climactic, containing the longest sustained orchestral fortissimo of the whole scene, the culmination of a gradual crescendo from bar 702. Earlier, the crescendo from bar 687 leading to the first embrace at bar 692 is similar in shape but on a somewhat smaller scale. Lesser actions at bars 669 and 685 have a similar if less powerful treatment: Berg's sense of proportion in structuring the music on the action is perfect, as is the unity of procedure he achieves by the large number of crescendos to *fp* (marked on the chart as vertical lines), a device which also has the practical virtue of clearing the sound for the singer without loss of emotional intensity.

The very striking silence in bar 699 must mean two things. Musically, it gives a moment's respite to focus our attention on the Drum Major's final onslaught. But because of the close relationship of action to music throughout the scene it must surely also be a time of dramatic stillness, the two characters braced for action, but facing each other, like two fighting animals poised for action but with no movement until the strident brass entry of bar 700 (as in the second sketch).

By the same token the sudden momentary dip in intensity in bar 696 not only gives a moment's dynamic respite for the Drum Major to get his short three-note phrase across, but can also be just a moment free of actual struggle. At the end of the section the final second-beat chord of bar 698 can be the instant when Marie, with a huge effort, pushes herself clear of him. At the end, the actual moment of their disappearing through the door is not articulated in the music, Berg's only stipulation being that they should be out of sight by the time the loud music finishes in bar 714. The point here is that for the moment the music continues to refer to the seduction which we understand to be continuing off-stage, and it is not relevant to the music whether we see it or not. However, when the seduction music stops on the empty stage we know that is because Berg is about to transfer our attention elsewhere, in this case to a short passage of general comment and then closure.

It may well be felt that the idea of structuring a scene round its actions, as Berg does here, is a more natural way of writing an opera than adhering to some of the earlier operatic conventions. For one thing, it brings opera much closer to the spoken theatre by enabling a stage play to be used as a libretto without the kind of adaptation which the conventions of operatic vocal levels would require. *Wozzeck* in this respect has become a model for a good deal of twentieth-century opera. Yet, scrupulously as the action may be delineated in the music, this is more than just a realist opera, for Berg imposes in the symphonic comment a dimension which may embrace moral outrage, a sense of impending doom, or compassion for the characters quite over and above what they, ensnared by their lowly circumstances, may be feeling at the time.

This apparent dichotomy has been criticised, notably by Joseph Kerman who writes of another scene of the opera, the great D minor interlude between scenes 4 and 5 of Act III, 'There is only one trouble . . . the great emphatic orchestral emotion is disconnected from the characters of the play; it is not *of* the action but *about* the action'.[16] In thinking about this one must remember that the interlude is one of many such interpretative passages in *Wozzeck*, perhaps outstanding for its scope and emotional depth, but not in the sense that by its nature it is at all exceptional in the opera. Act I, Scene 5, as we have seen, ends with a short meditative coda, and we can now further note the relationship of this to the music at the very beginning of the scene, before the curtain rises. Over the same G–D pedal point as in the coda and using a similar rocking rhythm, Berg presents the Seduction motif in a comparatively gentle way, as if suggesting that we can sympathise with the warm humanity of Marie's vulnerability. The effect of this is to project forwards into the scene so that when for instance in bars 693–6 we hear the same motif made more frenetic and combined with the Drum Major's motif, the music, in reminding us of a richer dimension to Marie's character, prevents our looking entirely dispassionately at the action on the stage. I believe that the singer playing the part of Marie (or Wozzeck too, for that matter) can feel her character to embrace that richer dimension.

Thus the short epilogue as the curtain falls on Act I brings us back again to the G–D bass of the opening and repeats a figure from the Seduction motif in such a way as to invite us to explore our deepest feelings towards Marie and her unhappy circumstances. Action has been at the very nerve centre of the music, but has not been its sole concern: that is one of the features which raises *Wozzeck* above many of its imitators later in this century.

V Operatic Action and the Dimension of Time

It is evident from these various scenes that the relationship between operatic time and real time is complex. There are scenes, certainly, where opera moves at about the same pace as the real world. The seduction of Marie in the last example is a case in point, and a good deal of classical recitative too would proceed at about the same pace as comparable passages in the spoken theatre; and that, in prosaic passages, is near to realism. On rare occasions opera may move faster than real time, and paradoxically this is often when music and action are at their slowest, in musical passages suggesting the passing of time. Butterfly's nocturnal vigil in Act II of Puccini's opera, as she waits for Pinkerton's arrival, has to represent a much longer passage of time than the actual duration of the music, and the transition between foggy night and grey dawn in the last act of *Peter Grimes*, Example 7.2, is a similar case. The slow pace of the music in these instances, backed up by appropriately slow actions or stasis on the stage can easily deceive us into accepting the passing of more time than has actually elapsed.

More usually, though, the dimension of time in opera is elongated rather than contracted and frequently the opera singer has the difficulty of spinning out the action over a longer time span than is realistic, and to an even greater extent than is normal even in the poetic spoken theatre. This is true of many arias, particularly the slow ones like 'Dove sono' (Example 1.3) and it can be true in a more general sense of whole operas: Dent puts it in his usual picturesque way, referring to *Lohengrin* which 'suffers from the fact that most of it goes at what Wagner himself called the 'German *andante*', which is the normal breathing rate of a corpulent man.'[17]

All this is only to be expected in a medium more concerned to explore the deeper meanings of situations than simply to narrate them and it may in part be a reflection of the sheer physical effort that has to go into singing and which precludes too vigorous action at the same time. It was in the very first opera *Dafne* of 1598 that when the librettist Rinuccini was faced with the problem of an operatic representation of Apollo killing a dragon, he arranged for an actor and a singer to be dressed in exactly the same way. The former did the killing and then the latter took his place to sing the song, and this was said to have been done at every performance without anyone in the audience being aware of the ruse.

In dividing up the action in this way Rinuccini divided up the time too, for the dance/mime could be understood to occupy a credibly realistic duration for such an action, but the singing could stretch the time out for commentary in a different, almost timeless, dimension. Even as late as 1940 Dent could reaffirm something of the same approach to the pacing of action by referring to 'a generally accepted standard rule' for singers 'to remain still while actually singing and to make (their) movements between the vocal phrases'.[18] This would hardly be strictly adhered to nowadays, though there are many arias like 'Non Disperar' (Example 1.1) where for musical even more than physical reasons such action as there is can most appropriately take place in the ritornelli.

In matters of pacing there is a certain correspondence between the recitative/aria division of classical opera and the prose/poetry of the Shakespearean theatre, the proportions over the whole in each case being about one to three. In Shakespeare the division between the two is very flexibly handled. Even the most prosaic of the speeches in prose can, like recitative, include occasional passages of greater (poetic) intensity. But one big difference is that in the spoken theatre it is the prerogative of the actor to control the pacing of the words as well as the action throughout the whole play, and indeed the exercise of that control is one of the most difficult aspects of his art.

The matter has been explored by John Barton,[19] who is very concerned as a producer that in the prose passages his actors should maintain a good pace: '(go for) the sweep and drive and surge of the whole, . . . don't try to characterise it particularly'.[20] On the use Shakespeare makes of the two contrasting styles he suggests an approach which could well be adapted to opera: 'concentrate . . . (on) the way Shakespeare keeps ringing the changes between the two within a given scene. . . . I suppose we should expect him to use verse for romantic, heightened passages and prose for naturalistic ones, and indeed he often does so. But not always, . . . so let's start asking why. There's always a good dramatic reason.'[21] Of course, the set speeches and soliloquies (generally in verse) go more slowly and elicit from him comments on such matters as the placing of pauses, the slowing for monosyllables and the moving forwards to the final couplet of a speech.[22]

The remarks on prose interpretation are of direct relevance to the performance of recitative because this is the area of opera where the singer has the most complete control of the pacing. However, for the musically most important parts of opera, including the arias, it is the composer who assumes the role of controlling the pace, and the task of the performers is to understand what this is and to co-operate with it. It is very hard to give any general guidelines as to how this can be done because they would vary from one type of opera to another. One might just, perhaps, posit the notion that the pace of the music itself may suggest the amount and pace of the action, and this is generally true of slow music; on the other hand increase of musical intensity can, according to the context, lead either to more action, as in *Wozzeck*, or to less, as in those classical and romantic set pieces where the dramatic reference is specifically to an inner intensity.

Perhaps the most interesting aspects of operatic pacing concern not so much what happens at any individual moment – that can vary enormously from production to production – but how the pacing and the implied stage movement changes over longer periods of time. 'Dove Sono' gives a pattern which is valid for countless arias across the whole field of opera. The most action (the Countess looking for Susanna and only gradually settling into her deeper thoughts) will be at the beginning of the recitative when the music is more declamatory and less stable in key. Once the aria has begun the intensity of the music is of an inward nature and demands little further action, and so the operatic structure in time is to be realised more in purely musical than in visual ways: it is the control of the singer's voice over the whole movement which will give the crown to the climactic top A's at the end. However, we noted in Example 1.4 that the gesture of standing for the final Allegro had the effect of reinforcing the climax. In other arias, like 'Non Disperar', the more lively music and situation will call for more action. It is almost as if the singer here is trying to disguise the convention that once the ritornello announces the start of the aria there can be no further important action on the stage for several minutes. The discussion of the scene in Example 1.1 was concerned in part to show how the action could be paced so as to bring out the ritornello structure of the aria and also, belying its apparently strict ternary form on paper, its growth to the end.

Another recurring pattern of stage pacing concerns those moments of structural action which take place between musical set pieces: Mercury's intervention as the storm disrupts Dido's hunting party, Susanna's appearance at the door, or the off-stage trumpet call in Act II of *Fidelio* announcing the arrival of the ambassador. Here, very commonly, the musical intensity will build up to the moment when the break comes, to be matched in intensity of movement or stance, and then immediately after the action there is a period of comparative stasis, generally to be realised in the actions as well as in the music, while the music allows the characters to come to terms with the new situation. Sometimes the voice may have responsibility for the timings across the gap, as in some of the joins between the *Rigoletto* Act I dances and in the little cadenzas before reappearances of the ritornelli in *La Bohème* or in the pub scene of *Peter Grimes*. Then it is an urgency of voice as well as gesture which will propel the opera forwards into the next section.

That moving forwards to the end of a section, movement, scene or act is one thing that is common to virtually all opera, for it derives from the very nature of music itself, which is at once the most free of the arts and yet in its own way the one most under the control and restraints of the continuing passage of time; as Auden put it 'A verbal art . . . is reflective; it stops to think. Music is immediate, it goes on to become.'[23] It is the art of the opera performer to understand this and to make the inevitable compromise seem natural.

Notes

1 See Winton Dean, 'The True Carmen', *The Musical Times*, (1965), pp. 846–55.
2 For example on the Rosi-Maazel video recording.
3 See Winton Dean, op. cit. p. 851.
4 See Susan McClary, (1992), p. 109.
5 Reprinted with critical commentary in C. Price, (1986), pp. 63–75.
6 See C. Price, op. cit. pp. 239–52 for contributions to the controversy by Geoffrey Bush, Benjamin Britten and Ellen Harris.
7 Reprinted in C. Price, op. cit., p. 183.
8 See Frits Noske, (1990), p. 34.
9 See J. Kerman, (1956), pp. 102–8, for perhaps the most profound of the many commentaries on this famous scene. Kerman relates it to other moments of resolution in this and other operas of Mozart.
10 David Freeman, 'Telling the Story', in J. Whenham, (1986), p. 158.
11 For a scholarly discussion of what is known of staging opera in the early seventeenth century see Philip Pickett, (1992), Chapter 5.
12 E.g. Benjamin Britten, *Curlew River*, Faber 1964, pp. 143–60 in the 1983 edition.
13 See D. Jarman, (1979), for a good discussion of the overall harmonic structure of the opera.
14 See George Perle, (1980), pp. 96–117.
15 See Berg's own lecture on *Wozzeck*, reprinted in an English translation in H. Redlich (1957).
16 J. Kerman, (1952), p. 231 in the edition of 1956.
17 Dent, (1940) p.133.
18 Dent, op. cit., p. 140.
19 John Barton, (1984).
20 John Barton, op. cit., pp. 68–9.
21 John Barton, op. cit., p. 70.
22 See Chapter 9 'Rehearsing the Text' in John Barton, op.cit.
23 Quoted from 'Notes on Music and Opera' in Auden (1963), p. 466.

Bibliography

Abbate, Caroline (1989), 'Opera as Symphony, a Wagnerian Myth' in Abbate and Parker (eds), *Analysing Opera: Verdi and Wagner*, Berkeley, California.

Abbiati, F. (1959), *Guiseppe Verdi*, Milan.

Abraham, G. (1974), *A Hundred Years of Music*, (4th edn), Duckworth, London.

Anderson, Emily (ed. and tr.) (1938, rev. 1966, ed. King, A.H. and M. Carolan), *The Letters of Mozart and His Family*, 3 vols, Macmillan, London.

Auden, W.H. (1963), *The Dyer's Hand*, Faber, London.

Barnett, Dene (May 1977, ff.) 'The Performance Practice of Acting': the Eighteenth Century', *Theatre Research International.*

Bartlett, Clifford (ed.) (1993), *Monteverdi L'Orfeo*, England, King's Music Gmc.

Barton, John (1984) *Playing Shakespeare*, London, New York, Methuen.

Boulez, Pierre (1986), *Orientations*, tr. M. Cooper, Faber, London.

Breckbill, David (1992), 'Performance Practice' in Millington, Barry, *The Wagner Compendium*, London, Thames and Hudson.

Brett, Philip, (ed.) (1983), *Benjamin Britten, Peter Grimes*, Cambridge University Press.

Britten, Benjamin (1945), *Introduction* in Brett, Philip, (ed.) (1993), *Benjamin Britten, Peter Grimes*, Cambridge University Press.

Bukofzer, M. (1947), *Music in the Baroque Era*, Norton, New York.

Burney, Charles (1796), *Memoirs of the Life and Writings of Abate Metastasio*, London.

Bush, Geoffrey (1986), 'The Missing Music Controversy: Another Point of View', in Curtis Price, *Purcell, Dido and Aeneas, An Opera*, Norton, New York, London.

Carner, Mosco (1974), *Puccini: a Critical Biography*, Duckworth, London.

Chailley, Jacques (1972), *The Magic Flute, Masonic Opera*, Gollancz, London.

Chused, Martin (1980), 'Notes on the Performance of Rigoletto', *Verdi Newsletter*, No.8.

Curtis, Alan (1989), Preface to *Claudio Monteverdi, L'Incoronazione di Poppea*, Novello, London.

Dahlhaus, Carl (1979), tr. M. Whittall, *Richard Wagner's Music Dramas*, Cambridge University Press, England.

Darcy, Warren (1992), 'Autograph Manuscripts', in *The Wagner Compendium*, Thames and Hudson, London.

Dean, Winton (1965), 'The True Carmen', *The Musical Times*, pp. 846–55.

——— (1969), *Handel and the Opera Seria*, University of California Press, Berkeley and Los Angeles.

——— (1975), *Georges Bizet, His Life and Work*, (3rd edn), Dent, London.

——— (ed.) (1976), *G.F. Handel, Three Ornamented Arias*, Oxford University Press, London.

——— (1977), 'The Performance of Recitative in Late Baroque Opera', *Music and Letters*, lviii (389).

Deane, Basil (1965), *Cherubini*, Oxford University Press, London.

Dent, Edward J. (1940, rev. 1949), *Opera*, Penguin, London.

Donington, Robert (1963), *Wagner's Ring and its Symbols*, Faber, London.

——— (1973), *A Performer's Guide to Baroque Music*, London.

——— (1990), *Opera and its Symbols*, Yale, New Haven and London.

Drummond, J.D. (1980), *Opera in Perspective*, Dent, London.

Einstein, Alfred (1946), *Mozart*, Cassell, London.

Ellis, W.A. (tr.) (1892–9, repr. 1972), *Richard Wagner's Prose Works*, London.

Erber, James, (ed.) (1978), *Marco da Gagliano, La Dafne*, London.

Evans, Peter (1979), *The Music of Benjamin Britten*, Dent, London.

Fenlon, Iain and Peter Miller (1992), 'Public Vice, Private Virtue' in N. John (ed.), *The Operas of Monteverdi*, Calder: London, Riverrun: New York.

Forsyth, Michael (1985), *Buildings for Music*, MIT Press, Cambridge Massachusetts.

Fortune, Nigel (1986), 'The Rediscovery of Orfeo' in Whenham (ed.) (1986).

Freeman, David (1986), 'Telling the Story' in Whenham (ed.) (1986).

Glover, Jane (1986), 'Solving the Musical Problems' in Whenham (ed.) (1986).

Goldman, A. and E. Sprinchorn (eds) (1964, rev. 1977) *Wagner on Music and Drama: a Compendium of Richard Wagner's Prose Works* tr. Ellis, W.A., Dutton, New York.

Graham, Colin (1965), 'Production Notes' in Benjamin Britten, *Curlew River*, Faber, London.

Grey, T.S. (1992), 'Reminiscence Motif' in Millington, Barry (ed.) (1992).

Grout, Donald J. (1988), *A Short History of Opera*, Columbia University Press, New York.

Higgins, John (1978), *The Making of an Opera*, Secker and Warburg, London.

Jarman, D. (1979), *The Music of Alban Berg*, University of California Press.

John, Nicholas (ed.) (1992), *The Operas of Monteverdi*, Calder, London and Riverrun, New York.

Kerman, Joseph (1956), *Opera as Drama*, Vintage, New York.

Kimbell, David R.B. (1981), *Verdi in the Age of Italian Romanticism*, Cambridge University Press.

Knight, Wilson (1953), *The Shakespearian Tempest*, London.

Kobbé, G. (1954 and frequently since), ed. and rev. The Earl of Harewood, *Kobbé's Complete Opera Book*, Putnam, London and New York.

Kurth, E. (1920), *Romantische Harmonik und ihre Krise in Wagners Tristan*, Berne and Leipzig.

Long, J.H. (1961), *Shakespeare's Use of Music, The Final Comedies*, Da Capo, London.

McClary, Susan (1992), *Georges Bizet, Carmen*, Cambridge University Press.

Mann, William (1977), *The Operas of Mozart*, Cassell, London.

Mattheson, J. (1739), *Das Vollkommene Capellmeister*, Hamburg.

Matthews, David (1983) 'Act II scene I : an examination of the music', in Brett (ed.) *Benjamin Britten, Peter Grimes*, Cambridge University Press.

Millington, Barry (ed.) (1992), *The Wagner Compendium*, Thames and Hudson, London.

Mozart, W.A., for letters see Emily Anderson (1938).

Newman, Ernest (1934), *More Opera Nights*, Putnam, London.

——— (1949), *Wagner Nights*, The Bodley Head, London.

Noske, Frits (1977), *The Signifier and the Signified*, Nijhoff, The Hague, also Oxford University Press, New York and London.

Osborne, Charles, (ed.) (1971), *The Letters of Verdi*, Gollancz, London.

Palmer, Christopher (ed.) (1984),*The Britten Companion*, Faber, London.

Parker, R. (1982), 'The Music of Rigoletto' in *Rigoletto, Verdi*, Calder, London.

Pears, Peter (1984), 'On Playing Peter Grimes' in Palmer (ed.) *The Britten Companion*, Faber, London.

Perle, George (1980), *The Operas of Alban Berg, Vol.I. Wozzeck*, University of California Press.

Pickett, Philip (1992), *Behind the Mask, Monteverdi's L'Orfeo*, King's Music Gmc.

Porges, H. (1876), *Wagner Rehearsing the Ring*, tr. Jacobs, (1983), Cambridge University Press.

Price, Curtis (1986), *Dido and Aeneas, an Opera*, Norton, New York and London.

Redlich, Hans (1957), *Alban Berg, the Man and his Music*, London.

Robinson, Michael F. (1966), *Opera before Mozart*, Hutchinson, London.

Rosen, Charles (1971), *The Classical Style*, Faber, London.

Sadie, Stanley (ed.) (1980), *The New Grove Dictionary of Music and Musicians*, MacMillan, London, Grove's Dictionaries of Music Inc., Washington.

——— (ed.) (1984), *The New Grove Wagner*, MacMillan, London.

Schrade, Leo (1950), *Monteverdi, Creator of Modern Music*, Norton, New York.

Shafer, Murray (1963), *British Composers in Interview*, Faber, London.

Shaw, Bernard (1898), *The Perfect Wagnerite*, Constable, London.

Spencer, Stewart (1992), 'Wagner as Librettist' in Barry Millington, *The Wagner Compendium*, Thames and Hudson, London.

Stanislavski, K. and P. Rumyantsev, (1975) *Stanislavski on Opera*, Theater Arts Books, New York.

Sternfeld, F. (1986) 'The Orpheus Myth and the Libretto of Orfeo' in Whenham (ed.) *Claudio Monteverdi, Orfeo*, Cambridge University Press, London and New York.

Strunk, Oliver (1950), *Source Readings in Music History*, Norton, New York.

Toye, Francis (1931), *Giuseppe Verdi*, Heinemann, London, Knopf, New York.

Tyrrell, John (1982), *Leos Janacek, Kat'a Kabanova*, Cambridge University Press, London and New York.

Wagner, Richard (1983), *My Life*, ed. Whittall, tr. Grey, Cambridge University Press.

Whenham, John (1978), *Italian Secular Duets and Dialogues c. 1600 to 1643*, diss. University of Oxford, reprinted UMI.

——— (ed.) (1986), *Claudio Monteverdi, Orfeo*, Cambridge University Press.

Zaslaw, Neal (ed.) (1989), *Man and Music, The Classical Era*, London.

List of Illustrations

Jacket illustration
Kiri Te Kanawa as The Countess and Reri Grist as Susanna in *The Marriage of Figaro*, Mozart.

Full page plates
(the singers are listed in the captions)

Video stills and principal singers

The Marriage of Figaro

The Count	Benjamin Luxon
The Countess	Kiri Te Kanawa
Figaro	Knut Skram
Susanna	Ileana Cotrubas
Basilio	John Fryatt

The Magic Flute

Act I scenes 1–4		206–12
Duet *Bei Männern*		89–90
Act II No. 9, Temple scene		213–15
Finale, March		257
Tamino	Leo Goeke	
Pamina	Felicity Lott	
Papageno	Benjamin Luxon	
The Queen of the Night	May Sandor	
Sarastro	Thomas Thomaske	

Carmen

Act I No. 9, Melodrama scene		221–2
Act IV final scene		237–9
Carmen	Maria Ewing	
Don José	Barry McCauley	
Zuniga	Xavier Depraz	

La Bohème

Act I opening scene		164–8
Mimi's entry		70–5
Act IV final scene		225–6
Rodolfo	Neil Shicoff	
Marcello	Thomas Allen	
Colline	Gwynne Howell	
Mimi	Ileana Cotrubas	

Peter Grimes

Act I scene 1, Grimes' Narration		78–82
Scene 2, Pub scene		171–5
Act II Ellen with boy		152–6
Act III transition into final scene		240–3
Grimes	Jon Vickers	
Balstrode	Norman Bailey	
Auntie	Elizabeth Bainbridge	
Mrs Sedley	Patricia Payne	
Boles	John Dobson	
Ellen	Heather Harper	

Sketches by Sylvia Bramley

Index